HIDDEN POTENTIAL

Hidden Potential

The Science of Achieving
Greater Things

ADAM GRANT

VIKING

VIKING
An imprint of Penguin Random House LLC
penguinrandomhouse.com

Grateful acknowledgment is made for permission to reprint
the following:

Lines from "Dreams" by Langston Hughes from *The Collected
Poems of Langston Hughes*. Copyright © 1994 by the Estate of
Langston Hughes. Reprinted by permission of Harold Ober
Associates and International Literary Properties LLC.

Lines from "The Rose That Grew from Concrete,"
written by Tupac Shakur. Reprinted by permission of King,
Holmes, Paterno & Soriano, LLP.

Image credits may be found on page 279

LIBRARY OF CONGRESS CATALOGING-IN-PUBLICATION DATA
Names: Grant, Adam, 1981– author.
Title: Hidden potential: the science of achieving
    greater things / Adam Grant.
Description: [New York, NY] : Viking, [2023] |
    Includes bibliographical references and index.
Identifiers: LCCN 2023020778 (print) | LCCN 2023020779 (ebook) |
    ISBN 9780593653142 (hardcover) | ISBN 9780593653159 (ebook)
Subjects: LCSH: Achievement motivation. | Motivation (Psychology)
Classification: LCC BF503 .G736 2023 (print) | LCC BF503 (ebook) |
    DDC 153.8—dc23/eng/20230722
LC record available at https://lccn.loc.gov/2023020778
LC ebook record available at https://lccn.loc.gov/2023020779

Printed in the United States of America
1   3   5   7   9   10   8   6   4   2

Book design by Daniel Lagin

In memory of Sigal Barsade, who saw the potential in everyone

CONTENTS

HIDDEN POTENTIAL

Prologue

Growing Roses from Concrete

Did you hear about the rose that grew
from a crack in the concrete
Proving nature's law is wrong it
learned 2 walk without having feet
Funny it seems but by keeping its dreams
it learned 2 breathe fresh air

—"THE ROSE THAT GREW FROM CONCRETE,"
WRITTEN BY TUPAC SHAKUR

On a chilly spring weekend in 1991, some of America's sharpest young minds gathered in a hotel outside Detroit. The hall buzzed with chatter as students worked their way to their assigned seats. The moment the clocks started, the room fell silent. The only sound was *click, click, click*. All eyes were locked on rows of black and white squares. It was the National Junior High Chess Championships.

In recent years, the tournament had been dominated by teams from fancy private schools and magnet schools. They had the resources to make chess part of the school curriculum. The defending champion was Dalton, an elite prep school in New York City that had won three straight national titles.

Dalton had built the chess equivalent of an Olympic training center.

Each kindergartner took a semester of chess, and every first grader studied the game for a full year. The most talented students qualified for lessons before and after school with one of the country's best chess teachers. Dalton's crown jewel was the child prodigy Josh Waitzkin, whose life story would become the basis for the hit movie *Searching for Bobby Fischer* just two years later. Even though Josh and another star player weren't competing this year, Dalton had a formidable team.

No one saw the Raging Rooks as contenders. As they walked nervously into the hotel, heads turned. They had very little in common with their wealthy white opponents. The Raging Rooks were a group of poor students of color—six Black boys, one Latino, one Asian American. They lived in neighborhoods ravaged by drugs, violence, and crime. Most of them grew up in single-parent homes, raised by mothers, aunts, or grandmothers with incomes less than the cost of Dalton tuition.

The Raging Rooks were eighth and ninth graders hailing from JHS 43, a public middle school in Harlem. Unlike their adversaries at Dalton, they didn't have a decade of training or years of competition under their belts. Some of them had only learned the game in sixth grade. The team captain, Kasaun Henry, had picked up chess at age twelve and practiced in a park with a drug dealer.

At nationals, teams got to keep their highest scores and throw out the rest. Teams as large as Dalton's could drop as many as six scores. But the Raging Rooks barely fielded enough players to compete. Every score would count—they had no insurance policy. To have any shot at success, they would all have to perform at their peak.

The Raging Rooks started strong. Early on, their weakest player upset an opponent ranked hundreds of points above him. The rest of the team rose to the occasion, checkmating foes who were far more seasoned. Going into the semifinals, of 63 teams competing, the Raging Rooks were in third place.

Despite their inexperience, they had a secret weapon. Their coach was a young chess master named Maurice Ashley. A Jamaican immigrant in his midtwenties, Maurice was on a mission to shatter the stereotype that darker-skinned kids weren't bright. He knew from experience that although talent is evenly distributed, opportunity is not. He could see potential where others had missed it. He was looking to grow roses in concrete.

But in the penultimate round of nationals, Maurice watched his team begin to slip. After gaining a lead, Kasaun blundered and barely squeaked out a draw. Another player was on the brink of victory when his opponent managed to capture his queen and beat him. He broke down in tears and bolted out of the room. One game got off to such an ugly start that Maurice walked out of the playing hall altogether. It was too painful to watch. By the end of the round, the Raging Rooks had fallen from third to fifth place.

Maurice reminded them they could control only their decisions—not their results. To catch up, the Raging Rooks would have to win their four final games and pray for the top teams to lose theirs. But regardless of what happened, they were now among the best in the country. They didn't have to win the tournament to win people's hearts. They had already smashed all expectations.

Chess is known as a game of genius. The top young players tend to be whiz kids with the raw brainpower to memorize sequences, rapidly analyze scenarios, and see many steps ahead. If you want to build a championship chess team, your best bet is to do what Dalton did: recruit a bunch of child prodigies and put them through intensive training from an early age.

Maurice did the opposite: he started coaching a group of middle schoolers who happened to be interested and available. One was the class bully. They were mostly B students, and they weren't selected for any special chess aptitude. "We didn't have any stars on our team," Maurice recalls.

Yet as the final round played out, the Raging Rooks managed to hold their own. Two players scored big checkmates, and Kasaun was hanging in there against a much higher-rated opponent. Even if he could pull off an upset, though, the Rooks knew it probably wouldn't be enough. Their first match that round had ended in a draw.

A few minutes later, Maurice heard shouts at the end of the hallway. "Mr. Ashley, Mr. Ashley!" After a long battle in the endgame, Kasaun had defied the odds and beaten Dalton's top player. To everyone's shock, the leading teams had faltered, paving the way for the Raging Rooks to tie for first place. The players erupted in high fives, hugs, and cheers. "We won! We won!"

In just two years, the poor kids from Harlem traveled the distance from novices to national champions. But the biggest surprise isn't that the underdogs won—it's why they won. The skills they developed would eventually earn them much more than chess titles.

———

Everyone has hidden potential. This book is about how we unlock it. There's a widely held belief that greatness is mostly born—not made. That leads us to celebrate gifted students in school, natural athletes in sports, and child prodigies in music. But you don't have to be a wunderkind to accomplish great things. My goal is to illuminate how we can *all* rise to achieve greater things.

As an organizational psychologist, I've spent much of my career studying the forces that fuel our progress. What I've learned might challenge some of your fundamental assumptions about the potential in each of us.

In a landmark study, psychologists set out to investigate the roots of exceptional talent among musicians, artists, scientists, and athletes. They conducted extensive interviews with 120 Guggenheim-winning sculptors, internationally acclaimed concert pianists, prizewinning mathematicians, pathbreaking neurology researchers, Olympic swimmers, and world-class tennis players—and with their parents, teachers, and coaches. They were stunned to discover that only a handful of these high achievers had been child prodigies.

Among the sculptors, not even one was identified as having special abilities by elementary school art teachers. A few of the pianists won big competitions before turning nine, but the rest only seemed gifted when compared to their siblings or neighbors. Although the mathematicians and neurologists generally did well in elementary and middle school, they didn't stand out among the other strong students in their classes. Hardly any of the swimmers set records early on; the majority won local meets but not regional or national championships. And most of the tennis players lost in the early rounds of their first tournaments and took several years to emerge as top local players. If they were singled out by their coaches, it was not for unusual aptitude but unusual motivation. That motivation wasn't innate; it tended to begin with a coach or teacher who made learning fun. "What any person in the world can learn, *almost* all persons ᵃ ⸗ learn," the lead psychologist concluded, "*if* provided with appropriate . . . conditions of learning."

Recent evidence underscores the importance of conditions for learning. To master a new concept in math, science, or a foreign language, it typically takes seven or eight practice sessions. That number of reps held across thousands of students, from elementary school all the way through college.

Of course, there were students who excelled after fewer practice sessions. But they weren't faster learners—they improved at the same rate as their peers. What set them apart was that they showed up to the first practice session with more initial knowledge. Some students got a boost from already having a grasp on related material. Others had parents teach them early or got a head start teaching themselves. What look like differences in natural ability are often differences in opportunity and motivation.

When we assess potential, we make the cardinal error of focusing on starting points—the abilities that are immediately visible. In a world obsessed with innate talent, we assume the people with the most promise are the ones who stand out right away. But high achievers vary dramatically in their initial aptitudes. If we judge people only by what they can do on day one, their potential remains hidden.

You can't tell where people will land from where they begin. With the right opportunity and motivation to learn, anyone can build the skills to achieve greater things. Potential is not a matter of where you start, but of how far you travel. We need to focus less on starting points and more on distance traveled.

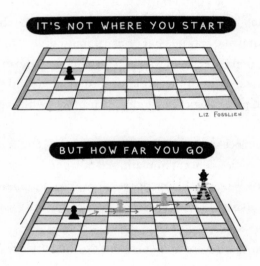

For every Mozart who makes a big splash early, there are multiple Bachs who ascend slowly and bloom late. They're not born with invisible superpowers; most of their gifts are homegrown or homemade. People who make major strides are rarely freaks of nature. They're usually freaks of nurture.

Neglecting the impact of nurture has dire consequences. It leads us to underestimate the amount of ground that can be gained and the range of talents that can be learned. As a result, we limit ourselves and the people around us. We cling to our narrow comfort zones and miss out on broader possibilities. We fail to see the promise in others and close the door to opportunities. We deprive the world of greater things.

Stretching beyond our strengths is how we reach our potential and perform at our peak. But progress is not merely a means to the end of excellence. Getting better is a worthy accomplishment in and of itself. I want to explain how we can improve at improving.

This book is not about ambition. It's about aspiration. As the philosopher Agnes Callard highlights, ambition is the outcome you want to attain. Aspiration is the person you hope to become. The question is not how much money you earn, how many fancy titles you land, or how many awards you accumulate. Those status symbols are poor proxies for progress. What counts is not how hard you work but how much you grow. And growth requires much more than a mindset—it begins with a set of skills that we normally overlook.

THE RIGHT STUFF

In the late 1980s, around the same time that the Raging Rooks were learning chess in Harlem, the state of Tennessee launched a bold experiment. At 79 schools—many of which were low income—they randomly assigned over 11,000 students to different classrooms in kindergarten through third grade. The original goal was to test whether smaller classes were better for learning. But an economist named Raj Chetty realized that since both students and teachers were randomly assigned to classrooms, he could go back to the data to analyze whether other features of classrooms made a difference.

Chetty is one of the world's most influential economists. He's the winner of a MacArthur genius grant. And his research suggests that excellence depends less on our natural talents than we might expect.

The Tennessee experiment contained a startling result. Chetty was able to predict the success that students achieved as adults simply by looking at who taught their kindergarten class. By age 25, students who happened to have had more experienced kindergarten teachers were earning significantly more money than their peers.

Having an Experienced Kindergarten Teacher Predicts Higher Adult Income

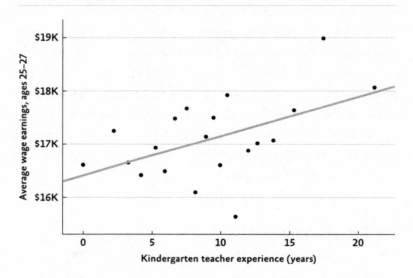

Chetty and his colleagues calculated that moving from an inexperienced kindergarten teacher to an experienced one would add over $1,000 to each student's annual income in their twenties. For a class of 20 students, an above-average kindergarten teacher could be worth additional lifetime income of $320,000.*

---

*For their next study, with over a million children, Chetty and his colleagues found that more experienced teachers added more value, as measured by gains in their students' test scores over the year. Students who had effective teachers between third and eighth grade were more likely to go to college, earned higher salaries, and saved more for retirement. When an effective teacher left their school, the students in that grade the following year suffered: their odds of attending college dropped. Teacher quality was especially important for the future success of women, in part because they reduced the odds of teenage pregnancy. Replacing a teacher in the bottom 5 percent of student gains with an average one would increase the undiscounted lifetime earnings of a classroom by $1.4 million. If you ever need proof that teachers are underpaid, that number might do the trick.

Kindergarten matters in many ways, but I never would have expected teachers to leave such a visible mark on their students' salaries two decades later. Most adults hardly even remember being five years old. Why did kindergarten teachers end up casting such a long shadow?

The intuitive answer is that effective teachers help students develop cognitive skills. Early education builds a solid foundation for understanding numbers and words. Sure enough, students with more experienced teachers scored higher on math and reading tests at the end of kindergarten. But over the next few years, their peers caught up.

To figure out what students were carrying with them from kindergarten into adulthood, Chetty's team turned to another possible explanation. In fourth and eighth grade, the students were rated by their teachers on some other qualities. Here's a sample:

- *Proactive*: How often did they take initiative to ask questions, volunteer answers, seek information from books, and engage the teacher to learn outside class?
- *Prosocial*: How well did they get along and collaborate with peers?
- *Disciplined*: How effectively did they pay attention—and resist the impulse to disrupt the class?
- *Determined*: How consistently did they take on challenging problems, do more than the assigned work, and persist in the face of obstacles?

When students were taught by more experienced kindergarten teachers, their fourth-grade teachers rated them higher on all four of these attributes. So did their eighth-grade teachers. The capacities to be proactive, prosocial, disciplined, and determined stayed with students longer— and ultimately proved more powerful—than early math and reading skills. When Chetty and his colleagues predicted adult income from fourth-grade scores, the ratings on these behaviors mattered 2.4 times as much as math and reading performance on standardized tests.

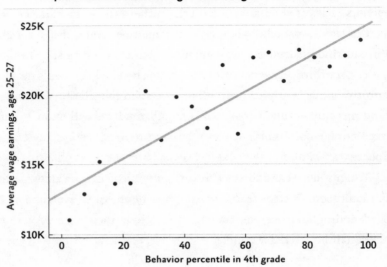

4th Grade Behavior Ratings Predict Higher Adult Income

Think about how surprising that is. If you want to forecast the earning potential of fourth graders, you should pay less attention to their objective math and verbal scores than to their teachers' subjective views of their behavior patterns. And although many people see those behaviors as innate, they were taught in kindergarten. Regardless of where students started, there was something about learning these behaviors that set students up for success decades later.

ACTING OUT OF CHARACTER

When Aristotle wrote about qualities like being disciplined and prosocial, he called them virtues of character. He described character as a set of principles that people acquired and enacted through sheer force of will. I used to see character that way too—I thought it was a matter of committing to a clear moral code. But my job is to test and refine the kinds of ideas that philosophers love to debate. Over the past two decades, the evidence I've gathered has challenged me to rethink that view. I now see character less as a matter of will, and more as a set of skills.

Character is more than just having principles. It's a learned capacity to live by your principles. Character skills equip a chronic procrastinator to meet a deadline for someone who matters deeply to them, a shy introvert to find the courage to speak out against an injustice, and the class bully to circumvent a fistfight with his teammates before a big game. Those are the skills that great kindergarten teachers nurture—and great coaches cultivate.

When Maurice Ashley assembled his chess team for the national championships, a student named Francis Idehen wasn't one of the best eight players. Maurice picked him anyway due to his character skills. "Another kid was a superior chess player," Francis tells me, "but he hadn't developed the emotional self-regulation that Maurice felt was important."

And when the Raging Rooks fell behind in the penultimate round of nationals, Maurice Ashley didn't pull out a book of secret plays. He didn't talk to them about strategy at all. "I reminded them about discipline," he notes—a skill they'd been practicing together for two years.

Their character skills caught the eye of the legendary chess coach Bruce Pandolfini, who had guided multiple protégés to national and world championships. After watching the Raging Rooks march to victory, Pandolfini marveled:

> Nothing fazed them. Most kids under pressure will start hurrying a little bit or showing their feelings, but not them. They took their time, and they were absolutely poker-faced at the board. I've never seen kids that age so cool. They were like professionals.

If a knight on the chess board was a Trojan horse, inside it Maurice had smuggled an army of character skills. They helped the Raging Rooks surge as their opponents floundered. "He was always conveying life lessons without being heavy-handed," Francis says. "It was less about executing a chess plan than understanding of self and mastery of self. That was pivotal in my life."

Maurice had seen the value of character skills in his own life. Growing up, he watched his mother sacrifice everything to move to America while his grandmother stayed behind in Jamaica to raise him and his siblings. When they finally made it to New York a decade later, they knew opportunity wouldn't just come knocking—they'd have to build their own doors.

After stumbling onto a book about chess in his high school library, Maurice decided to join the school team. But he quickly discovered he wasn't good enough. He poured himself into improving and went on to become the captain of his college team. When he got an offer to teach chess in Harlem schools for $50 an hour, he jumped at the invitation.

Today, if you ask anyone in the chess world about Maurice, they'll tell you he's a brilliant strategist. In the middle of a game, if you castle instead of moving your bishop, he can tell you the number of moves it will take him to checkmate you, and whether you'll lose your queen in the process. He's played ten games simultaneously against ten different opponents and won them all—blindfolded. But he believes character matters more than talent.

Sure enough, evidence shows that although kids and novices learn chess faster if they're smarter, intelligence becomes nearly irrelevant in predicting the performance of adults and advanced players. In chess— like in kindergarten—the early advantages of cognitive skills dissipate over time. On average it takes over 20,000 hours of practice to become a chess master and over 30,000 to reach grandmaster. To keep improving, you need the proactivity, discipline, and determination to study old games and new strategies.

Character skills do more than help you perform at your peak—they propel you to higher peaks. As the Nobel laureate economist James Heck-man concluded in a review of the research, character skills "predict and produce success in life." But they don't grow in a vacuum. You need the opportunity and motivation to nurture them.

IF YOU BUILD IT, THEY WILL CLIMB

When people talk about nurture, they're typically referring to the ongoing investment that parents and teachers make in developing and supporting children and students. But helping them reach their full potential requires something different. It's a more focused, more transient form of support that prepares them to direct their own learning and growth. Psychologists call it scaffolding.

In construction, scaffolding is a temporary structure that enables work crews to scale heights beyond their reach. Once the construction is complete, the support is removed. From that point forward, the building stands on its own.

In learning, scaffolding serves a similar purpose. A teacher or coach offers initial instruction and then removes the support. The goal is to shift the responsibility to you so you can develop your own independent approach to learning. That's what Maurice Ashley did for the Raging Rooks. He set up temporary structures to give them the opportunity and motivation to learn.

When he started teaching chess, Maurice saw other instructors line up all the pieces to teach the standard opening moves: king's pawn forward two spaces, followed by knight up one and diagonal one. But he knew learning the rules could be boring, and he didn't want kids to lose interest. So when he first showed up to introduce the game to a group of sixth graders, he did it backward. He put a handful of pieces on the board and began at the endgame. He taught his students different ways to checkmate their opponents. That structure was their first bit of scaffolding.

It's often said that where there's a will, there's a way. What we overlook is that when people can't see a path, they stop dreaming of the destination. To ignite their will, we need to show them the way. That's what scaffolding can do.

By teaching the game in reverse, Maurice lit a fire of determination. Once students knew how to corner a king, they had a route to victory. Once they had a way to win, they had a will to learn. "You don't tell kids, 'Well, you're going to learn patience and determination and fortitude,' 'cause they'll fall asleep right away." He laughs. "You say this: 'This game is fun. Let's go—I'm gonna beat you'. . . . stir their spirit, their competitive fire. They sit down, they start learning the game, and as they become hooked, and they lose a game, they want to win." It wasn't long before Kasaun Henry would lie in bed at night, imagine 64 squares on his ceiling, and play out entire matches in his mind.

Maurice also introduced scaffolding for the players to support one another's development. He taught them creative ways to share techniques: they drew cartoons about chess moves, wrote science fiction stories about chess matches, and recorded rap songs about commanding the center of the board. They were learning to treat a solitary game as a prosocial exercise in teamwork. When a player cried at nationals, it wasn't because he lost; he was devastated that he had let his teammates down.

As they gelled into a team, the players started taking the motivation and opportunity to learn into their own hands. They held one another accountable for recording every move of their games on score sheets so the whole group could learn from individual mistakes. They weren't worried about being the smartest player in the room—they were aiming to make the room smarter.

The previous year, at their first nationals, the Raging Rooks had finished in the top 10 percent despite being short on players due to budget constraints. When Maurice set a goal for them to win the following year, it was the players who took the initiative to plan. Now that they had the skill, they had the will. They created their own makeshift chess camp, spending the summer practicing and reading books. They cajoled Maurice into dedicating his summer off to their training. They had moved into the driver's seat.

In an ideal world, students wouldn't have to rely on one coach for these opportunities. The scaffolding Maurice created was a substitute for a broken system.* One parent told him that when she saw her son play chess, she realized she hadn't believed in him. Maurice wasn't just helping his players reach their potential—he was helping their parents and teachers recognize it too.

———

Few of us are lucky enough to have a coach like Maurice Ashley. We don't always have access to the ideal mentors, and our parents and teachers aren't always equipped to provide the right scaffolding. My aim is for this book to be that scaffolding.

Hidden Potential is divided into three sections. The first section explores the specific character skills that catapult us to greater heights. You'll learn about them from a professional boxer who taught himself the trade of architecture, a woman who escaped poverty by becoming a human sponge, and a pair of people who struggled in a particular subject in school but now rank among the world's best.

The second section is about creating structures to sustain motivation. Even with strong character skills, no one is immune to burnout, doubt, or stagnation. But making significant gains doesn't require you to be a workaholic, and it doesn't have to push you to the edge of exhaustion. To shed light on the scaffolding for maintaining momentum, I'll introduce you to a musician who built a temporary structure to overcome a perma- nent disability, a trainer who helped to turn an underwhelming athlete into a star, and an unheralded class of military officer candidates who

---

* Empirically, character skills matter more for individuals from disadvantaged backgrounds. As Mau- rice put it, "Structural and cultural oppression amplify the need for the skills learned through char- acter building. You've got to be strong when the proverbial knee has been on your neck for generations."

proved everyone wrong. You'll find out why practice is incomplete without play, going in circles may be the best way to move forward, and bootstraps aren't meant to be pulled alone.

The third section focuses on building systems to expand opportunity. The very doors that societies are supposed to open to people with great potential are often wrongly closed to those who have faced the greatest obstacles. For every longshot who breaks through after being underrated or overlooked, there are thousands who never get a chance. You'll learn how to design schools, teams, and institutions that nurture potential instead of squandering it. Through a visit to a tiny country that built one of the world's most successful education systems, you'll see how we can help every child get ahead. Studying one of the most miraculous rescues in human history will reveal what it takes to make groups more than the sum of their parts. And to figure out how we can fix broken selection processes, I'll take you behind the curtain of NASA's astronaut selection process and of Ivy League admissions. By changing systems that prematurely write people off, it's possible to improve the odds for underdogs and late bloomers.

I care about unlocking hidden potential because I've lived it. My most meaningful accomplishments have come in areas where I started with serious shortages of talent. Thanks to stellar coaches, I went from being the worst diver in my school to ranking among the best in the country—and from bombing in small lectures to a standing ovation on the TED stage. If I had judged my potential by my early failures, I would have given up. What I learned along the way helped me create my own scaffolding for future leaps. It left me determined to demystify how we surpass our supposed limits.

As a social scientist, I started with the data: randomized experiments, longitudinal studies, and meta-analyses (studies of studies) that quantify cumulative results. Only then did I turn to my personal reflections and search for stories to bring the research to life. I met people who progressed far beyond their starting points and uncovered their hidden potential in a wide range of settings—from underwater and underground to mountaintops and outer space. My hope was to learn how they traveled great distances by transforming themselves or others—and sometimes the world around them.

That's what the Raging Rooks did. Their success played a role in changing the face of chess. Coaches estimate that since they burst onto the scene, the proportion of racial minorities at national tournaments has quadrupled. Maurice has become an international spokesman for chess as a vehicle for building character, and the movement he helped to fuel now features chess programs in low-income schools across America. One chess nonprofit has single-handedly taught more than half a million kids.

There's no reason to believe the magic is limited to chess. If debate happened to be Maurice's passion, he'd be guiding students to anticipate counterarguments and help one another refine rebuttals. What makes a difference is not the activity but the lessons you learn. As Maurice says, "The achievement is in the growing."

Thanks to the opportunity and motivation that Maurice set in motion, the Raging Rooks applied their character skills beyond chess. The discipline they exercised to resist the pull of shortsighted moves came in handy for resisting gangs and drugs. The determination and proactivity they marshaled to memorize patterns and anticipate moves also applied to studying for tests. The prosocial skills they developed practicing together and critiquing each other helped them become great collaborators and mentors themselves.

Most of the players managed to rise above their circumstances. Jonathan Nock came from a rough neighborhood where he was mugged on a basketball court during the winning season; he's now a software engineer and the founder of a cloud solutions company. Francis Idehen had dodged stabbings and shootings on his walk to school; he landed an economics degree from Yale, an MBA from Harvard, and jobs as the treasurer of America's largest utility company and COO of an investment firm. Kasaun Henry went from being homeless and being recruited by a gangster to earning three master's degrees and becoming an award-winning filmmaker and composer. "Chess developed my character," Kasaun reflects. "Chess increased my concentration and focus. . . . Chess ignited me. Someone lit a star that will keep burning as long as I live."

Along with building successful careers, chess encouraged the Raging Rooks to create opportunities for others. Growing up around the corner from four crack houses, Charu Robinson had multiple friends who were murdered and a number who went to jail. After beating one of Dalton's best players at nationals in 1991, Charu won a full scholarship to Dalton. He ended up earning a criminology degree and becoming a teacher. He wanted to pay forward what he'd learned.

In 1994, the principal of another Harlem middle school three blocks away from JHS 43 begged Maurice to coach their Dark Knights. Over the next two years, their teams of boys and girls won back-to-back national championships. By then Maurice was ready for the next step on his mission to make history. He took a break from coaching to work on his own game. In 1999, Maurice became the first African American chess grandmaster ever.

That year, with a new coach, the Dark Knights won their third national title. Their assistant coach was Charu Robinson—who went on to teach chess to countless children in schools throughout the city. The Raging Rooks weren't just single roses growing from cracks in the concrete. They tilled the soil for many more roses to bloom.

When we admire great thinkers, doers, and leaders, we often focus narrowly on their performance. That leads us to elevate the people who have accomplished the most and overlook the ones who have achieved the most with the least. The true measure of your potential is not the height of the peak you've reached, but how far you've climbed to get there.

PART I

Skills of Character

Getting Better at Getting Better

n the late 1800s, the founding father of psychology made a bold claim. "By the age of thirty," William James wrote, "character has set like plaster and will never soften again." Kids could develop character, but adults were out of luck.

Recently a team of social scientists launched an experiment to test that hypothesis. They recruited 1,500 entrepreneurs in West Africa—a mix of women and men in their 30s, 40s, and 50s—who were running small startups in manufacturing, service, and commerce. They randomly assigned the founders to one of three groups. One was a control group: they went about their business as usual. The other two were training groups: they spent a week learning new concepts, analyzing them in case studies of other entrepreneurs, and applying them to their own startups through role-play and reflection exercises. What differed was whether the training focused on cognitive skills or character skills.

In cognitive skills training, the founders took an accredited business course created by the International Finance Corporation. They studied finance, accounting, HR, marketing, and pricing, and practiced using what they learned to solve challenges and seize opportunities. In character skills training, the founders attended a class designed by psychologists to teach personal initiative. They studied proactivity, discipline, and determination, and practiced putting those qualities into action.

Character skills training had a dramatic impact. After founders had spent merely five days working on these skills, their firms' profits grew by an average of 30 percent over the next two years. That was nearly triple the benefit of training in cognitive skills. Finance and marketing knowledge might have equipped founders to capitalize on opportunities, but studying proactivity and discipline enabled them to generate opportunities. They learned to anticipate market changes rather than react to them. They developed more creative ideas and introduced more new products. When they encountered financial obstacles, instead of giving up, they were more resilient and resourceful in seeking loans.

Along with demonstrating that character skills can propel us to achieve greater things, this evidence reveals that it's never too late to build them. William James was a very wise man, but in this case he was very wrong. Character doesn't set like plaster—it retains its plasticity.

Character is often confused with personality, but they're not the same. Personality is your predisposition—your basic instincts for how to think, feel, and act. Character is your capacity to prioritize your values over your instincts.

Knowing your principles doesn't necessarily mean you know how to practice them, particularly under stress or pressure. It's easy to be proactive and determined when things are going well. The true test of character is whether you manage to stand by those values when the deck is stacked against you. If personality is how you respond on a typical day, character is how you show up on a hard day.

Personality is not your destiny—it's your tendency. Character skills enable you to transcend that tendency to be true to your principles. It's not about the traits you have—it's what you decide to do with them. Wherever you are today, there's no reason why you can't grow your character skills starting now.

HOW TO GET BETTER AT SOMETHING

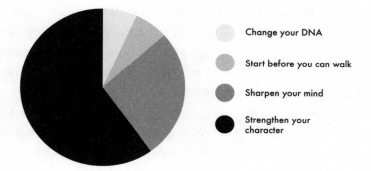

Change your DNA

Start before you can walk

Sharpen your mind

Strengthen your character

For too long, character skills like proactivity and determination have been dismissed as "soft skills." The term can be traced back to the late 1960s, when psychologists were tasked with expanding U.S. Army training beyond a narrow focus on operating tanks and guns. Recognizing the importance of human skills, they introduced a broader emphasis on the leadership and teamwork capabilities that enabled groups to become more than the sum of their parts and troops to come home safe and sound. They needed labels to describe the two sets of skills, and that's when they made an unfortunate decision.

The psychologists called the tank and gun skills "hard skills" because they involved working with weapons made from steel and aluminum. "Soft skills" were the "important job-related skills that involve little or no interaction with machines." These were actually the social, emotional, and behavioral skills that soldiers needed to succeed in any role; they were only called "soft" because they didn't apply to working with metal. *By this definition, even finance is a soft skill.* A few years later, the psychologists recommended discontinuing the term: calling a skill soft made it sound weak, and soldiers wanted to be strong. They didn't realize character skills might be their greatest source of strength.

If our cognitive skills are what separate us from animals, our character skills are what elevate us above machines. Computers and robots can now build cars, fly planes, fight wars, manage money, represent defendants in court, diagnose cancer, and perform cardiac surgery. As more and more cognitive skills get automated, we're in the midst of a character revolution. With technological advances placing a premium on interactions and relationships, the skills that make us human are increasingly important to master.

When we say success and happiness are our most important goals in life, I'm curious about why character isn't higher on the list. What if we all invested as much time in our character skills as we do in our career skills? Imagine what America would look like if the Declaration of Independence granted every citizen the right to life, liberty, and the pursuit of character.

After studying the character skills that unleash hidden potential, I've identified specific forms of proactivity, determination, and discipline that matter. Traveling great distances requires the courage to seek out the right kinds of discomfort, the capacity to absorb the right information, and the will to accept the right imperfections.

CHAPTER 1

Creatures of Discomfort

Embracing the Unbearable
Awkwardness of Learning

Character cannot be developed in ease and quiet. Only through
experiences of trial and suffering can the soul be strengthened,
vision cleared, ambition inspired, and success achieved.

—HELEN KELLER

When she first developed her superpower, Sara Maria Hasbun
didn't know anyone else who shared it. Then she stumbled
across a whole community of strangers who made her feel
less alone. In 2018, she started traveling around the world to meet them.
On the surface, they had little in common. They all hailed from different
countries and held different day jobs. But they bonded around a mission
as uncommon as their aptitude.

As Sara Maria made her way into her new community, she took on
a challenge. She would introduce herself to people as an entrepreneur
from California in a language that matched her setting. In Bratislava, she
said hello in Slovak: *Ahoj, volám sa Sara Maria!* In Fukuoka, she addressed
people in Japanese: *Konnichiwa! Watashi no namae wa Sara Maria desu!*
When she was stranded in China during the pandemic, she volunteered
with the deaf community in Beijing and greeted people in Chinese Sign
Language.

It might sound like a parlor trick, but Sara Maria's understanding went far beyond basic introductions. On one trip she hit it off with an Irish engineer named Benny Lewis. Over the course of an hour, they were able to dialogue in Mandarin, Spanish, French, English, and American Sign Language.

Sara Maria and Benny are polyglots: people who can talk—and think—in many languages. She can speak five languages fluently and four more conversationally; he's achieved fluency in six languages and intermediate proficiency in four others. When they cross paths at an annual polyglot gathering, if they want to go beyond the five languages they share, they don't have to look far. Sara Maria usually bumps into someone who can shoot the breeze with her in Korean and Indonesian and help her dust off her rudimentary Cantonese, Malay, or Thai (she has less luck finding a partner to refresh her Nicaraguan Sign Language). It's only a matter of time before Benny finds a friend who can yak with him in German, Irish, Esperanto, Dutch, Italian, Portuguese, or, yes, Klingon.

What's impressive about these polyglots is not just how much they know—it's how fast they learn. In less than a decade, Sara Maria learned six new languages from scratch. Meanwhile, it took Benny just a couple months of living in the Czech Republic to speak passable Czech, three months in Hungary to become conversational in Hungarian, another three months to pick up Egyptian Arabic (while living in Brazil), and five months in China to communicate at an intermediate level and conduct an hour-long discussion entirely in Mandarin.

I've always assumed polyglots were freaks of nature. They're born with an extraordinary ability that manifests when they have the opportunity to absorb a new foreign language. One of my college roommates belonged to that breed—he spoke six languages and often used his linguistic prowess to invent new idioms. *My personal favorite, for whenever someone dumps their baggage on you: "Stop suitcasing on me."* I marveled at how rapidly he mastered new tongues and how fluidly he switched between them.

When I came across Sara Maria and Benny, I figured they were wired the same way. I could not have been more wrong.

Growing up, Benny was convinced that he lacked the aptitude to even become bilingual. In school, he took eleven years of Irish and five of German, but couldn't hold a conversation in either tongue. After college, he moved to Spain, but six months later he still couldn't speak Spanish. By the time he turned twenty-one, English was still the only language he spoke fluently, and he was ready to give up: "I kept telling myself that I didn't have the language gene."

Sara Maria also had a rough start. Despite studying Spanish for six years, she remained monolingual. She was certain that she missed the critical window for language acquisition. Although her father was from El Salvador, she didn't get much exposure to Spanish early on because he spoke excellent English:

> That's the language we used at home. When I started learning Spanish in high school I was really stunned at how difficult it was for me. . . . It's supposed to be one of the easiest languages for English speakers to learn . . . but I really struggled with it. Even my high school teachers were flustered at my inability to learn it. . . . People came up to me all the time speaking Spanish and it really broke my heart that I couldn't respond to them. . . . Why couldn't I learn this language when so many people around me seemed to be learning other languages so effortlessly?

After years of bringing her homework to her father for help, he gently told her she was never going to be able to speak Spanish, but she didn't need it in America anyway. She might as well move on and spend her time on something she did well.

Many people wish they could learn a new language, but believe the distance is too great to travel. Some, like Benny, conclude that they simply lack the natural ability. Others, like Sara Maria, believe they missed the opportunity—if only they had started learning as toddlers, they might have picked it up. But according to a growing body of evidence, the decline in the rate of language learning around age 18 is not a feature of our biology. It's a bug in our education.

Polyglots prove that it's possible to master new languages well into adulthood. As soon as I came across Sara Maria and Benny online, I knew I had to get to the bottom of their methods, because they're professional learners. I was surprised to discover that when they finally picked up their first foreign tongue, it wasn't due to overcoming a cognitive block. It was because they cleared a motivational hurdle: they got comfortable being uncomfortable.

Becoming a creature of discomfort can unlock hidden potential in many different types of learning. Summoning the nerve to face discomfort is a character skill—an especially important form of determination. It takes three kinds of courage: to abandon your tried-and-true methods, to put yourself in the ring before you feel ready, and to make more mistakes than others make attempts. The best way to accelerate growth is to embrace, seek, and amplify discomfort.

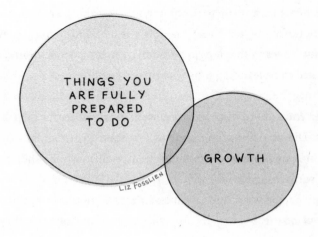

GOING OUT OF STYLE

There's a popular practice in schools that has dissuaded many learners from seeking discomfort. It arose as a well-intentioned solution to a pervasive problem in the American education system. For decades, many schools were run like assembly lines in a factory. Students were treated as interchangeable parts in the mass production of young minds. Despite having different strengths, they were stuck absorbing uniform knowledge through the same standardized lessons and lectures.

In the 1970s, a new wave of thinking upended the world of education. The core premise was that when students struggled, it was because the method of instruction wasn't tailored to their learning style—the cognitive mode in which they were best at acquiring and retaining information. To grasp new concepts, verbal learners needed to read and write them; visual learners needed to see them illustrated in images, diagrams, and charts; auditory learners needed to hear them out loud; and kinesthetic learners needed to experience them through acting them out with body movements.

The theory of learning styles exploded in popularity. Parents were thrilled that their children were being recognized for their individuality. Teachers loved having the freedom to vary their methods and personalize their material.

Today, learning styles are a foundational element of teacher training and student experience. Around the world, 89 percent of teachers believe in matching their instruction to students' learning styles. Many students have told me they prefer podcasts to books because they're auditory learners. Did you decide to read this book with your eyes because you identify as a verbal or visual learner?

There's just one small problem with learning styles. They're a myth.

When a team of experts conducted a comprehensive review of several decades of research on learning styles, they found an alarming lack of support for the theory. In controlled experiments with specific lessons and longitudinal studies over the course of a semester, students and adults didn't do any better on tests when their teachers or study habits aligned with their abilities or their preferences. "There is no adequate evidence base to justify incorporating learning styles assessments into general educational practice," the researchers conclude. "The contrast between the enormous popularity of the learning-styles approach within education and the lack of credible evidence for its utility is . . . striking and disturbing."

We don't want to go back to the rigid factory model of learning. But people shouldn't be pigeonholed in a rigid learning style either. Of course, you might still have a preferred style of acquiring new knowledge and skills. What we now know is that your preference isn't fixed, and playing only to your strengths deprives you of the opportunity to improve on your weaknesses.

The way you like to learn is what makes you comfortable, but it isn't necessarily how you learn best. Sometimes you even learn better in the mode that makes you the most uncomfortable, because you have to work harder at it. This is the first form of courage: being brave enough to embrace discomfort and throw your learning style out the window.

One of the best examples I've seen is in comedy. When Steve Martin first started doing stand-up performances in the 1960s, he bombed over and over. During one show a heckler actually stood up and threw a glass of red wine at him. "I was not naturally talented," Steve reflects. His early critics agreed: one wrote that he was "the most serious booking error in the history of Los Angeles."

If you think about how great performers master their craft, it seems natural that they would learn through listening, watching, and doing. That's what Steve did: he would listen to other people's material, watch their mannerisms, mix in some of his own stories, and practice delivering the concoction. Despite pouring countless hours into preparing for them, his performances were lackluster. One night he went five minutes without a single laugh . . . and another five minutes . . . and another. As he sweated onstage, there wasn't even a chuckle for twenty straight minutes. Watching, listening, and doing weren't enough to drive his growth.

The one approach to comedy that Steve had written off was writing—it wasn't his style. He hated writing, because it didn't come naturally to him: "It was hard, so hard."

If you feel that way about writing too, you're not alone. Even some of the best writers I know will do almost anything to put off writing.* Procrastination is a common problem whenever you're pushing yourself beyond your comfort zone. As blogger Tim Urban describes it, your brain gets hijacked by an instant gratification monkey, who picks what's easy and fun over the hard work that needs to be done. All you have to show for your time is a profound sense of inadequacy and idleness. You've burned your self-esteem to ashes of shame.

Many people associate procrastination with laziness. But psychologists find that procrastination is not a time management problem—it's an emotion management problem. When you procrastinate, you're not avoiding effort. You're avoiding the unpleasant feelings that the activity stirs up. Sooner or later, though, you realize that you're also avoiding getting where you want to go.

For a while, Steve Martin procrastinated on writing his own jokes. Why would he sit down alone to do something he hated when it was

---

* If writing isn't your preferred mode of learning, the greatest discomfort of putting your thoughts on a page is probably writer's block. As Steve Martin joked, "Writer's block is a fancy term made up by whiners so they can have an excuse to drink alcohol." There's a reason we don't talk about dancer's block or carpenter's block. Writer's block is actually a thinking block: you're stuck because you haven't figured out what to say. Some novelists get in the groove by typing sentences from fiction they've loved. I get my ideas churning by answering a few emails: it's like a warm-up to give me momentum. If writing becomes a regular routine, eventually words start to flow as fluidly on the page as they do out of your mouth. Psychologists have found that when people were randomly assigned to schedule daily writing sessions, their output quadrupled—and even scheduling 15 minutes a day was enough to make progress. And now we have artificial intelligence (AI) chatbots to help. In preliminary experiments, randomly assigning professionals to use tools like ChatGPT and Bing boosts both the quality and quantity of their writing—especially for poor writers—by shifting effort from rough drafting to idea generating and editing. *For the record, I didn't write a word of this book using AI. Though that's probably what an AI would tell you.*

so much more fun to borrow other people's material and improvise onstage? His instant gratification monkey was in the driver's seat. But after a few years of struggling at stand-up, he recounts, he had a "horrible revelation that if I was going to be successful as a comedian, I'd have to write everything myself."

Steve worked up the nerve to venture beyond his comfort zone. He would learn to write jokes. When he heard that a variety show was looking for young writers, he submitted some material, but it didn't make the cut. "I didn't know how to write," Steve told me. The head writer took a chance on him anyway—he'd seen Steve play the banjo, found him quirky, and paid him out of his own salary. When Steve was asked to write an intro for a bit, he froze. His writer's block was so bad that after failing to type a single word, he called his roommate to borrow a joke. It was good enough that they hired him.

For the next few years, Steve wrote for TV by day and did stand-up by night. Writing was a slog, but he was becoming more comfortable with it. Meanwhile, he kept crashing and burning onstage. His agent told him, "Stick to writing."

What his agent didn't know was that Steve was growing as a performer through writing. Onstage, speaking off-the-cuff made it easy to ramble. On paper, writing forced him to trim the fat. The painful process of jotting down his material taught him to strip his humor down to the basic elements, "because it's all about the bare bones of something," he said. "The way a joke's structured, it can't be too elaborate." It wasn't until he embraced the discomfort of writing that he honed his ability to develop killer punch lines like this one:

I handed in a script last year and the studio didn't change one word. The word they didn't change was on page 87.

By the mid-1970s, Steve was one of the most popular stand-up comedians in America. He was selling out huge arenas on national tours, hitting platinum with a comedy album, and doing stand-up on *Saturday Night Live*. Along the way, he grew to love writing, and it also opened the door to his acting career—if not for his newfound writing skills, he would never have written and starred in his breakout movie, *The Jerk*.

I've seen many people shy away from writing because it doesn't come naturally to them. What they overlook is that writing is more than a vehicle for communicating—it's a tool for learning. Writing exposes gaps in your knowledge and logic. It pushes you to articulate assumptions and consider counterarguments. Unclear writing is a sign of unclear thinking. Or as Steve himself quipped, "Some people have a way with words, and other people, uh . . . oh, not have a way."

The lesson is not that everyone who hates writing should do it any-way. It's that if we avoid the discomfort of learning techniques that don't come easily to us, we limit our own growth. In the words of the great psychologist Ted Lasso, "If you're comfortable, you're doin' it wrong." That was the discovery that launched our polyglots into language learning.

GETTING IN THE ARENA

Fans of learning styles would have us believe that verbal learning is good for one person and auditory learning is good for another person. But learning is not always about finding the right method for you. It's often about finding the right method for the task.

A fascinating demonstration comes from an experiment where students were given just over 20 minutes to go through a science article. Half were randomly assigned to read it; the other half listened to it. The listeners enjoyed the lesson more than the readers, but when they were quizzed two days later, it was clear that they had learned less. The listeners scored 59 percent; the readers scored 81 percent.

Although listening is often more fun, reading improves comprehension and recall. Whereas listening promotes intuitive thinking, reading activates more analytical processing. It's true in English and Chinese—people display better logical reasoning when the same trivia questions, riddles, and puzzles are written rather than spoken. With print, you naturally slow down at the start of a paragraph to process the core idea and use paragraph breaks and headers to chunk information. Unless you have a reading disability or learning disorder that makes it difficult to parse text, when it comes to critical thinking, there's no substitute for reading.*

Learning a foreign language requires a different approach. In school, Sara Maria Hasbun learned vocabulary and grammar by reading textbooks and making endless stacks of index cards. Her classes didn't require much speaking, and she didn't feel ready to talk until she had committed a great deal of vocabulary to memory. She was afraid of sounding stupid, so she avoided the discomfort altogether and stuck to English.

In college, Sara Maria ended up majoring in linguistics. She realized that her approach was similar to reading a bunch of books about piano or figure skating, and then expecting to be able to play concertos like Clara Schumann or do a triple axel like Kristi Yamaguchi. But no matter how hard you concentrate, you can't see a Castilian accent with your eyes, visualize a diagram of it in your mind, or internalize it through an interpretive dance. If you want to understand it, you have to listen to it with your ears. If you want to speak it, you have to practice saying the words out loud.

Sure enough, in meta-analyses of dozens of experiments, students and adults were more adept at understanding and speaking a new language

---

* If you're aiming to improve your social and emotional intelligence, you're probably better off paying attention to audio than visual cues. Research reveals that if you can hear the voice of a friend or stranger, closing your eyes doesn't make you any less accurate in reading their emotions. We're constantly misreading facial expressions and misinterpreting body language. The tone of voice is a more accurate, purer signal of what people are feeling. The trouble you have reading emotions in text messages is because you can't hear their tone, not because you can't see their face. The same is true of lie detection: if you want to figure out whether a criminal suspect is telling you the truth, verbal clues are more reliable than nonverbal signals. When they smile, it doesn't necessarily mean they're trustworthy—they may be feeling duping delight, the rush of getting away with a lie. The real red flags to listen for include a shaky voice, a rise in pitch, and inconsistencies in stories.

over time when they had been taught to produce it rather than only to comprehend it. They also learned better in "flipped classrooms" that challenged them to study vocabulary before class and then practice communicating during class. The popular adage "use it or lose it" doesn't go far enough. If you don't use it, you might never gain it in the first place.

It's not enough to simply accept minimal discomfort when it arises. Surprisingly, we're better off actively seeking out discomfort. Sara Maria did that by moving to Madrid for a job teaching English and deliberately choosing to live with a family that only spoke Spanish. By the end of the summer, she was speaking fluently. She realized that if she could keep getting comfortable being uncomfortable, she could learn any language.

As I talked with Sara Maria about her breakthrough, a light bulb went off for me. Comfort in learning is a paradox. You can't become truly comfortable with a skill until you've practiced it enough to master it. But practicing it *before* you master it is uncomfortable, so you often avoid it. Accelerating learning requires a second form of courage: being brave enough to use your knowledge as you acquire it.

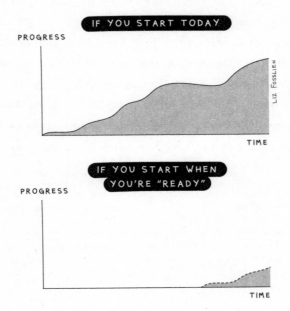

DELIBERATELY AWKWARD

In a clever experiment, psychologists Kaitlin Woolley and Ayelet Fishbach studied hundreds of people taking improv comedy classes and randomly assigned them to focus on different goals. The ones who persisted the longest—and took the most creative risks—weren't the ones who were encouraged to focus on learning. They were the ones who had been advised to intentionally pursue discomfort. "Your goal is to feel awkward and uncomfortable . . . it's a sign the exercise is working," the instructions said. Once people saw discomfort as a mark of growth, they were motivated to stretch beyond their comfort zones.

It worked for political rivals too. We usually try to motivate Democrats and Republicans to escape their echo chambers by urging them to seek new information. But in the research, if partisans were nudged to seek discomfort instead, they were more likely to download articles from across the aisle.* When discomfort is a signal of progress, you don't want to run away from it. You want to keep stumbling toward it to continue growing.

Seven months before her wedding, Sara Maria decided to surprise her husband and his family by giving her wedding toast in their native tongue of Cantonese. The thought was terrifying—and that made it exciting. She wrote a draft in English and enlisted a tutor to translate it into Cantonese and record it for her. Then she treated the recording of the toast like a song on a playlist. She listened to it on repeat until she

---

*Getting comfortable with discomfort is vital for groups too. In a series of experiments led by management scholar Kathy Phillips, people in racially diverse groups generated more creative solutions to problems and made wiser decisions than those in racially similar groups. Despite doing better, they thought they did worse—diversity made them uncomfortable. Ironically, that discomfort was one of the engines of their success: it pushed them to think more systematically, prepare more thoroughly, explain themselves more clearly, and listen more carefully. As Kathy and her colleagues concluded, embracing discomfort can help people "convert affective pains into cognitive gains."

knew it by heart. She recited it on her way to the grocery store, hiding it from her husband to keep him in the dark.

Knowing her in-laws would test her after the toast, she started doing what she calls "spamming your brain." She listened to podcasts in Cantonese and watched Cantonese-language movies. She practiced talking daily in secret lessons with a Cantonese tutor, embracing the pain of introducing herself with the wrong words and the embarrassment of reciting her monologue with the wrong tones. She had nightmares about choking and stumbling, but she reminded herself that feeling awkward and making mistakes was a sign of learning. She delivered the wedding toast beautifully, pronouncing nine different tones correctly. Afterward, she joked with her husband's grandmother, who spoke only Cantonese, and her in-laws told her how much it meant to them that she took the time to honor their culture by learning their language.

You don't have to wait until you've acquired an entire library of knowledge to start to communicate. Your mental library expands as you communicate. When I asked Sara Maria what it takes to begin, she said she no longer waits to talk until she has a basic level of proficiency. She starts talking on the first day, discomfort be damned. "I'm always trying to convince people to start speaking," she tells me. "Just memorize a few sentences—a short monologue introducing yourself and explaining why you're learning the language."

That advice was life-changing for Benny Lewis. During his time in Spain, he bought *The Lord of the Rings* in Spanish and sat down with a dictionary to translate a story he loved. It took him a week to finish the first page. *One down, 700 to go.* After six months of failing to learn Spanish, he realized he'd tried everything except actually speaking the language. That took a third form of courage—not just embracing and seeking discomfort, but amplifying it by being brave enough to make more mistakes.

BITING YOUR TONGUE

I once traveled to Costa Rica with a cousin. When we walked into a restaurant after a long hike, he mentioned that the fresh-squeezed orange juice looked delicious. When he placed his order in Spanish, the server burst out laughing. Instead of *jugo de naranja*, he'd asked for *fruto de periódico*. He'd tried to order a glass of newspaper fruit.

When you've tried to use a new language for the first time, you've probably felt a pang of anxiety. If you fumble with a foreign word, you'll embarrass yourself. If you commit a faux pas, you might offend others. My wife, Allison, studied Japanese in high school, and the final exam included a class trip to a restaurant to order in Japanese. She had so much anxiety about making mistakes and failing the test that she pretended to be sick. That's where courage comes in: to get practice speaking a language, you need to be brave enough to make many mistakes. The more, the better.

Sara Maria thinks this is one of the reasons why kids tend to absorb foreign languages faster than adults. Yes, they benefit from greater brain plasticity (the developing mind rewires more quickly than the developed one) and less interference from prior knowledge (they're not entrenched in the grammatical rules of one language). But they're also largely immune to the fear of embarrassment and the discomfort of making mistakes. Children don't hold back on communicating—they start babbling as soon as they know some new words. They're not scared of feeling stupid or being judged. They love newspaper fruit.

The thought of making mistakes is especially distressing if you're shy. Shyness is the fear of negative evaluation in social situations, and Benny Lewis felt it intensely. As a socially awkward teenager at parties, he'd head for a corner and play games on his phone. In language classes, he wouldn't raise his hand to participate. When he moved to Spain, he steered clear of his fear by gravitating to people who spoke English.

When therapists treat phobias, they use two different kinds of exposure therapy: systematic desensitization and flooding. Systematic desensitization starts out with a microdose of the threat and gradually amps it up over time. If you're afraid of spiders, you draw a picture of one and then see one in a closed cage across the room. Before you get up close and personal with the daddy longlegs in your bathtub, you learn to manage your fear in less threatening situations. Flooding is the opposite: a therapist might just drop a creepy-crawly on your arm. Sure, you might freak out, but having survived the ordeal unscathed, your visceral terror melts away.

Exposure therapy reduces discomfort by amplifying it. An extreme example happens with pilots learning to fly, where there are few situations more frightening than an aircraft stalling. Stalling is when a plane starts hurtling toward the ground—usually when a pilot makes the mistake of flying too slowly or too steeply. Stalls are responsible for 15 percent of fatal commercial airline accidents and nearly a quarter of private fatal crashes. Many pilots have nightmares about their planes falling out of the sky.

If you start training to be a pilot, you'll first go through systematic desensitization in a flight simulator. The simulator can familiarize you with the mechanics and sensory input of a stall—what to do with your hands, what the horizon looks like as you begin to fall. But when you're in the real cockpit, there will come a moment when your flight instructor gives you a terrifying instruction. Slow your speed and pull back on the controls to raise the nose until the plane stalls.

This is the part you can experience only through full-on flooding. Your amygdala doesn't care how many times you've run the flight simulator or that you're several thousand feet in the air with plenty of time to course-correct. You're trapped in a huge, heavy metal cage, tumbling fast toward the earth in an uncontrolled nosedive. And there's nothing that can prepare a human being for the pure horror of deliberately causing an aircraft to drop like a rock.

If you want to get a pilot's license in America, you have to demonstrate that you can maneuver out of a stall and land your plane safely. Effective training programs are intentionally designed to introduce new and unexpected threats. Evidence suggests that this element of surprise is critical: if stall training becomes a predictable routine, it no longer prepares pilots for real-life emergencies. You can't be ready for anything if you haven't trained for everything. Pilots learn to cope with discomfort by intensifying it, and they build their skills as they navigate it.

Amplifying discomfort was pivotal for Benny Lewis to learn new languages. To overcome his shyness, Benny started out with systematic desensitization: he put himself in mildly uncomfortable situations. He motivated strangers to approach him by wearing a leprechaun hat on the streets and showing up at concerts with a laser pointer that had a disco filter for dancing. He got used to initiating interactions by handing out earplugs at loud events and clinking glasses with people at bars. After another six months in Spain, he was speaking solid Spanish and relocating to Italy to learn his next language. It was only a matter of time before he became a professional language hacker. His purpose was to become conversational in new languages in a matter of months to communicate with strangers—and teach others to do the same. And that led him to flooding.

Benny calls it social skydiving. When he arrives in a new country, he commits to approaching anyone who's near him for more than five seconds. Instead of leading with small talk, he takes a bigger leap to elicit a more meaningful response.* When he crossed paths with someone from Valencia, where he lived in Spain, he burst out into a local song. When he checked in at a hostel in Brazil, he told the receptionist about his experience being overworked and underpaid as a receptionist in Rome. "One of the biggest mistakes I see language learners make is believing that studying languages is about acquiring knowledge," Benny notes. "It's not! Learning a new language is about building a communication skill."

Learning is often understood as the process of recognizing, correcting, and preventing mistakes. But Benny believes that if you want to become proficient in a language, rather than aiming to reduce your mistakes, you should strive to increase them. It turns out that he's right. Many experiments have shown that when students are learning new information, if they're randomly assigned to guess wrong before being given the right answer, they're less likely to make errors later on tests. When we're encouraged to make mistakes, we end up making fewer of them. Early mistakes help us remember the correct answer—and motivate us to keep learning.

---

*Although we often stick to small talk to avoid awkwardness, deep talk is surprisingly enjoyable. Across seven studies, people felt happier, more connected, and less uncomfortable in deep conversations with strangers than they expected. When I took a bus from Boston to Mexico after years of letting my Spanish skills collect dust, I had more delightful conversations—and got much better practice—when I shifted from *Qué haces?* to *Qué te encanta hacer?* Instead of asking what they do, I was asking what they love to do.

MAKING MORE MISTAKES

THEORY

REALITY

Looking stupid

Feeling shame

Being laughed at

Experiencing discomfort

Getting smarter

Gaining courage

Laughing at yourself

Expanding your comfort zone

When Benny is ready to start learning a new language, he sets an ambitious goal: to make at least 200 mistakes a day. He measures his progress by the number of errors he makes. "The more mistakes you make, the faster you will improve and the less they will bother you," he observes. "The best cure to feeling uncomfortable about making mistakes is to *make more mistakes.*"

Along the way, Benny has put himself in some awkward positions. He's introduced himself with the wrong gender, said he was attracted to a bus, and accidentally complimented someone for having a nice arse. But he doesn't beat himself up, because his goal is to make mistakes. Even when he fumbles, people generally commend him for making an effort. And that motivates him to keep trying.

Psychologists call that cycle learned industriousness. When you get praised for making an effort, the feeling of effort itself starts to take on secondary reward properties. Instead of having to push yourself to keep trying, you feel pulled toward it.

The idea of speaking from day one has changed how I think about learning. You can code from day one, teach from day one, and coach from day one. You don't need to get comfortable before you can practice your skills. Your comfort grows as you practice your skills.

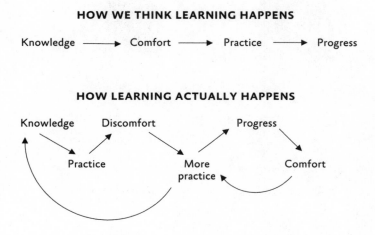

Today, Sara Maria is the founder and managing director of a language and translation services company. She believes that as long as you're willing to be a little uncomfortable, it's never too late to learn. And that courage can be contagious.

A few years ago, Sara Maria Hasbun noticed that someone was watching Korean dramas on her family's Netflix account. It was her dad. After visiting her in Korea, he became enamored with the culture and decided to secretly start learning the language. At age 77, he's rapidly working his way through vocabulary and grammar, and she's able to teach him. "He actually had a lot of Korean knowledge already—he was writing a lot and reading a lot," she says. "But he was really nervous about speaking. He's finally at the point that we can speak a little bit."

Today, Sara Maria is the founder and managing director of a language and translation services company. She believes that as long as you're willing to be a little uncomfortable, it's never too late to learn. And that courage can be contagious.

If we wait until we feel ready to take on a new challenge, we might never pursue it all. There may not come a day when we wake up and suddenly feel prepared. We become prepared by taking the leap anyway.

CHAPTER 2

Human Sponges

Building the Capacity to Absorb and Adapt

It is not the most intellectual of the species that survives;
it is not the strongest . . .

the species that survives is the one that is able best to adapt.

—LEON C. MEGGINSON

Nearly half a billion years ago, the forces of nature wreaked havoc on our planet. Volcanic eruptions spewed ash into the air and phosphorus into the oceans, massive glaciers formed and melted, and oxygen levels plunged and then spiked. More than three quarters of all species died. It was one of the first and worst mass extinction events in history—more devastating than the one that decimated the dinosaurs.

Strangely, though, there was at least one species that didn't just survive—it thrived. Entire forests of sea sponges grew and flourished. Long before SpongeBob memes ruled the internet, sponges ruled the oceans.

Upon discovering sea sponges, scientists assumed they were plants. They're often shaped like bushes, they're almost entirely stationary, and they have no brains, nerves, organs, or muscles. But they don't subsist on sunlight—they consume food like animals. Sea sponges are now recognized as one of the earth's oldest animals.

When you think of a sea sponge, you're probably picturing a creature that's like your kitchen sponge—it soaks up everything around it. But sea sponges don't just passively absorb food and oxygen. They're adept at filtering out toxic substances and unhealthy particles. Their flagella, which look like tiny hairs, create currents that catch nutrients and expel bacteria. They take in water through their outer walls and eject it through what looks like a miniature mouth. They can even sneeze out mucus through their pores.

Some sea sponges can live more than 2,000 years. Despite having bodies that are soft and porous, they have skeletal structures that are strong and durable. When sponges are damaged by strong currents or munched on by predators, they don't necessarily float away or die. Some can regenerate via survival pods: cells that allow a new sponge to develop once conditions improve. This capacity to absorb, filter, and adapt enables sponges to grow and thrive. And it's a capacity that matters a great deal for humans too.

Being a sponge is more than a metaphor. It's a character skill—a form of proactivity that's vital to realizing hidden potential. Improving depends not on the quantity of information you seek out, but the quality of the information you take in. Growth is less about how hard you work than how well you learn.

BOOSTING THE RETURN ON EFFORT

As the youngest of six kids to a single mother in Chicago, Mellody Hobson had a stressful childhood. Her mom often couldn't afford to pay the bills. Sometimes the only way to take a bath was to warm up water on a hot plate and pour it into the tub. Mellody frequently came home from school to find that the electricity had been cut off or the phones had been disconnected. As her mom juggled bills, financial crises erupted. Along with losing basic utilities, the family had their car repossessed and had to move regularly after being evicted.

Mellody had her heart set on attending an Ivy League university. But she started out lagging behind her peers. When she got to first grade, she struggled to concentrate and adapt, and she didn't know how to read. She was placed in a remedial class.

Today Mellody is the co-CEO of a successful investment firm. She chairs the board of Starbucks. She's been named one of *Time*'s 100 Most Influential People. She not only got into Princeton—she will soon become the first Black person to have a residential college named after her there.

If you ask people how Mellody beat the odds, it won't be long before you hear about her legendary work ethic. When she was in elementary school, her bus was in an accident. As her classmates waited to be picked up, Mellody walked to school. In high school, she repeatedly earned straight As, served on the student council executive board, edited the spirit page of the yearbook, and volunteered as the treasurer and vice president of the substance abuse prevention club as well as a tutor to local elementary schoolers.

Mellody's rise seems like a quintessentially American rags-to-riches story. A century ago, the great sociologist Max Weber traced extraordinary gains in achievement to the Protestant work ethic. He argued that before the Protestant Reformation, labor had been a necessary evil. Thanks to Martin Luther's teachings in the 1500s, it was transformed into a calling. Being a good Protestant meant that you had a moral obligation to serve society through productive work. Determination and discipline became virtues; idleness and wastefulness became vices. That might be why many people today worship at the altar of hustle and pray to the high priest of persistence. But the distance we travel is due less to how much labor we do than the fruit it bears.

Not long ago, the economists Sascha Becker and Ludger Woessmann decided to test the impact of the Protestant Reformation on a grand scale: Did it affect what a population accomplished? They found that as Protestant beliefs spread, entire countries had higher economic growth. But it wasn't necessarily because people were suddenly working harder.

In most areas where Protestantism took hold, the historically dominant religion was Catholicism. At the time, the Catholic Church maintained careful control over the Bible, and Catholics typically absorbed its teachings orally at church. Martin Luther changed that: he wrote the first influential German translation of the Bible and preached that every school in every town should teach children to read scripture. That meant people had to learn to read. And once they could read, a whole world of information was at their fingertips. They could learn everything else at a much faster rate. Becker and Woessmann argued that the engine of the Protestant Reformation wasn't work ethic so much as literacy.

Look at these two graphs of the proportion of Protestants in different countries as of 1900. The one on the left shows GDP per capita, and the one on the right shows the literacy rate. With the exception of a few Nordic outliers (more on them later in the book), the positive correlations are nearly identical:

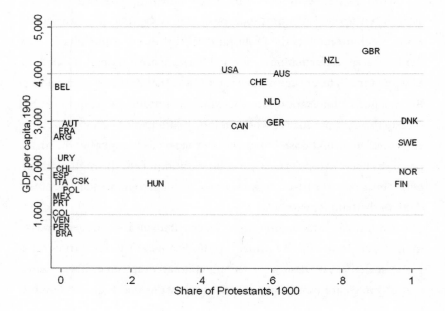

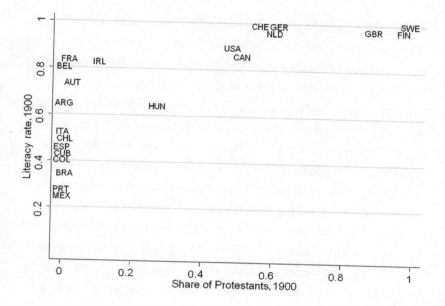

The countries with few Protestants—like Brazil, Italy, and Mexico—tended to have both low economic growth and low literacy rates. The countries that were swept up in the Protestant Reformation—from Germany to Great Britain to Sweden—trended toward higher economic growth and greater literacy.

Of course, it's impossible to draw causal conclusions from correlations with a small sample of countries that differ in countless ways. So Becker and Woessmann capitalized on a natural experiment with more than 450 counties in the German empire. They identified the heart of the Protestant Reformation as Martin Luther's city of Wittenberg. Before the Protestant Reformation, whether a county was near or far from Wittenberg had no bearing on its educational or economic progress. Since communities closer to Wittenberg were more likely to be drawn into Protestantism, the economists were able to test whether that truly set them on different trajectories.

The result: the closer counties were to the center of the Protestant movement, the higher their average incomes were—and the higher their literacy rates too. And after controlling for literacy rates, distance from Wittenberg no longer predicted higher income. To the extent that living near the origin of the Protestant Reformation raised people's incomes, it was entirely attributable to gains in the ability to read and write.*

The lesson here is layered. The progress we normally chalk up to working harder may actually be due to working smarter. Cognitive skills aren't sufficient for learning, but they're necessary. Basic literacy makes it possible to leverage character skills more effectively—to be proactive in learning more and learning faster. Prosperity rises as people become more capable of absorbing new ideas and filtering out old ones.

Cognitive skills that amplify our ability to take in and understand information lay the groundwork for becoming a sponge. As we become more spongelike, we become better equipped to achieve greater things. To paraphrase a verse from *Hamilton*, you get a lot farther by being a self-starter. That's what Mellody Hobson did.

A HERO AND A SCHOLAR

In second grade, Mellody learned to read. That year she won a short-story-writing contest, and the prize was a copy of *Charlotte's Web*. Although her first chapter book was a big leap, she was determined to read it cover to cover and learn the meaning of the words she didn't know.

Mellody's desire to soak up the words and world around her only

---

* Although debate continues about whether, where, and when the Protestant Reformation drove economic growth, there's consensus that around the world, it wasn't the only factor driving gains in reading and writing. For example, research reveals that after towns built libraries in the early 1900s, children advanced more in their education—and landed jobs that were safer, more entrepreneurial, and more prestigious. And in a study of towns that won Carnegie library grants and got preliminary construction approval, following through to build a library paid dividends over the next two decades. Patent rates climbed by 8 to 13 percent (primarily in the technology categories covered by library holdings), and the number of female and immigrant inventors rose too. Literacy is no panacea, but it's an important source of opportunity to learn.

grew with age. That desire eventually landed her a summer internship with John Rogers, who had founded one of the country's largest minority-owned investment firms. John used to read the newspaper at McDonald's on Saturday mornings, and Mellody would meet him there even when she'd already eaten breakfast. This was how she started studying the stock market. "Once she got the investment bug, she knew as much about Warren Buffett as I did," John tells me. "She was committed to learning all about this world that she was interested in. She was a sponge."

Sponginess was the first thing that stood out to me about Mellody too. I first met her a decade ago, when I was invited to give a presentation on my research to a group of VIPs. When I walked into the room, I recognized multiple Oscar-winning filmmakers and tech billionaires. It was Mellody who asked the most questions—and she was the only one to take notes. When it came to seeking and soaking up information, she was in a league of her own. Her engagement was more than curiosity: she had unusual levels of what social scientists call absorptive capacity.

Absorptive capacity is the ability to recognize, value, assimilate, and apply new information. It hinges on two key habits. The first is how you acquire information: Do you react to what enters your field of vision, or are you proactive in seeking new knowledge, skills, and perspectives? The second is the goal you're pursuing when you filter information: Do you focus on feeding your ego or fueling your growth?

Being reactive and ego driven is a surefire way to short-circuit learning. It traps people in a protective bubble. They limit their access to new information and reject any input that threatens their image. Their thin skin leaves them with thick skulls.

When people are proactive and ego driven, it opens the door to more information. Rather than being passive consumers, they're active seekers of feedback—but if it's negative, it gets weeded out. It's too uncomfortable. They're impervious to constructive criticism. They become like Teflon: nothing sticks.

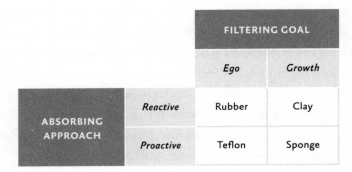

		FILTERING GOAL	
		Ego	*Growth*
ABSORBING APPROACH	*Reactive*	Rubber	Clay
	Proactive	Teflon	Sponge

Learning is more likely when people are reactive and growth oriented. Responding with an eye toward improvement makes people moldable, like clay. They're often praised as coachable or teachable. They're not worried about whether criticism will hurt their egos; they embrace the discomfort and internalize whatever input might help their development. The problem is that they don't seek information beyond what's easily available. They don't make much progress until someone picks them up and shapes them. Their growth depends on guidance from others—they rarely take their learning into their own hands.

The sweet spot is when people are proactive and growth oriented. That's when they become sponges. They consistently take the initiative to expand themselves and adapt. That character skill is especially valuable when the deck is stacked against you—as a pair of young athletes in Africa learned.

REBEL WITHOUT A COACH

Growing up in a rural Kenyan village without electricity or cars, Julius Yego enjoyed competing with his older brother to see who could throw a stick farther. By the time he reached high school, he had set his sights on becoming a great javelin thrower. But he didn't have access to the right facilities, the ideal training routines, or the key equipment. Julius didn't even have a coach—he practiced on his own and did his best to teach himself. He was at a major disadvantage against his biggest rival.

Ihab Abdelrahman was raised in a poor village in Egypt by a family that wasn't into sports. Until he was seventeen he had only played soccer. When a teacher encouraged him to try the javelin, he won the first competition he entered. Just two years later he made the world junior championships and won a silver medal.

On paper, Julius and Ihab had plenty in common. Both hailed from African communities where opportunities were limited, and sport was a ticket to a better life. Both loved soccer before shifting to track and field and discovering the javelin. But physically, it was David against Goliath.

Throwing the javelin is a feat of strength. Early on, a top coach called Ihab's arm "one of the best I've ever seen. He is big and strong and has a natural gift for throwing." Ihab was built for the sport, towering at 6'4" and weighing 212 pounds. Julius didn't have those physical advantages. He stood just 5'9" and weighed only 187 pounds—he wasn't a freak of nature. If he wanted to defeat Ihab, he would have to become a freak of nurture.

In 2010, after seven years of training, Julius finally got to face off against Ihab at the African championships. He managed to win a bronze medal. But Ihab claimed the gold, and even his worst throw sailed farther than Julius's best.

The following year at the All-Africa Games, Julius bent down to pick up a metal spear. He stood up, cocked his arm back, and sprinted to the line. As he cranked his arm forward and launched his javelin into the air, he stumbled.

Julius caught his balance in time to watch his javelin sail nearly the length of a football field. It wasn't just a personal best—it was a new national record. Ihab finished fifth, and Julius won the gold. This time, his worst throw was good enough to beat Ihab's best. David had toppled Goliath.

Look at his trajectory compared with Ihab's—and with the other top finishers from the 2008 world junior championships who kept competing annually in the javelin. Over time, their progress slowed, plateaued, or even reversed. During the same period, Julius did more than just attain steady gains—he actually increased his rate of improvement.

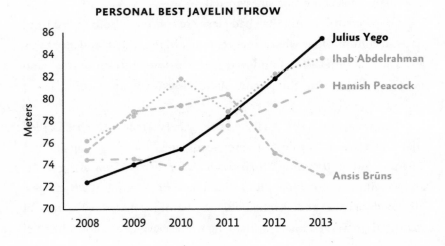

PERSONAL BEST JAVELIN THROW

Ihab was coachable. After receiving a scholarship to train in Finland— widely regarded as the javelin capital of the world—he worked with a top coach there. He listened to advice and improved his technique and his speed. But he was more like clay than a sponge. His approach was reactive, not proactive. When he couldn't get funds from the Egyptian federation for another trip to Finland, he didn't take the initiative to teach himself. He quit training altogether and didn't resume until five months later.

By contrast, Julius took charge of his own growth. When people asked who his coach was, he said: "YouTube."

In 2009, Julius went to an internet café and started watching videos of top javelin throwers on YouTube. By scrutinizing their skills, he was able to start coaching himself. "Everything began to change in my training," Julius says. "Javelin requires technique, power, flexibility, and speed and there were many of these aspects which I'd never looked at."

In 2015, Julius won the world javelin championship. At 92.72 meters, his was the farthest throw in fourteen years—only two humans had ever hurled a javelin farther.

Other than a few months of training in Finland, Julius was self-taught. He had actively sought the information he needed to grow. His form was still unconventional. As he released his javelin, he was often the only athlete to fall face-first with his legs up in the air—like he was about to do the break-dancing move known as the Worm. He had absorbed what he saw, filtered out what didn't apply to his unique style, and adapted his release to become the best in the world.

Julius arrived in Rio in 2016 with high hopes for an Olympic victory. Unfortunately, he sustained a groin injury and only managed to complete one of the six throws during the finals. At 88.24 meters, it was still good enough to land him an Olympic silver medal.

A do-it-yourself approach can be effective for certain kinds of learning. If you're doing a relatively mechanical task like throwing the javelin, you can make great strides by absorbing objective techniques. But in many walks of life, becoming a sponge depends on filtering more subjective guidance from others. As I learned early in my career, that feedback may not even arrive at all—and gathering it is not as simple as it seems.

GETTING THE COLD HARD TRUTH

The message from my body came through loud and clear: *You do not belong here.* Between the sweat drenching my shirt and the butterflies in my stomach, I had no business being onstage. As a shy introvert, just raising my hand to speak in class was enough to give me jitters. In the days before caller ID, I even got nervous answering the phone.

As a graduate student, I was determined to get over my fear of public speaking the fast way. I didn't have time to dip my toe in the shallow end of exposure therapy; I dove right into the deep end of flooding. I volunteered to give a series of guest lectures in my friends' undergraduate classes. I needed their input to learn. But when I asked those friends for feedback afterward, they came back with vague compliments. *Interesting content. Enthusiastic delivery.*

When they have helpful input, people are often reluctant to share it. We even hesitate to tell friends they have food in their teeth. We're confusing politeness with kindness. Being polite is withholding feedback to make someone feel good today. Being kind is being candid about how they can get better tomorrow. It's possible to be direct in what you say while being thoughtful about how you deliver it. *I don't want to embarrass you, but I realized it would be a lot more embarrassing if no one told you about the broccoli sprouting from your gums.*

When you kick off a presentation, you know you're in trouble if you say, "Good morning!" and multiple people respond, "Great point!" To help students overcome their hesitations, I gave out anonymous feedback forms. I wanted to become a sponge: I would absorb everything I could from the audience and then filter out what wasn't useful. Little did I know I was going about it the wrong way.

The students panned my performance. *Your nervous breathing sounds like Darth Vader.* Then I interviewed for my first job at a top university, and the hiring committee rejected me. No one told me why until months later, when a colleague finally came clean. *You lack the confidence to command the respect of our students.* The following year, when I delivered my first session for U.S. Air Force leaders, the colonels crucified me. *I gained nothing from this session, but I trust the instructor gained useful insight.* It was a crash course in demoralization by useless criticism.

It's easy for people to be critics or cheerleaders. It's harder to get them to be coaches. A critic sees your weaknesses and attacks your worst self. A cheerleader sees your strengths and celebrates your best self. A coach sees your potential and helps you become a better version of yourself.

If I wanted to master the art of public speaking, I needed a better filter. I decided to turn my critics and cheerleaders into coaches. I'd tried to do that in the past by asking for feedback. But research suggests that's a mistake.

Instead of seeking feedback, you're better off asking for advice. Feedback tends to focus on how well you did last time. Advice shifts attention to how you can do better next time. In experiments, that simple shift is enough to elicit more specific suggestions and more constructive input.* Rather than dwelling on what you did wrong, advice guides you toward what you can do right.

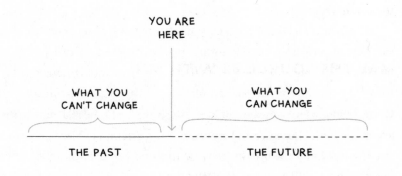

LIZ FOSSLIEN

---

* People sometimes worry about coming across as insecure, but seeking advice doesn't reveal a lack of confidence. It reflects respect for another person's competence. When you seek their guidance, people judge you as more capable. *You're a genius! You knew to come to me!*

I replaced my usual feedback questions with a basic request for advice.* *What's the one thing I can do better?* Suddenly people started giving me useful tips. *Don't lead with a joke unless you're confident it will land.* The audience wasn't always ready for my dry humor, and hearing crickets amplified my anxiety. *Open with a personal story—it humanizes you.* I was trying to make it about the audience, not myself, but I was distancing myself from them instead of connecting with them.

After a decade of practice, I got an invitation to give a TED talk. I opened with a story about the time I failed to invest in Warby Parker, and managed to wait a full 42 seconds to unveil my first joke, which got laughs. A later joke did bomb, and you can hear my nerves at several points, but all things considered, the talk went over well. Over the next five years, I was invited to stand in the red circle three more times, and Darth Vader only made a cameo.

After every talk I give, I ask the hosts what I can do better. It reminds me that not all advice is created equal, and the more suggestions you collect, the more important filtering becomes. How do you know which sources to trust?

MAY THE SOURCE BE WITH YOU

When Mellody Hobson sent off her college applications, she was thrilled to get into both Harvard and Princeton. In an attempt to lure her, Princeton invited her to a breakfast with high-powered alumni. She was seated next to Bill Bradley, the NBA star turned U.S. senator. As she

---

* If you're new to a skill, asking for advice isn't always helpful. Psychologists find that novices are more likely to seek and listen to praise than criticism. The opposite is true for experts: they're more attuned and responsive to suggestions for improvement than encouragement. It's not just for learning—it's also for motivation. If you're a novice, discovering a strength is affirming: it energizes you to invest more time in the activity. With experience, you gain confidence that you can excel. At that point, you're looking for information, not validation. What propels you to action is finding out that you haven't made as much progress as you hoped. You want to learn how to close the gap.

bombarded him with questions, he was taken with her curiosity and started mentoring her.

One day at lunch, Bill gave Mellody some tough feedback. He told her that in his basketball days, he had seen talented players take all the shots themselves instead of passing the ball to others. She had a tendency to dominate the room, and if she wasn't careful, she would become a ball hog. Mellody felt tears welling up.

There's nothing wrong with taking criticism personally. Taking it personally shows you're taking it seriously. Getting upset isn't a mark of weakness or even defensiveness—as long as your ego doesn't stand in the way of your learning.

A key to being a sponge is determining what information to absorb versus what to filter out. It's a question of which coaches to trust. I like to break trustworthiness down into three components: care, credibility, and familiarity.

WHICH SOURCES TO TRUST

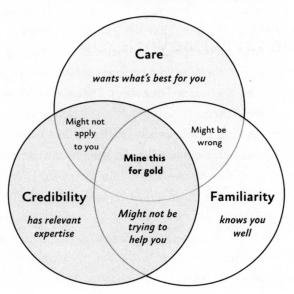

If they don't care about you, they haven't earned the right for you to care about their reactions. If they're not qualified to judge the task or close enough to know your potential, you can discount their views and prove them wrong. But if they've demonstrated that you matter to them and they know the domain and your skills, they're offering information to improve yourself. That doesn't mean you have to accept every bit of constructive criticism they give. You also don't have to agree with it to learn from it. By trying to understand what provoked their reactions, you can glean insights about how to elicit a different response next time.

As Mellody processed Bill Bradley's warning not to be a ball hog, she remembered that no one is entitled to receive feedback or advice. She thought to herself, *If I cry, he won't ever give me feedback again.* She realized he was taking the time to give her tough love because he believed in her potential and cared about helping her grow. There was also no question about Bill's credibility—from his basketball past and his political present, he knew what a ball hog looked like. And he had plenty of familiarity: their mentoring relationship gave him a clear understanding of her skills and shortcomings.

Instead of letting the tears flow, Mellody sought advice about how she could improve. She discovered that being a ball hog was not so much a weakness as a strength overused—or misused. Her absorptive capacity could suck the air out of a room, and her quest to learn could inadvertently silence other voices. She learned that she had to adapt how she expressed her thirst for information.

Mellody's constructive response motivated Bill to keep coaching her, and the connection blossomed. Years later, he introduced her to the Starbucks founder, who invited her to join their board. When she got married, Bill walked her down the aisle, and Mellody called him the father she never had.

Many people fail to benefit from constructive criticism because they overreact and under-correct. Mellody made a resolution to do the opposite: she told herself that champions adapt. She would go out of her way to show an interest in others and use her absorptive capacity to ask them questions and learn more about them. Just as her coaches had done for her, she would help people grow by dishing out tough love. That became a signature strength. Mellody gained a reputation as the board member who challenged everyone else to think more broadly and deeply, and as the mentor who never hesitated to tell the truth. I've seen it firsthand.

Recently, Mellody happened to be in the audience when I gave a new talk. Afterward, as her peers gave generic praise, I knew I could count on her for coaching. Sure enough, when I reached out, she called me with notes. My big takeaway was that I needed a clearer throughline so the attendees didn't lose the message. She wasn't just there to absorb and apply information for herself—she wanted to make sure the audience could absorb and apply it too. That speaks to my favorite property of a sponge.

At some point in the past, sea sponges branched off on their own evolutionary tree. We're not their descendants. But that hasn't stopped them from being good ancestors.

As I read far and wide about sea sponges, I was delighted to discover something even more remarkable than their capacity to absorb. It's their capacity to create. Sea sponges don't just expunge toxins. They also produce biochemicals that protect and promote life with anticancer, antibacterial, antiviral, and anti-inflammatory properties. Substances from a Caribbean sea sponge spurred breakthroughs in the treatment of HIV, herpes, and leukemia. Compounds from a Japanese sea sponge have been developed into a chemotherapy drug that has extended the lives of women with advanced breast cancer by blocking cell division. And a peptide from an Antarctic sea sponge offers a promising lead in the treatment of malaria.

Despite these recent developments, the greatest life-giving impact of sea sponges may have taken place about half a billion years ago. For decades, scientists believed that new animal species emerged as oxygen arose in the oceans. The latest evidence suggests that sea sponges actually contributed to this process. By filtering organic matter out of the water, they helped to oxygenate the oceans, which enabled animals to evolve. This means sponges may be partly responsible for all complex life as we know it. If not for sponges, the human race might not exist.

Being a sponge is not only a proactive skill—it's a prosocial skill. Done right, it's not just about soaking up nutrients that help us grow. It's also about releasing nutrients to help others grow.

CHAPTER 3

The Imperfectionists

Finding the Sweet Spot between Flawed and Flawless

There is a crack, a crack in everything
That's how the light gets in

—LEONARD COHEN

When he got word of the earthquake rocking his home in Japan, Tadao Ando was halfway across the world. With a heavy heart he dashed to the airport and boarded the first flight back from Europe. As he took a boat to the city of Kobe, he felt every second pass by. It wasn't concern for his own house that was weighing on his mind. He was anxious to check on whether the community was safe. They had entrusted him to design a number of their buildings, from a housing complex on a steep hill to a Buddhist temple.

Ando had good reason to be nervous. He didn't have any formal training as an architect. Born in poverty in the early 1940s, he was raised by his grandmother in a *nagaya*—a small, one-story row house made of wood. As broken windows left them shivering through icy winters, Ando escaped to the small carpentry shop across the street. He spent countless afternoons and evenings building wooden boats, blowing glass, and working with metal. He dreamed of creating his own buildings.

Without the means to go to college, Ando decided to learn architecture on his own. While doing odd jobs to pay the rent, he scrutinized the structures around him. He borrowed architecture books from friends and read about the evolution of materials, techniques, and styles. He honed his drawing skills by tracing directly over sketches of buildings until the pages were black.

Eventually, Ando had taught himself enough to earn an architecture license. By the time the earthquake hit Kobe in 1995, he had designed dozens of buildings there—on an active fault line. Tragically, when the aftershocks subsided, more than 6,000 people had lost their lives. Entire neighborhoods were destroyed and over 200,000 buildings were in shambles.

Arriving heartbroken, Ando somberly surveyed the devastation. He ventured over roads that had split in half and maneuvered around power lines that were still in flames. He climbed through the rubble of ten-story buildings that had crumbled to the ground. Remarkably, not a single one of Ando's 35 buildings had collapsed. As he inspected them, he couldn't find even a visible crack.

Tadao Ando is the only architect ever to win all four of the field's most prestigious prizes. Known as the master of light and concrete, he's revered for pioneering minimalist, sturdy structures—from homes to temples to museums—that amplify the natural world around them. His buildings have been described as earthquake-proof, and his designs have been called visual haikus.

When I considered the traits of great architects, the first quality that came to mind was perfectionism. It takes painstaking attention to detail to create an aesthetic masterpiece—let alone a structure that can withstand an earthquake. If you're not fastidious about getting every element right, your designs will be flawed and your buildings could collapse. But then I learned that to be uncompromising, architects have to make compromises. And I kept hearing that no one did this better than Tadao Ando.

Ando is esteemed for his ability to make the most of limited spaces with limited budgets. He's only able to do this because he fully rejects the notion of perfectionism. He knows that to be disciplined in some areas, we have to let others go. One of his specialties is being disciplined in deciding when to push for the best and when to settle for good enough. For him, this often means prioritizing durability and design while compromising on comfort. His signature style is meticulous on form but less exacting on function.

When Ando designed his second house, the entire lot was less than 200 square feet. The constraints of the space meant that even if he sought perfection, it would be unattainable. He had to settle for a design with some fundamental flaws. He built a tiny concrete box without any windows—there was only a skylight at the top. "After satisfying the minimum conditions of ventilation, lighting, and exposure to sunlight," Ando reflected, "I thought the question of functionality could be left to the inhabitant."

To get from one bedroom to the other, you had to walk through a courtyard without a ceiling and brave the elements. On rainy days, you had to carry an umbrella in your own house. When the project was submitted for an architecture prize, a judge wrote, "The award should be given to the brave owner who is living and surviving in this environment."

Ando accepted those shortcomings because he was unwilling to sacrifice his vision of being an urban guerilla. He wanted to create a well-designed, durable oasis smack in the center of a city. By closing off the walls to the outside world, he was protecting the home from ugliness and uproar. By opening an interior patio to the sky above, he was connecting the home with the splendor and simplicity of nature. Despite the deficiencies, the row house won a major prize and launched his career.

We usually associate aesthetic and technical prowess with a drive for flawless results. As I've studied the habits of great designers, dancers, and divers, though, I've come to understand that unlocking hidden potential is not about the pursuit of perfection. Tolerating flaws isn't just something novices need to do—it's part of becoming an expert and continuing to gain mastery. The more you grow, the better you know which flaws are acceptable.

WHAT STRAIGHT-A STUDENTS GET WRONG

When I was growing up, my mom often said that no matter what grades I got in school, as long as I did my best, she'd be proud of me. Then she added, "But if you didn't get an A, I'll *know* you didn't do your best." She said it with a smile, but I took it seriously: I shouldn't settle for anything less than perfect.

It's one thing to care about attaining success and avoiding failure. I'm guessing you wouldn't want a heart surgeon who was content with doing an adequate job. But perfectionism takes expectations to a whole different level. I'm not talking about the line people use in job interviews. *My greatest weakness is that I'm too much of a perfectionist.* It's much more extreme than that.

Perfectionism is the desire to be impeccable. The goal is zero defects: no faults, no flaws, no failures. It's my college classmate who was so enamored with his perfect SAT score that his email handle was IGot1600. It's the students who still display their 4.0 GPAs on their resumes and LinkedIn profiles a decade after graduation. It's the friends who appear to be living their best lives online but hide their physical and emotional scars in shame.

There's strong evidence that perfectionism has been rising for years across the United States, the United Kingdom, and Canada. Social media clearly hasn't helped, but the spike started in the 1990s—a full generation before anyone was posting curated images on Instagram. In an increasingly competitive world, kids face growing pressure from parents to be perfect and harsh criticism when they fall short. They learn to judge their worth by the absence of inadequacies. Every flaw is a blow to their self-esteem. I've lived it myself.

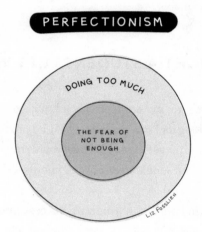

When I won the fifth-grade quiz bowl on world explorers, I beat myself up afterward for missing one question. *How could I forget that the sea route to India was discovered by da Gama, not Magellan?* When I made the finals of a Mortal Kombat tournament and won a lifetime pass to a local movie theater, I didn't celebrate. *Third place is the second loser.* When I set the curve on a math test, I was disappointed. *Only a 98? Not good enough.*

Perfectionists excel at solving problems that are straightforward and familiar. In school, they ace multiple-choice tests that have a single right answer and fill-in-the-blank questions that allow them to regurgitate facts they've committed to memory. *Michelangelo's marble architectural membering was set within a thin, blue-gray pietra serena molding.* That line is still emblazoned in my brain from the weekend I spent studying for a final exam as a college freshman, and I have no idea what it means.

The real world is far more ambiguous. Once you leave the predictable, controllable cocoon of academic exams, the desire to find the "correct" answer can backfire. In a meta-analysis, the average correlation between perfectionism and performance at work was zero. When it came to mastering their tasks, perfectionists were no better than their peers. Sometimes they even did worse. The skills and inclinations that drive people to the top of their high school or college class may not serve them so well after they graduate.

The people who go on to become masters in their fields often start out with imperfect transcripts in school. In a study of world-class sculptors, it turned out that they were mostly average students. Two thirds graduated high school with Bs and Cs. A similar pattern emerged in a comparison of America's most influential architects with peers who had fallen short of transforming the field. The great architects had rarely been great students: they typically finished college with a B average. Their perfectionistic colleagues had gleaming grades but went on to build far fewer glistening buildings.

In their quest for flawless results, research suggests that perfectionists tend to get three things wrong. One: they obsess about details that don't matter. They're so busy finding the right solution to tiny problems that they lack the discipline to find the right problems to solve. They can't see the forest for the trees. Two: they avoid unfamiliar situations and difficult tasks that might lead to failure. That leaves them refining a narrow set of existing skills rather than working to develop new ones. Three: they berate themselves for making mistakes, which makes it harder to learn from them. They fail to realize that the purpose of reviewing your mistakes isn't to shame your past self. It's to educate your future self.

THE PERFECTIONISM SPIRAL

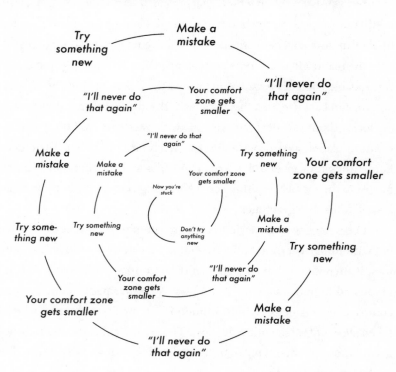

If perfectionism were a medication, the label would alert us to common side effects. *Warning: may cause stunted growth.* Perfectionism traps us in a spiral of tunnel vision and error avoidance: it prevents us from seeing larger problems and limits us to mastering increasingly narrow skills.

Even if you don't consider yourself a perfectionist, you've probably experienced those tendencies on tasks that are important to you. On the projects that matter deeply to us, we've all felt the urge to keep revising and refining until it's exactly right. But traveling great distances depends on recognizing that perfection is a mirage—and learning to tolerate the right imperfections.

CONCRETE POSSIBILITIES

According to legend, a young man once sought out a master to teach him the Japanese tea ceremony. The master tested him by asking him to clean up a garden. The young man removed the weeds and raked the leaves until the grounds were pristine. As he reviewed his flawless work, he decided something was missing. He walked over to a cherry tree and shook it so that some flower petals fell to the ground. By finding the beauty in imperfection, he showed he was ready to become a master.

This legend traces back to the sixteenth century, when the Japanese tea ceremony underwent a seismic shift. Immaculate dishes were replaced with chipped bowls. People drank from pottery that was worn and weathered. They called this practice *wabi sabi*.

Wabi sabi is the art of honoring the beauty in imperfection. 'I' not about creating intentional imperfections. It's about accepting that flaws are inevitable—and recognizing that they don't stop something from becoming sublime. That's been a dominant theme in Tadao Ando's architecture and his life. He's an imperfectionist: he's selective about what he decides to do well.

If you ask Ando about his school days, he'll tell you his academic performance was inadequate. He was perfectly willing to accept imperfect scores. Despite his passion for the subject, he didn't even excel in the architecture class he took in high school. Even if he'd been able to afford the tuition, his grades weren't good enough to get into architecture school. He became a professional boxer.

Ando's comfort with imperfection solidified further in the boxing ring. In a fight, there was no such thing as a flawless performance—he was going to get hit. If he wanted to win, he couldn't get stuck in the weeds, hide from his weaknesses, or avoid challenges. There was no need to beat himself up; his opponents would do plenty of beating. If he wanted to protect his face and head, he had to leave his body exposed and take some punches. "In boxing, you must risk moving into danger in order to fully take advantage of your skills and eventually win the match," Ando observes. "New building projects require the same mentality. . . . Taking that extra step forward into the unknown is vital."

After two years, Ando quit boxing. He started teaching himself architecture and honed his vision. He would strive not for perfection but for "perfectly acceptable." He chose to build walls out of concrete—a material his peers avoided due to its aesthetic limitations. He was drawn to concrete for its toughness and "intricate roughness." Since his early projects lacked the budgets to cover it up, he ended up leaving it exposed.

The exposed concrete became Ando's signature look. There are visible imperfections on every wall. You can see lines from the seams and holes that are only partially filled with mortar. To make sure it didn't distract from the beauty around it, he would carefully smooth the concrete until it felt like silk or cashmere. As one contractor put it, Ando wanted the concrete "vibrated till it looked like butter." The material was still imperfect to the eye, but it became acceptable once it was perfectly smooth to the touch.

The iconic concrete walls are on vivid display in the Church of Light, one of Ando's most famous projects. He anchored the design on what most architects would consider an obvious flaw: gaps in the concrete that leave the back wall open to the outdoors. But they serve a stunning purpose, allowing light to beam through in the shape of a cross. After the church deemed the open air too cold, Ando compromised by installing glass. He still hopes to remove it one day, joking that every time he visits, priests beg: "No glass removal, please."

Wabi sabi is a character skill. It gives you the discipline to shift your attention from impossible ideals to achievable standards—and then adjust those standards over time. But finding beauty in imperfection is often easier said than done. As a recovering perfectionist, I know from experience.

IN SEARCH OF THE RIGHT IMPERFECTIONS

After I spent almost an entire summer playing video games indoors, my exasperated mom dragged me to a local swimming pool. As I looked toward the deep end, I saw a lifeguard walking down the diving board with unusual grace. He leapt into the air, folded his body into a ball, and spun in a blur. After two flips and a dive, he vanished into the water without a splash. I was in awe.

I spent the rest of the summer learning a few basic dives and showed up at fall tryouts as a high school freshman. The team coach, Eric Best, would go on to train multiple Olympic medalists. Eric said he had good news and bad news. The bad news: diving required grace, flexibility, and explosive power. I walked like Frankenstein, I couldn't touch my toes without bending my knees, and his grandmother could outjump me. *Sorry, did you say there was good news?*

There was good news: Eric didn't care how bad I was. He would never cut a diver who wanted to be there. And diving was a nerd sport—it mostly attracted athletes who lacked the size, speed, or strength to star in more mainstream sports. He predicted that if I put in the effort, by my senior year, I would become a state finalist in diving.

That lit a fire under me. Although I was only doing beginner dives,

I was determined to get them exactly right. When it was time for me to move on, I would beg, "One more!"

At the end of practice, Eric had to kick me out of the pool. I didn't want to leave until I'd erased every defect.

Dives are judged against an ideal of perfection. Every flaw is a possible deduction from your score. You lose points for under-rotating or over-rotating, for finishing too close to the board or too far from the board, for failing to touch your toes or point your toes, for making even a small splash. You want a perfect takeoff and a perfect pike and a perfect entry.

I thought my perfectionism would be an asset, but it turned out to be a liability. I spent hours trying to eliminate tiny droplets from my entry into the water instead of working on the larger hurdle of improving my lackluster vertical leap into the air. And along with focusing on the wrong problems, I had a problem with balking.

I would start my approach, walk down the board, and jump to the end. But just before takeoff, I'd stop. I had a long list of excuses. I was leaning too far forward or too far back. I was either too quick or too slow for the rhythm of the board. I was tilting slightly to the left or the right. I was Goldilocks: I expected everything to be just right.

My balking was especially bad when it came time to try new dives. At one practice, I went back and forth on the board for 45 minutes without making a single attempt. As I stood there frozen, I wasn't just wasting time—I was freezing my progress. I was failing to learn hard dives and only making small refinements to easy ones. I needed to get over my perfectionism.*

---

*Perfectionists are also at greater risk for mental blocks. Think of when Simone Biles got lost in midair in Tokyo. Gymnasts and divers call it the twisties, when your body suddenly fails to execute routines that your brain used to initiate automatically. It's known by different names in different sports—lost move syndrome in trampolining, and the yips in golf and baseball. Preliminary research suggests that this mental block is more common among perfectionists, who are prone to performance pressure and anxiety that deactivate autopilot and distort muscle memory. It happened to me once on a dive I'd been doing for years—a full-twisting one and a half. Instead of diving in headfirst, I smacked flat on my back facing the opposite direction, having done an extra half twist without the slightest intent or awareness of it. Even though I was only hitting the water, it was terrifying.

But how do we change? Perfectionists don't know any other way to be. Even if you're not one, when you care about a goal, it's hard to be disciplined in choosing what to prioritize, what to minimize, when to stop, and how to accept inescapable flaws.

Extensive evidence shows that it's having high personal standards, not pursuing perfection, that fuels growth. Many people interpret that as advice to shift from *be the best* to *do your best*. But aiming for your best is not the best alternative. Across hundreds of experiments, people who are encouraged to do their best perform worse—and learn less—than those who are randomly assigned to goals that are specific and difficult.

Do your best is the wrong cure for perfectionism. It leaves the target too ambiguous to channel effort and gauge momentum. You're not sure what you're aiming for or whether you've made meaningful progress. The ideal foil for perfectionism is an objective that's precise and challenging. It focuses your attention on the most important actions and tells you when enough is enough.

Eric told me that when announcers rave about dives getting perfect 10s, they're making a mistake. There's no such thing as a perfect dive. Even in the Olympic judging rules, a 10 doesn't stand for perfection—it stands for excellence. He was teaching me the art of wabi sabi.

The lesson hit home: I didn't need to be perfect. I just needed to aim for a clear, high target. Eric worked with me to set goals for each dive at the edge of my abilities. On my bread-and-butter basic dive, a front dive pike, we started off aiming for a 6.5. But on my more complicated, shaky flip with a twist, all I needed was a 5. And if I was learning a new dive, we'd settle for anything above a 0. In other words, not a failure: I'd made the dive. Every time I came out of the water, Eric gave me a score. Then he gave me a change to make and reminded me that if I wanted to get closer to right, it had to feel wrong.

I stopped waiting for the perfect approach and started going on the first one that was good enough. I stopped avoiding hard dives and started pushing the limits of my abilities—within a few years I was doing two flips with a full twist and a dive at the end. I stopped beating myself up for past failures and focused on recent progress. *Mostly.* At our team banquet, the captains gave me the "If Only" award. They drew a cartoon of me saying, "If only I'd pointed my left pinky toe on that entry, I would've gotten an 8.5 instead of an 8."

If I didn't do my best, I still felt frustrated. When divers tell him they had a bad day, Eric likes to ask two questions: Did you make yourself better today? Did you make someone else better today? If the answer to either question is yes, it was a good day. *His last name may be Best, but he's all about better.*

I learned that even when I wasn't satisfied with my diving, there was a version of me that could be. There's another technique that I've found helpful for dumping perfectionism. In psychology, it's known as mental time travel. Yes, that's a thing.

Expectations tend to rise with accomplishment. The better you're performing, the more you demand of yourself and the less you notice incremental gains. Appreciating progress depends on remembering how your past self would see your current achievements. If you knew five years ago what you'd accomplish now, how proud would you have been?

The 14-year-old kid who could barely do a flip would have been amazed by the progress I'd made in a few years. I started watching videos of my early diving days. It melted away my shame and marked my growth.

Beating yourself up doesn't make you stronger—it leaves you bruised. Being kind to yourself isn't about ignoring your weaknesses. It's about giving yourself permission to learn from your disappointments. We grow by embracing our shortcomings, not by punishing them. *Make it feel wrong.*

Perfectionists often worry that failing even once will make them a failure. But take it from eight studies: people don't judge your competence based on one performance. It's called the overblown implications effect. If you cook one bad dish, people rarely think you're a terrible chef. If you leave a finger over the camera lens, they don't conclude you're a bad photographer. They know it's only a snapshot from a single moment in time.

It turns out that when people assess your skills, they put more weight on your peaks than on your troughs. Even if you happened to see Serena Williams repeatedly double-fault on her serve, you'd recognize her excellence if you witnessed just one of her aces. When Steve Jobs flopped with the Apple Lisa, people still deemed him a visionary for his feats with the Mac. And we judge Shakespeare's genius by his masterpieces (think *Hamlet* and *King Lear*), forgiving his forgettable plays (I'm looking at you, *Timon of Athens* and *The Merry Wives of Windsor*). People judge your potential from your best moments, not your worst. What if you gave yourself the same grace?

In diving, my performance had a clear ceiling. I never got anywhere near making the Olympic team. But I did manage to exceed my goals. Before I finished high school, I made the All-American list and qualified twice for the Junior Olympic nationals. My proudest moment, though, was when Eric told me I'd gotten further with less talent than any diver he'd coached. I realized that success is not so much how close you come to perfection as how much you overcome along the way.

THE SHOW MUST GO ON

In sports, excellence is fairly objective. Diving has a formula for degree of difficulty and a rule book for judging execution. But in many domains, success is more subjective. One person's beautiful mess can be another's ugly duckling. That makes it challenging to decide which imperfections to accept.

In the summer of 2002, over a thousand people filed into a Chicago theater to see the debut of a dance musical. During the first act, the audience looked so miserable and confused that the creator worried they'd leave after intermission. In a scathing review, theater critic Michael Phillips called it "strenuous, chaotic . . . crazily uneven . . . ill-conceived."

The show was the brainchild of Twyla Tharp, best known for her choreography of ballets for Mikhail Baryshnikov—and of dances in films like *Hair* and *Amadeus*. She had dreamed up a "two-hour dance extravaganza" of Billy Joel songs without any dialogue. She'd raised $8.5 million to fund it, hoping to deliver a hit that would finally be profitable for the dancers themselves—a group long undervalued in the performing arts.

The big Broadway premiere was just around the corner. The devastating feedback raised serious questions in Tharp's mind about whether it was fatally flawed: "Whether I or anybody else could make it work was a gamble." It wasn't clear whether she should reimagine the plot, introduce dialogue, develop characters, or subtract songs. Whatever adjustments she made would need to be learned and rehearsed by the performers.

Just a month after the disastrous debut, Tharp unveiled a revamped show for the end of their Chicago run. When the critic Michael Phillips came back, he was pleasantly surprised at the distance traveled. "Extensive revisions . . . have made for a clearer, more satisfying show" that was "often exhilarating," he wrote. "Tharp's changes may give the show a better chance at Broadway success." She hadn't choreographed a perfect performance, but the blemishes no longer overshadowed the strengths—thanks to her quick pivot.

Pivoting is a popular concept in Silicon Valley, where it's often said that done is better than perfect. To rapidly iterate and improve, entrepreneurs and engineers are advised to build a minimum viable product. But excellence is a higher standard: for me, that means aiming for a minimum lovable product.

To create a minimum lovable show, Tharp needed to pinpoint what people were hating. It was time to be a sponge, but she didn't know which critics and comments to trust. She needed to absorb and adapt to the key reactions while filtering out the rest. Her son, Jesse, made a grid categorizing the substantive comments by theme.

Research indicates that one of the best ways to gauge the value of other people's judgments is to look for convergence between them. If one person raises a red flag, it might be idiosyncratic. If a dozen people independently have the same issue, it's more likely to be an objective problem. You have inter-rater reliability.

Tharp and her son came up with a filter to find the signal in the noise. They decided that any concern raised independently by more than two critics wasn't a matter of taste—it was a quality control issue. "The critics turned out to be enormously useful," Tharp recalls, quipping: "Bless their coal-black little hearts."

The grid revealed that the consistent complaints were about the first act, not the second. Tharp was trying to do too much. One audience member was so overwhelmed by the different sources of stimulation that she covered her eyes during one song and her ears in the next. It was up to Tharp to fix it, and she knew time was running out. "I didn't need the perfect solution to every problem, but I did need a workable solution—a lot of them."

A MINIMUM LOVABLE PRODUCT

Perfecting the show would have required Tharp to go back to the drawing board and intersperse dialogue between the songs and dances. But she was an imperfectionist—she was aiming for excellence, not flawlessness. For minimum lovable, she just needed to simplify the story, clarify the characters, and manage expectations. She did that with a simple addition familiar to fans of musical theater: a prologue.

Adding a prologue meant she had to choreograph a new opening number in a matter of days. Rather than scrambling to design a perfect arrangement from scratch, she borrowed something from her own shelf. Her production designer noticed striking similarities between some Billy Joel beats and a dance Tharp had created for another show decades earlier. It took Tharp just a few hours to teach the recycled routine to the two dozen dancers. Now they had an opening that introduced the characters and dazzled visually. The following spring, *Movin' Out* was nominated for ten Tony Awards, and Tharp won for best choreography. She had found wabi sabi: the audience and the critics appreciated that a beautiful dance musical could be set to an imperfect story.

Identifying which imperfections to fix doesn't have to be a last-minute scramble. These days, Twyla Tharp isn't content to leave her fate in the hands of critics with coal-black little hearts. After she launches a new project, she invites a small group of people to review her work in progress. They help her spot and solve the problems she's too close to see. But they're not just coaches—they're judges. Their role is to gauge whether she's on a promising track. She recommends that we all set up a committee of judges to help us with quality control. Mine is based on my diving days.

After I retired from diving, I missed the clarity of knowing exactly where my performance stood on the spectrum from failure to excellence.

I decided that when I finished a first draft of an article or book chapter, I would send it to a group of trusted colleagues.

For every project that matters to me, I've had judging committees for over a decade now. They're not permanent structures; they're temporary scaffolding. I think of them as pop-up workshops. For each project, I pull together a different mix of five to seven insiders and outsiders with complementary skills. The group bands, disbands, and morphs as relevant.

My first request isn't for feedback or advice. It's for a score. I ask the judges to independently rate my work on a scale from 0 to 10. No one ever says 10. Then I ask how I can get closer to 10.

My target score varies with my skill and the importance of the task. For a major project like this book, I set two targets: an aspirational goal (9) and an acceptable result (8). When I get 8s across the board, I know I can be satisfied with my progress. *But if only I'd pointed my left pinky toe on that sentence . . .*

Getting a precise score isn't just information—it's motivation. When multiple judges come in below 7, it nudges them to start coaching me and me to be coachable. I know I can't settle for minor tweaks—it needs a major overhaul. I want to close the gap. There's nothing that fires me up as much as a 4.5 on a first draft. It helps me brace myself for the feedback and advice that follows. My personal favorite: *"not a page-turner."* Then I keep revising until every judge gives at least an 8 and some give 9s. That's minimum lovable. I've accepted that life is like diving: if you're ever lucky enough to get a 10, it's not for perfection but for excellence.

We have to be careful about how much weight we put on judges' scores. A great deal of research shows that perfectionists tend to define excellence on other people's terms. This focus on creating a flawless image in the eyes of others is a risk factor for depression, anxiety, burnout, and other mental health challenges. Striving for social approval comes with a cost: across 105 studies with over 70,000 people, valuing extrinsic goals like popularity and appearance over intrinsic goals like growth and connection predicted lower well-being. Seeking validation is a bottomless pit: the craving for status is never satisfied. But if an external assessment serves as a tool for growth, it may be worth using.

Ultimately, excellence is more than meeting other people's expectations. It's also about living up to your own standards. After all, it's impossible to please everyone. The question is whether you're letting down the right people. It's better to disappoint others than to disappoint yourself.

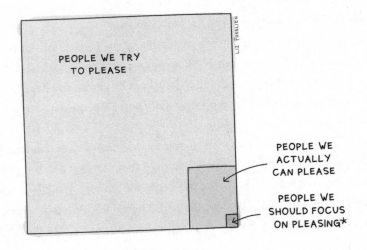

Before releasing something into the world, it's worth turning to one final judge: you. If this was the only work people saw of yours, would you be proud of it?

Tadao Ando asks himself this question regularly. "What some other people think of my work" is "not my prime mover," he says. "It's my desire to satisfy me, and to challenge myself."

After the earthquake rocked Kobe, Ando wanted to preserve the artifacts of the past and renew hope for the future. On the waterfront overlooking the mountains, he designed an art museum. The deck features a sculpture of his own: a giant green apple. "In life, it's better to be green—and the greener the better," Ando declares. "The green apple is a symbol of youth." Ando is now in his eighties, and his youth is reflected in his ongoing desire to grow.

Aspiring to stay green is a commitment to continued growth, to staying unfinished. An apple that isn't ripe is not fully formed—it's incomplete and imperfect. That's what makes it beautiful.

PART II

Structures for Motivation

Scaffolding to Overcome Obstacles

On the path to any goal, roadblocks are inevitable. When we run into external barriers, they often take an internal toll. The daily grind starts to bore us and eventually burns us out. Stagnation leaves us discouraged. Difficult tasks lead to failure, dejection, and doubt. We begin to question whether we can bounce back, let alone move forward.

Character skills aren't always enough to travel great distances. Many new skills don't come with a manual, and steeper hills often require a lift. That lift comes in the form of scaffolding: a temporary support structure that enables us to scale heights we couldn't reach on our own. It helps us build the resilience to overcome obstacles that threaten to overwhelm us and limit our growth.

When psychologists study resilience in experiments, they often create an overwhelming experience by showing people distressing video clips.

Think about the last time you saw an intense or unsettling scene on TV or in a movie. Your favorite character gets decapitated in outer space by a lightsaber—or devoured in the Upside Down by Demobats. If you're anything like my kids (and my wife), those scenes keep replaying in your mind, continuing to haunt you long after the end credits stop rolling. *Thank you, Duffer Brothers.* But psychologists have discovered that it's possible to stop those unwanted flashbacks in their tracks with a special kind of scaffolding.

At first, I assumed it would be a form of therapy. Maybe they'd show you the clip repeatedly to systematically desensitize you (exposure therapy) or help you reframe the scene as something that can't hurt you (cognitive reappraisal). But I was wrong. The scaffolding that psychologists offer to boost resilience is a game of Tetris.

Yes, Tetris.

After people watch an especially upsetting film clip, over the next week they typically have six or seven disturbing flashbacks. But if they're randomly assigned to play a few rounds of Tetris right after watching the scene, it cuts their flashbacks in half over the next week. Somehow, the act of rotating, moving, and dropping geometric blocks shields us from intrusive thoughts and aversive emotions.

To be clear, playing Tetris won't cure your addiction or heal your PTSD. A game is not a substitute for therapeutic or pharmacological interventions. But the effect has been replicated by different research teams. At first, I just found it fascinating. As I dove further into the evidence, I came to see that the Tetris effect illustrates four key features of scaffolding.

One: Scaffolding generally comes from other people. It would never have occurred to me to ward off unwelcome images by playing Tetris—the idea came from people with relevant experience and expertise. When our circumstances threaten to overpower us, instead of only looking inward, we can turn outward to mentors, teachers, coaches, role models, or peers. The scaffolding they provide looks and feels different depending on the type of challenge we're facing, but it has the same effect: giving us a foothold or a boost.

Two: Scaffolding is tailored to the obstacle in your path. When psychologists suggest Tetris, it's because it has a specific benefit: it changes how your brain constructs mental imagery. Brain scans suggest that Tetris blocks intrusive images by activating our visual-spatial circuits— we're too busy processing falling shapes to attend to the threat of unnerving images. Different kinds of games, like trivia, don't reduce the flashbacks. Tetris is effective scaffolding because it helps you bypass a particular challenge.

Three: Scaffolding comes at a pivotal point in time. It doesn't do any good to play Tetris before you watch the movie—there's no imagery yet to disrupt. The structure becomes useful after the disconcerting scene, and the critical period seems to be the next 24 hours. If you wait longer, the memory has already consolidated, so you need to first reactivate the memory of the scene before you turn to Tetris to block it.

Four: Scaffolding is temporary. It doesn't take a lifetime of Tetris therapy to recover from a horror movie. Playing for just ten minutes is enough to interfere with memory consolidation and curtail flashbacks. Once you've gotten the support you need, you're no longer dependent on it—you can move forward without it.

Since the type of scaffolding we need varies from one day to the next, we'll find support from different sources at different times for different challenges. We might look to a coach or a mentor to show us that what looks like an insurmountable block can be rotated into a stairway. We might rely on a teammate or a mentee to show us that the key missing piece is right around the corner. And we might have to work together to reach the next level when the odds are stacked against us.

Too often, it feels like our mistakes pile up, while our accomplishments disappear. With the right support at the right moments, we can overcome obstacles to growth. To learn how to build these support structures, I went to people who traveled extraordinary distances in the face of extreme physical and emotional challenges. Mountain climbers, musicians, military recruits, and athletes who beat the odds changed how I see scaffolding. You don't have to be a sports fan to appreciate their insights—they apply to every walk of life.

Scaffolding unleashes hidden potential by helping us forge paths we couldn't otherwise see. It enables us to find motivation in the daily grind, gain momentum in the face of stagnation, and turn difficulties and doubts into sources of strength.

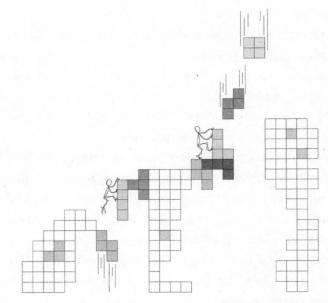

@RESEARCHDOODLES BY M. SHANDELL

CHAPTER 4

Transforming the Daily Grind

Infusing Passion into Practice

It is neither work nor play, purpose nor purposelessness that
satisfies us. It is the dance between.

—BERNARD DE KOVEN

A s she put the finishing touches on her application, a teenager
named Evelyn Glennie felt butterflies in her stomach. Growing up
on a farm in Scotland, she had dreamed of becoming a musician.
She was drawn to the rhythm of the sounds around her: the beat of the
tractor, the low hum of the cows, the clanging of the blacksmiths, the
rustling of the trees in the wind. After four years honing her percussion
skills and several more practicing the piano, Evelyn felt ready. She applied
to one of the most prestigious conservatories in the United Kingdom.

The Royal Academy of Music accepted only the cream of the crop.
Alumni included Elton John and Annie Lennox. When Evelyn arrived in
London for her audition, she had twenty minutes to demonstrate her skills.
She played the Overture to *William Tell* on the timpani, various pieces on
the snare drum and the xylophone, and a Mozart sonata on the piano.

The Academy didn't accept her. Multiple expert panelists voiced concerns about a lack of ability. They concluded she had no hope of making
it as a professional musician.

Less than a decade later, Evelyn became the world's first full-time percussion soloist.

Normally, drummers aren't the musicians crowds flock to see. They play in the background of an orchestra or band, like Ringo sitting in the shadow of John and Paul. But Evelyn was so talented that when she toured the world alone, she routinely sold out 100 concerts a year.

She's won three Grammy Awards, for Best Classical Instrumental Solo as well as Best Chamber Music Performance and Best Classical Crossover Album. She's performed with Björk, played on *Sesame Street*, and been knighted by the queen. In 2015, she was the first percussionist to win the Polar Music Prize—the musical equivalent of a Nobel Prize—joining the company of Elton John, Yo-Yo Ma, Paul McCartney, Joni Mitchell, Paul Simon, Bruce Springsteen, and Stevie Wonder.

When the Royal Academy of Music decided that Evelyn was lacking in ability, they weren't wrong. Technically, she didn't have an ear for music—she couldn't really hear it at all. The world's first and finest solo percussionist is profoundly deaf.

Evelyn's ears had begun failing her when she was eight. By the time she was twelve, when people spoke to her, she could barely make out a sound. An audiologist diagnosed her with degenerating nerves and said it would be impossible for her to play music. The degree of difficulty was too high and the distance to travel too far.

Being profoundly deaf made mastering music unusually hard work. But Evelyn didn't slave over scales for endless, cheerless hours. Her school's percussion teacher, Ron Forbes, didn't push her through a tedious practice schedule of drills. They worked together to create the scaffolding for her to enjoy the process of learning.

When Evelyn first visited Ron, he asked how she would hear music. She had no choice but to adopt a different learning style. She explained that although she couldn't hear all the different pitches with her ears, she could feel the vibrations in her arms, her stomach, her cheekbones, and her scalp. She started to think of her body as a giant ear. As Ron played the timpani, Evelyn put her hands on the wall, learning to associate different pitches with different body parts. Some of the higher notes resonated around her face and neck. The lower notes mostly reverberated in her legs and feet. She started practicing barefoot to feel the vibrations more intensely.

At the start of every lesson, Evelyn relished the challenge of sensing the sounds. As she gained mastery, Ron narrowed the pitch intervals. It was like leveling up in a video game: she was making increasingly fine distinctions between notes using only her fingertips. Soon Ron was stoking her enthusiasm by giving her a whole new set of challenges to master. "See this piece by Bach? Do you think you can play it on a snare drum?" Continually varying the task and raising the bar made learning a joy. "There was never a distinction between fun and hard work," she tells me. "I was like a sponge." She went on to develop her own versions of Bach's music in contemporary drum style.

We're often told that if we want to develop our skills, we need to push ourselves through long hours of monotonous practice. But the best way to unlock hidden potential isn't to suffer through the daily grind. It's to transform the daily grind into a source of daily joy. It's not a coincidence that in music, the term for practice is play.

GETTING IN HARMONY

If you want to become an expert in any field, it's not enough to be a freak of nature. No one is born with the innate ability to play "Amazing Grace" on the bagpipes, pull a bubbling Baked Alaska out of the oven, juggle seven balls at a time, or even spell words like *onomatopoeia* and *mayonnaise*. It takes practice to master a skill.

Ever since the notion of achieving mastery through 10,000 hours of practice took the world by storm, coaches, parents, and teachers have been fascinated by a particular kind of practice. Deliberate practice is the structured repetition of a task to improve performance based on clear goals and immediate feedback. How much of that you need, however, is more nuanced than the 10,000-hours idea would have us believe.

Research reveals that the actual number of hours required for excellence varies dramatically by person and activity. What's clear is that deliberate practice is particularly valuable for improving skills in predictable tasks with consistent moves—swinging a golf club, solving a Rubik's Cube, or playing a violin.

Even child prodigies have been known to dedicate long, obsessive hours to deliberate practice. Mozart's violinist father put him through rigorous drills and a performance schedule so grueling that one biographer called it "unconditional slavery." But that kind of fanatical practice takes a toll. Mozart wrote letters about how drained he felt, confessing as a teenager that "my fingers are aching from composing so many recitatives" and in his late twenties that he was "tired . . . from so much performing." There's reason to believe that he succeeded in spite of his compulsive practice, not because of it.

Research demonstrates that people who are obsessed with their work put in longer hours yet fail to perform any better than their peers. They're more likely to fall victim to both physical and emotional exhaustion. The monotony of deliberate practice puts them at risk for burnout—and for boreout. Yes, *boreout* is an actual term in psychology. Whereas burnout is the emotional exhaustion that accumulates when you're overloaded, boreout is the emotional deadening you feel when you're under-stimulated. Although it takes deliberate practice to achieve greater things, we shouldn't drill so hard that we drive the joy out of the activity and turn it into an obsessive slog.

In a study of concert pianists who attained international acclaim before turning forty, few were obsessed with their craft. In their early years, most practiced the piano only an hour a day. They weren't raised by slave drivers or drill sergeants; their parents responded to their intrinsic motivation with enthusiasm. As they became teenagers, they steadily increased their daily effort, but it didn't become an obsession or a chore. "They practiced because they were interested in what they were doing," psychologist Lauren Sosniak explains, and "because they enjoyed working with the teacher."

Elite musicians are rarely driven by obsessive compulsion. They're usually fueled by what psychologists call harmonious passion. Harmonious passion is taking joy in a process rather than feeling pressure to achieve an outcome. You're no longer practicing under the specter of should. *I should be studying. I'm supposed to practice.* You're drawn into a web of want. *I feel like studying. I'm excited to practice.* That makes it easier to find flow: you slip quickly into the zone of total absorption, where the world melts away and you become one with your instrument. Instead of controlling your life, practicing enriches your life.

The importance of passion isn't unique to music. Across 127 studies with over 45,000 people, persistence was more likely to translate into performance when passion was present.* The question is how to build the scaffolding to bring that passion into practice. My favorite answer is called deliberate play.

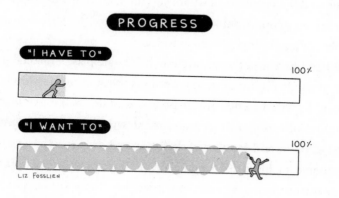

LIZ FOSSLIEN

---

*My colleague Nancy Rothbard finds that the toll of long hours depends on how you feel about them. People are at elevated risk for depression, sleep problems, and high blood pressure and cholesterol when they burn the midnight oil based on obsession—but not when they do it based on passion. There's also evidence that obsession predicts greater conflict between work and the rest of life: you struggle to disconnect from your job, which contributes to burnout. Meanwhile, harmonious passion is linked to gains in satisfaction and work-life balance—it's easier to keep different priorities in harmony when you don't feel pressure to work all the time.

PLAY BY PLAY

Deliberate play is a structured activity that's designed to make skill development enjoyable. It blends elements of deliberate practice and free play. Like free play, deliberate play is fun, but it's structured for learning and mastery along with recreation. It's built to break complex tasks into simpler parts so you can hone a specific skill.

When I asked Evelyn Glennie how she practices, she said she spends nearly all her time in deliberate play. When she gets bored, she switches instruments, gracefully bouncing back and forth between different percussion tools. "If I'm trying to stay interested in a new marimba skill, I'll transfer it to a drum kit," she tells me. Mixing it up breaks up the monotony and keeps her passion in harmony. "There is absolutely no routine," she says, laughing. "That spells hostage to me."

Deliberate play often involves introducing novelty and variety into practice. That can be in the ways you learn, the tools you use, the goals you set, and the people with whom you interact. Depending on the skill you're trying to build, deliberate play might take the form of a game, a role-play, or an improvisational exercise.

When I first read the research on deliberate play, it opened my eyes to the possibility of bringing harmonious passion into any kind of skill practice. I started wondering if I could transform the grind in more traditional job training. In an experiment with healthcare professionals, my colleagues and I found that their burnout dropped after we nudged them to inject a bit of deliberate play into their most stressful tasks. An allergy nurse started introducing herself as Nurse Quick Shot, which immediately put her young patients at ease. She let them time her, and when they came back for their next visit, they would ask for Nurse Quick Shot and challenge her to beat her previous time.

There's a movement to bring deliberate play into professional development. Medical schools have started offering improvisational comedy courses to bring levity into the challenge of learning to interpret nonverbal cues. In one exercise, Foreign Movie, students watch their classmates shout out nonsense words and try to decipher their meaning by observing their gestures and facial expressions. Students report that along with being enjoyable, deliberate play makes them better doctors—and the initial evidence is encouraging. After these kinds of improv sessions were added to a communication course in pharmacy school, students performed better on patient examinations. They were better equipped to identify a patient's chief complaint and empathize with a patient's concerns.

These benefits aren't limited to healthcare. In some sales classes, students were invited to learn through playing the role of salesperson and customer. In one exercise, the customer would walk up holding a box, and the salesperson would ask what was in it, with the objective of keeping the conversation going for three minutes without skipping a beat. Over the next month, when they were sent to sell tickets for a professional sports team, the students who participated in this role-play exercise sold 43 percent more tickets than a control group of students who had not completed this training. They also enjoyed the course more.

The scaffolding for deliberate play is often set up by a teacher or coach, but it's possible to make real strides on your own. If you want to improve your sight reading at the piano, you could challenge yourself to see how many notes you get right on new pieces and track your progress week by week. If you're a Scrabble player hoping to improve your anagram aptitude, you can practice drawing random sets of tiles and see how many words you can spell in a minute.

Deliberate play has become especially popular in sports. Extensive evidence shows that athletes who specialize early in a single sport tend to peak quickly and then flame out. Pounding the pavement from a young age puts them at greater risk for both physical and mental health challenges. With deliberate play, it's easier to sustain enjoyment and achieve greater things.

In sports, deliberate play is typically organized around a subcomponent of a performance or match. In tennis, for example, you might hone your serving skills by challenging yourself to see how many consecutive serves you can make. Success might be defeating an opponent, outdoing yourself, or beating the clock. You're not counting your hours; you're tracking your improvement. Your score is not a symbol of victory; it's a gauge of progress.

In a small experiment in Brazil, sports psychologists compared deliberate play and deliberate practice as strategies for teaching basketball to young players. Some of the athletes spent over half their training time in deliberate practice. Their coaches took them through dribbling, passing, and shooting drills with regular feedback, with and without defenders.

The remaining athletes spent nearly three quarters of their training time in deliberate play. To develop their skills, their coaches designed games instead of drills. Sometimes players had a teammate who was allowed to pass but not shoot. Other times they played at a disadvantage—one against two, or three against four. Several months later, the psychologists tested the basketball intelligence and creativity of both groups, measuring their ability to move to open spots on the court and make passes that eluded defenders. It was deliberate play—not deliberate practice—that propelled significant improvement.

By fueling harmonious passion, deliberate play can prevent boreout and burnout. Although it might sound similar to gamification, deliberate play is fundamentally different. Gamification is often a gimmick—an attempt to add bells and whistles to a tedious task. The aim is to offer a dopamine rush that distracts from boredom or staves off exhaustion. Sure, a leaderboard might motivate you to push through the pain, but it's not enough to trick you into liking a routine you hate.* In deliberate

---

*I learned recently that the first treadmills were invented as torture devices. In the early 1800s, British prisoners had to spend about six hours a day stepping on the spokes of a big wheel that pumped water or powered mills. A prison guard wrote that what "constitutes its terror" was not the "severity" but the "monotonous steadiness."

play, you actually redesign the task itself to make it both motivating and developmental. The best example I've seen was dreamed up by a basketball trainer.

PRACTICE WITHOUT PLAY

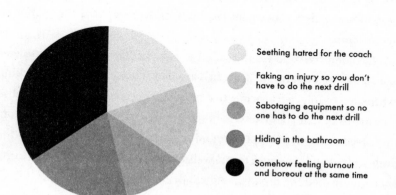

Seething hatred for the coach

Faking an injury so you don't have to do the next drill

Sabotaging equipment so no one has to do the next drill

Hiding in the bathroom

Somehow feeling burnout and boreout at the same time

OUT OF PRACTICE

As soon as I read about Brandon Payne's philosophy of practice, I had to call him. When Brandon was growing up in the Charlotte suburbs, his dreams were dominated by basketball. As the son of a basketball coach, he learned the fundamentals early. After spending afternoons, evenings, and weekends shooting hoops on his driveway, he became a sharpshooter known for swishing free throws and draining three-pointers. But after arriving at Wingate University with aspirations to walk onto the basketball team, Brandon ran into a problem. When he saw an open spot, he couldn't beat his opponents to it. When he faked to one side and dribbled to the other, they stayed with him. Eventually, Brandon's game hit a wall, and he was told his basketball career was over. "It crushed me," Brandon laments. "There's no worse feeling than someone telling you you're done when you still love to play."

Although Brandon loved to play, when it came to developing skills beyond shooting, he didn't love to practice. To leave defenders in the dust and create his own shot, he needed to work on his quickness and agility. "I was limited athletically," he admits, and "I didn't do the things I needed to do." He didn't do the necessary sprints to build his speed, the essential stretching exercises to boost his flexibility, or the required drills to improve his footwork.

Brandon transitioned to coaching. Now he had to motivate athletes to do some of the same drills he had avoided. They loathed the wheezing exhaustion of full-court sprints that burned their bodies and the repetitive humdrum of footwork exercises that bored their minds. Like Brandon, they loved to shoot. But that harmonious passion didn't spill over into the dullest drills—it seemed to make them even duller. The joy of jump shots intensified the dread of endless dribbling.

Passion for one task can lead us to neglect the less exciting ones on our plate. It's a pattern I've demonstrated in research with a former student, Jihae Shin. In one study of Korean salespeople, we found that the more they loved their favorite task in their job, the worse they performed at their least favorite task. We replicated that effect in an experiment, giving people the boring task of copying names and numbers from a phone book. They made more errors if we had randomly assigned them to watch fascinating YouTube videos first. The contrast between the two tasks made the data entry even more mind-numbing.

Practice involves multiple skills, and it's rare to love them all. Brandon started looking for ways to work harmonious passion into every element of practice. Although he couldn't subtract the pain from drills, he could add pleasure to the process. Instead of trying to push players through the most punishing parts of practice, he was going to reimagine practice to pull them in. "I wanted to create a system to make sure no players would fall victim to what I created for myself," Brandon reflects. He would build the scaffolding to help athletes reach their potential by harnessing their love of the game.

In 2009, Brandon set up a training center for basketball players. One day, he crossed paths with a young NBA player whose weaknesses had been readily apparent to scouts. One wrote that he was "extremely limited by his poor physical tools." Another lamented: "He doesn't have the size, the strength, or the lateral quickness/athleticism. . . . He probably is never going to end up being a star in the league because of a lack of explosiveness."

Brandon recognized some of his own shortcomings in the player and handed him his business card. They started working together the next morning. In his first full season after training with Brandon, the player set the NBA record for most three-pointers made. A few years later, he was named the NBA's most valuable player in back-to-back seasons. His name is Stephen Curry.

CHANGING THE GAME

Steph Curry is widely regarded as the best shooter in NBA history. It's often said that what Michael Jordan did for the slam dunk, Curry has done for the three-pointer—he's revolutionized the sport by turning it into a marksmanship contest. The two previous record holders for the most three-pointers in a career took over 1,300 games to set their standards. Curry eclipsed them in just 789 games.

Despite being the son of an NBA player, Curry didn't get a single scholarship offer from top college basketball programs. Coming out of high school, he was massively underrated: on a five-star scale, he was branded as only a three-star recruit. The summer before his senior year, the coach at Davidson College went to see him play. "He was awful. He threw the ball into the stands, he dropped passes, he dribbled off his foot, he missed shots," the coach recalls. "But never ever once during that game did he blame an official, or point a finger at a teammate. He was always cheering from the bench . . . and he never flinched. That stuck with me."

Those weren't the first signs of Curry's character skills. When he was a kid hanging around with his father's team, one of the players noticed that Curry "was like a little sponge . . . soaking up information everywhere he went." In high school, even when he was struggling, he had the determination to support his team and the discipline to keep his cool. But research suggests that the people with the most discipline actually use the least amount of it. My colleague Angela Duckworth finds that instead of relying on willpower to push through a strenuous situation, they change the situation to make it less strenuous.

A clear example comes from research on the marshmallow test. It's one of the most famous—and most misunderstood—studies in the history of psychology. You're probably familiar with the classic version: psychologists put a marshmallow on a plate and told four-year-olds that if they could wait a few minutes to eat it, they would get two marshmallows. Preschoolers who managed to resist the urge to gobble up the marshmallow now for a bigger fluffy treat later ended up scoring higher on the SAT as teenagers—a finding that's been replicated recently.

When I first watched the videos of the marshmallow test, I was expecting to see a subset of kids with superior willpower. What I saw instead was kids creating bits of scaffolding to remove the need for willpower. Some covered their eyes or the marshmallow. Others sat on their hands. One mushed the marshmallow into a ball and bounced it, turning it into a toy. They had improvised their own forms of deliberate play.* That's what Brandon Payne did for Steph Curry.

---

*The early marshmallow research assumed that delaying gratification is a sign of discipline—the capacity to prioritize long-term goals over short-term rewards. But a recent replication suggests that waiting for the extra marshmallow may be an even stronger signal of social support: kids raised in more nurturing environments may be more likely to trust the experimenter to deliver on the promise of a reward. Disproportionately, the kids who succumb to the immediate gooey delight come from socioeconomically disadvantaged families. When you grow up in a world of scarcity and uncertainty, you can't count on a bigger reward coming later.

FOR THE LOVE OF PRACTICE

Brandon has been training Curry for over a decade now. He told me he began with a basic principle: "There is no boring in our workouts." He set up the scaffolding to make the hardest parts of practice easier—to help Curry make more progress while relying less on sheer discipline.

To make practice fun while building technical skills, Brandon created a menu of deliberate play activities. In Twenty-One, you get a minute to score twenty-one points with three-pointers, jump shots, and layups (worth one). But after each shot, you have to sprint to the middle of the court and back. Getting out of breath during that game simulates the fatigue of the real game. "Every drill is a game," Brandon explains. "There's always a time to beat. There's always a number to beat. If you beat the number and you don't beat the time, you still lose."

The downside of competing against others is that you can win without improving. They might have a bad day, or you might benefit from a stroke of good luck. In Brandon's form of deliberate play, the person you're competing with is your past self, and the bar you're raising is for your future self. You're not aiming for perfect—you're shooting for better. The only way to win is to grow.

I assumed it would be ideal to practice one skill until you make progress, and only then move on to the next one. But rather than repeating the same challenges over and over, Brandon mixes them up. In twenty-minute intervals, Brandon has Curry bouncing from one shooting-and-quickness challenge to another. The variety isn't just motivating—it's also better for learning. Hundreds of experiments show that people improve faster when they alternate between different skills. Psychologists call it interleaving, and it works in areas ranging from painting to math, especially when the skills being developed are similar or complex. Even small tweaks, like shifting between thinner and thicker paintbrushes or slightly adjusting the weight of a basketball, can make a big difference.

Deliberate play is particularly valuable for transforming the grind of summer practice. When there are multiple games per week, many athletes have little trouble staying motivated. In the offseason, though, it's easy to lose interest. After rising star Luka Doncic showed up to preseason out of shape, he started training with Brandon and dropped weight while gaining speed. "Unless you're playing pickup, summers are sometimes long. The workouts can become a little monotonous if you let them," Steph Curry told a reporter. Deliberate play "creates a game-like situation with pressure," he said, which means "you have to stay locked in and focused."

Over a decade of training, Curry realized his hidden potential. What he lacks in size at 6' 2" and 185 pounds, he now makes up in explosiveness as well as accuracy. He gives much of the credit to the deliberate play that Brandon organizes—it brings harmonious passion into practice. And he gets more out of it because of his determination. "He loves the process. That's one of the things that ties all great athletes together," Curry's longtime coach Steve Kerr observes. "There's a routine . . . but it's really enjoyed each day. There's a passion that comes with it, and that's what sustains it over time. When you love something like those guys do, you work at it, you get better and you just keep going."

Although it may not turn you into a professional athlete, deliberate play can amplify your motivation and accelerate your development. One day I saw a video of a YouTuber who followed Steph Curry's training regimen for two hours a day. At the start, he made only 8 percent of his three-pointers. Over fifty days of deliberate play, he traveled a great distance, making 40 percent of those same shots.

It's clear that deliberate play can spark and sustain harmonious passion. But can that passion can be maintained over long periods of time? Evelyn Glennie thinks so—she's felt it for half a century. She knows what research shows: even deliberate play shouldn't be done all day every day. She learned this lesson the hard way.

YOU CAN TAKE A BREAK WHEN...

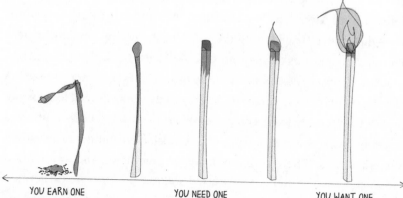

| YOU EARN ONE | YOU NEED ONE | YOU WANT ONE |
| TOXIC CULTURES | GOOD CULTURES | VIBRANT CULTURES |

@RESEARCHDOODLES BY M. SHANDELL

GIMME A BREAK

I first saw Evelyn play in 2012 during the opening ceremony of the Olympics. To build to a crescendo, she was invited to lead a thousand drummers. Standing in front of an array of multi-drums, she progressed from rhythmic taps to rapid pounds, and the stadium crackled with energy. Later, when a gold medalist entered the stadium carrying the Olympic torch, Evelyn introduced the world to a new sound on an instrument she helped design, the Glennie Concert Aluphone. It looked like a set of mushroom-shaped bells, and as she struck it with four mallets, it sounded like a warmer, more uplifting version of orchestral chimes. I had no idea she had a physical disability—let alone one that prevented her from hearing the music she made.

Back when Evelyn was a teenager auditioning for the Royal Academy of Music, the experts on the panel simply didn't believe a deaf girl could become a professional musician. She challenged them to pay attention to the caliber of the performance rather than the impairment of the person delivering it. After a second audition, the Academy didn't just admit her—they ended up changing the rules for the entire United Kingdom to evaluate applicants on their musical skills, not their physical abilities.

As a full-time music student at the Academy, Evelyn loved to practice. She started off playing two or three hours a day, but it wasn't long before she felt the pressure to take on more. When she saw her peers putting in longer hours, she noticed a sense of compulsion creeping into her mind. She asked herself how long she *should* be practicing, and wondered if she *should* practice more. She started waking up an hour earlier and practicing later into the evening. But the feeling of obligation sucked the playful rhythm out of percussion, and she saw her creativity and progress evaporate with it. She began to realize that there was such a thing as over-practice. To make sure music didn't become a grind, she decided to take regular breaks.

It turns out that taking breaks has at least three benefits. First, time away from practice helps to sustain harmonious passion. Research indicates that even micro-breaks of five to ten minutes are enough to reduce fatigue and raise energy. It's not just about preventing burnout: research reveals that when we work nights and weekends, our interest and enjoyment in our tasks drop. Even just reminding you that it's Saturday is enough to reduce your intrinsic motivation—you realize that you could be doing something fun and relaxing instead. Yo-Yo Ma limits his practice to between three and six hours a day and strives to avoid early-morning and late-night sessions. Chopin urged his students not to practice more than two hours a day in the summer.

Second, breaks unlock fresh ideas. In my own research with Jihae Shin, I've found that taking breaks boosts creativity when you feel harmonious passion toward a task. Your interest keeps the problem active in the back of your mind, and you're more likely to incubate new ways of framing it and unexpected ways of solving it. Lin-Manuel Miranda dreamed up his blockbuster musical *Hamilton* while daydreaming on vacation, sitting on a pool float with a margarita in his hand. It's why Beethoven, Tchaikovsky, and Mahler all regularly took walks nearly as long as their workdays.

Third, breaks deepen learning. In one experiment, taking a ten-minute break after learning something improved recall for students by 10 to 30 percent—and even more for stroke and Alzheimer's patients. Once about 24 hours have passed, information starts to fade from our memories—we fall down a forgetting curve. It's well established that we can avoid that forgetting curve with spaced repetition—interspersing breaks into practice. At first, you might practice once an hour, and then start taking longer breaks until you're practicing once a day.

Obsession leads us to see rest as taking a foot off the gas pedal. We don't stop until we've pushed ourselves to the edge of exhaustion—it's a price to pay for excellence. Under harmonious passion, it's easier to recognize that rest is a supply of fuel. We take regular reprieves to maintain energy and avoid burnout.

WHEN WE SHOULD
TAKE A BREAK

WHEN WE ACTUALLY
TAKE A BREAK

Relaxing is not a waste of time—it's an investment in well-being. Breaks are not a distraction—they're a chance to reset attention and incubate ideas. Play is not a frivolous activity—it's a source of joy and a path to mastery.

If you watch Evelyn today, you'll see that she exudes the same joy practicing alone as she expresses performing in front of the entire world. But she rarely practices in more than twenty-minute intervals before taking a break. "Sometimes I feel like I really want to pick up a pair of sticks and do something, and other times I think, 'No, I just want to sit here and stare at the walls.' Other times I might want to write a little something in my notebook, or read a good book."

She tells me that when she loses interest or focus, she just stops playing altogether. "Worthwhile practice is where progress is made. It's about quality, not quantity. You need to feel there's a shift—something is different when you walked out of the room."

Not long ago, a mother contacted Evelyn for a consultation. After going through a series of music exams, her daughter had lost interest in practicing the violin. The mother was hoping Evelyn would give her a pep talk and motivate her to keep practicing.

Instead, Evelyn improvised some deliberate play. She challenged the girl to play pieces backward, to come up with ten ways not to play the violin, and to incorporate sounds from her favorite TV show and her favorite animal. The girl left the session beaming. Before, her practice time was focused on "an outcome of being judged," Evelyn says. Deliberate play taught her that "the real outcome is her enjoyment." Without enjoyment, potential stays hidden.

CHAPTER 5

Getting Unstuck

The Roundabout Path to Forward Progress

Every limit is a beginning as well as an ending.

—GEORGE ELIOT

n seventh grade, people started calling him a phenom. By his sophomore year of high school, professional scouts were coming to his baseball games. As a college student, he won an Olympic bronze medal as a starting pitcher for Team USA. That same year, the Texas Rangers drafted him in the first round and offered a signing bonus over $800,000. He would start at the top of their minor-league system and make the big leagues in a year or two. R. A. Dickey was going somewhere.

Then all of a sudden, he wasn't.

When RA showed up to sign his contract in 1996, a team trainer noticed his arm hanging at an unusual angle and suggested an X-ray. Unbeknownst to him, RA was missing a ligament in his right elbow. It was a critical piece of tissue for a throwing arm, and it put a clear ceiling on his potential. His fastball might never get fast enough. The Rangers slashed his signing bonus to under $80,000 and sent him to the lowest tier of their minor-league system. *Strike one.*

This wasn't supposed to happen. Baseball was RA's escape from a bleak life. He grew up poor in Nashville, and by the time he was five, his mother was dragging him along to local bars and drinking until they closed. His parents divorced a few years later, and his father was largely absent. Feeling abandoned left him with something to prove.

For seven years, RA toiled away in minor-league baseball. It felt as if he was wasting the prime of his career. Since he couldn't throw a blazing fastball, he honed his ability to fool batters by varying speed and spin. Finally, in his late twenties, he got his big break: the Rangers brought him up to the majors full time.

It didn't take long for RA to realize he was out of his league. Scouts and journalists gave brutal assessments of his performance and potential. *Journeyman. Marginal. Mediocre.* He gave up too many runs and lost more games than he won. He knew what that meant. *Has-been. Never-was.*

Partway through his third major-league season with the Rangers, his managers brought him in for a tough conversation. They told him he was "going nowhere," he reflects, "an assessment that I could hardly argue with. I'd been going nowhere for a long time." They demoted him back down to the minors. *Strike two.*

RA was determined to return to the majors. In the offseason he threw countless pitches against cinder blocks and kept a baseball in his car to refine his grip while driving. He pushed himself harder than ever.

The following season, the Rangers gave him another chance. In his first game back, he tied a major-league record.

But not the good kind of record. RA gave up six home runs in just three innings—no pitcher had ever done worse. As the crowd booed, the Rangers yanked him out of the game and sent him down to the minors . . . again. *Strike three. You're out.*

Pitchers usually peak in their mid- to late twenties and retire by their early 30s. At 31, it was clearly too late for RA to make a comeback. The writing was on the wall he kept hitting: his baseball career was over.

One of the most frustrating parts of honing a skill is getting stuck.

Instead of continuing to improve, you start to stagnate. It feels as if you've reached the upper bound of your mental or physical capacities. Since stagnation marks the end of growth, it seems to spell the beginning of decline. *My best days are behind me. It's all downhill from here.* Surgeons expect to stagnate and decline as their eyesight and reflexes deteriorate. Scientists prepare to stagnate and decline as their neurons die. Athletes inevitably stagnate and decline as their strength and speed wane. Or at least that's what we assume. But the reality is less linear—and more uplifting.

At age 35, R. A. Dickey broke through his wall once and for all. After spending the bulk of fourteen years in the minor leagues, he made it back to the majors. That year, his earned run average made him one of the ten best pitchers in all of baseball, and he signed a multiyear, multimillion-dollar contract with the New York Mets. Of the nine pitchers who had outranked him in his draft class, eight had already retired, and the ninth would never make it back to the majors. Yet RA was just beginning to realize his hidden potential.

The key to his eventual triumph was the scaffolding others helped him build. It came from many different sources, and it took RA a while to put the pieces together. But he never would've gotten unstuck if his coaches hadn't started by sending him back to the drawing board.

A rut is not a sign that you've tanked. A plateau is not a cue that you've peaked. They're signals that it may be time to turn around and find a new route. When you're stuck, it's usually because you're heading in the wrong direction, you're taking the wrong path, or you're running out of fuel. Gaining momentum often involves backing up and navigating your way down a different road—even if it's not the one you initially intended to travel. It might be unfamiliar, winding, and bumpy. Progress rarely happens in a straight line; it typically unfolds in loops.

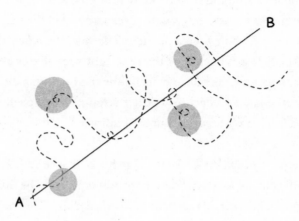

LEARNING EXPERIENCES

LIZ FOSSLIEN

BACKING UP TO MOVE FORWARD

Skills don't grow at a steady pace. Improving them is like driving up a mountain. As we climb higher and higher, the road gets steeper and steeper, and our gains get smaller and smaller. When we run out of momentum, we start to stall. It's not enough to step on the gas—our wheels are spinning, but we've stopped moving.

After poring over more than a century of evidence on progress, cognitive scientists Wayne Gray and John Lindstedt observed a fascinating arc. When our performance stagnates, before it improves again, it declines. When people's skills stalled in tasks ranging from Tetris to golf to memorizing facts, they didn't usually ascend again until after they had deteriorated.

When we reach a dead end, to move forward, we may have to head back down the mountain. Once we've retreated far enough, we can find another way—a path that will allow us to build the momentum needed to reach the peak.

It's often difficult to accept that we need to retreat. Backing up means scrapping our current plan and starting over. That's what causes a temporary decline in performance: we've chosen to give up the gains we've made. We're regressing in order to progress. "Performance suffers as new methods are being invented, tested, rejected, or accepted," Gray and Lindstedt explain. We ascend after "the implementation of a successful new method . . . to surpass prior levels of achievement."

Finding the right method involves trial and error. Some trials will just be plain errors: we spin our wheels on bad strategies. But even if we discover a better method, our inexperience with it will usually make us worse at first. Those backsteps aren't only normal—in many situations they're necessary.

In typing, if you hunt and peck, you'll probably level off around 30 to 40 words per minute. No matter how hard you practice, you'll hit that wall. If you want to double your pace to 60 to 70 words a minute, you have to try a new method: typing by touch instead of sight. But before you can speed up, you have to slow down. It takes time to learn the keys by heart.

More advanced skills come with steeper learning curves. If you're solving a Rubik's Cube, the easiest method is layer by layer. You make a blue cross on one side, then rotate it to fill in the corners and start working on the next side. About 130 moves later, you're done. If you want to do it faster, you'll need to memorize a list of algorithms. It will take you longer at first, but eventually you'll only need 60 moves. In the process, you'll also need to rebuild your muscle memory—shedding old habits in favor of new ones.

One of the surprising things about backing up is that it can set the stage for improvement even when you don't do it intentionally. In a study of over 28,000 NBA basketball games, researchers investigated what happened to teams after their star players got injured. As expected, teams got worse. But once the star returned, they won even more games than they had before he was hurt. Why did losing their best player ultimately help them get better?

Without their stars, teams had to go back to square one and search for new paths to success. They rearranged their roles to enable peripheral players to step up and drew up fresh plays to leverage their strengths. When the star came back, their shot balance improved. They were less dependent on one hero to carry the entire team.*

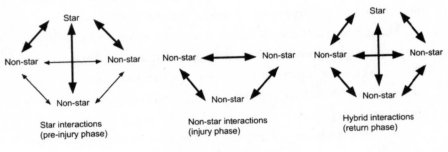

Star interactions
(pre-injury phase)

Non-star interactions
(injury phase)

Hybrid interactions
(return phase)

Thicker lines represent more passes

You can see a similar pattern in NHL hockey teams after a player got injured. The more teams experimented with their lineups to bring different players together on the ice, the better they performed.

It shouldn't take an extreme event like an injury to push us to stop, reverse, and switch routes. But the truth is we're often afraid to go backward. We see slowing down as losing ground, backing up as giving up, and rerouting as veering off course. We worry that when we step back, we'll lose our footing altogether. This means we stay exactly where we are—steady but stuck. We need to embrace the discomfort of getting lost.

---

*The duration of the injury matters. If an NBA star missed only a game or two, the team didn't improve once he returned—it seems there wasn't enough pressure or time for them to adopt new roles and learn new routines. And if the star was gone too long, missing half the season or more, there weren't any benefits either—possibly because teams got stuck in their new roles and routines and struggled to utilize their star effectively when he was back. Before you hope your favorite team will pull their star for a few games, you should know that for the benefits to outweigh the costs, an average team would need its star to play about 43 games after missing 15. But this does suggest a new rationale and approach for pulling stars out. Normally, load management involves resting players for a game here and there to avoid injury and exhaustion. When a team gets stuck, it might pay dividends to give stars several consecutive games off—it's an opportunity for the whole team to reset.

A SWING AND A MISS

Backing up puts us on new terrain—we're in uncharted territory. We're taking an unfamiliar path to a destination we've never visited, and the summit might not even be visible at the start. To find our way, we need scaffolding in the form of some basic navigational tools.

The bad news is that a perfect map won't exist. The exact route hasn't been plotted for us—there may not even be a road. We might have to pave our own way, figuring out the route as we go, one turn at a time.

The good news is that to start moving, we don't actually need a map. All we need is a compass to gauge whether we're heading in the right direction.

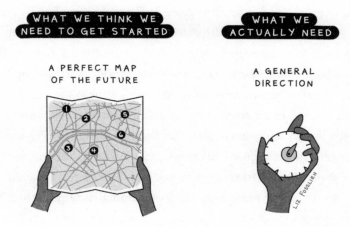

Depending on the skill you're trying to learn, you might discover a compass in a book, on the web, or in a conversation. A good compass signals when you're going off course and orients you in a better direction. If you begin to stall as you learn to code in C++, you can find a compass in a quick online search that points you toward Python: it's easier to learn and just as well suited to accomplish a wide variety of projects. If your oil paintings keep coming out lumpy, you might pick up a compass in a chat with a seasoned artist who suggests a solvent to thin your paints. And if you're a baseball pitcher trying to climb out of what feels like a permanent slump, your compass might come from a coach who tells you your fastball is too slow—and points you toward a new pitch.

That was the beginning of R. A. Dickey's transformation. I sought him out because I'd never seen someone make such a dramatic improvement after being stalled for so long and taking so many steps backward. If anyone knew how to get unstuck, it was the guy who transitioned from one of the worst in his field to one of the best.

After nearly a decade as a minor-league pitcher, RA was struggling to build a career and support his family. To pay the bills during the off-season, one spring he sold golf balls that he fished out of alligator-infested lagoons. In the span of a decade, he moved more than thirty times, only to find himself in the exact same place. It was as if he was stuck in quicksand: the harder he tried to pull himself out, the harder it became to escape.*

When RA made his final trip down to the minors at age 31, his pitching coaches handed him a compass. They told him he was heading in the wrong direction: he was never going to make it back to the majors on his current course. In an attempt to salvage his career, they pointed him toward a murky, mysterious path that few had navigated. For years, as part of his repertoire, RA had occasionally hurled a strange pitch—he named it the Thing. His coaches recognized the way he was holding the ball: it was similar to the grip for a rare pitch called the knuckleball. They encouraged RA to develop it and make it the centerpiece of his game.

---

*According to quicksand science (yes, that exists), it's impossible for humans to drown in quicksand. With the slightest pressure, the mixture of sand, clay, and salt water liquefies, dragging us down with it—but we're too dense to sink more than halfway. It's still hard to get unstuck, though: just pulling a foot out requires about as much force as it takes to lift a car. To break free, you wiggle your legs to let water drain through, dislodging the sand that's trapping you. Then you lie on your back to spread your weight across the surface, reducing the strain on the sand and causing you to float. From there, you can backstroke your way out.

Instead of flying with vicious speed and deadly spin, a knuckleball sails slower and as flat as possible. Rather than wrapping your fingers around the ball, you dig the nails of your index and middle fingers into it. Those two knuckles stick up in the air, giving the pitch its signature name. That unusual grip takes the rotation off the ball, allowing it to zigzag erratically in the air and befuddle batters.

The knuckleball is so unpredictable that catchers wear oversized mitts to snag it. Since it doesn't require great strength or cause unusual strain, it can add years of longevity to a pitcher's arm. But as difficult as it is to hit and catch, the knuckleball is even tougher to pitch—and as RA would find out, even tougher than that to master.

There was no obvious way for RA to develop his skills. His pitching coaches had never worked with a knuckleballer before—they couldn't give him a map, because they didn't have one. There weren't any knuckleball textbooks or tutorials. All they could offer was a compass pointing him in the general direction of throwing a pitch that doesn't spin.

Everything about the knuckleball felt backward for RA. To keep the ball from spinning, as he released it, he was supposed to keep his wrist as stiff as possible. But from the time he was a kid, he had been taught to rotate his wrist rapidly as he let the ball fly. Fastballs have backspin, curveballs have topspin, sinkers have sidespin. "I had to unlearn all of that," RA told me, and "relearn my mechanics. It took major deconstruction to be able to reconstruct. I had to tear it down to ground zero to rebuild." There was no guarantee that his effort would succeed.

Seeking discomfort was a character skill he fully embraced. But RA's early outings with knuckleballs did not go smoothly. In his first minor-league game throwing the pitch, he gave up twelve runs in six innings. After the debacle of debuting his knuckleball in the majors—the game where he tied the all-time worst record for homers given up—the Rangers let him go from their organization altogether. Still, he thought his knuckle-ball had the potential to go somewhere good. He just didn't know how to get there.

The drawback of a compass is that it only gives you direction—not directions. It can help you back away from the wrong path and point you toward a better one. But to navigate that path effectively, you need a guide.

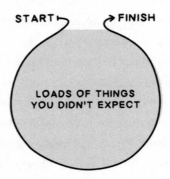

Janis Ozolins from OzolinsJanis.com

WHAT THOSE WHO CAN DO CAN'T TEACH

When we're unsure of the path to a goal, we often seek directions from an expert guide. It's a familiar mantra: if you want to be great, learn from the best. Take a master class in cooking from a top chef. Sign your kids up for a tennis lesson with a pro. Convince the biggest star in your field to be your mentor and learn how to follow in their footsteps. What could be better than taking your first physics class with Einstein?

Quite a bit, it turns out. In a clever study, economists wanted to find out whether students really learn more from experts. They collected data on every freshman at Northwestern University from 2001 to 2008. They investigated whether freshmen did better in their second course in a subject if their introductory class was taught by more qualified instructors.

You might assume that students would be better off learning the basics from an expert (a tenure-track or tenured professor) than a nonexpert (a lecturer with less specialized knowledge). But the data showed the opposite: students who took their initial class with an expert ended up with *poorer* grades in the next class.

The pattern was robust across fields: students learned less from introductory classes taught by experts in every subject. It held across years—with over 15,000 students—and in courses with tougher as well as easier grading. And the experts were especially bad at teaching students who were less academically prepared.*

It turns out that if you're taking a new road, the best experts are often the worst guides. There are at least two reasons why experts struggle to give good directions to beginners. One is the distance they've traveled—they've come too far to remember what it's like being in your shoes. It's called the curse of knowledge: the more you know, the harder it is for you to fathom what it's like to not know. As cognitive scientist Sian Beilock summarizes it, "As you get better and better at what you do, your ability to communicate your understanding or to help others learn that skill often gets worse and worse."

That was Einstein's curse in the classroom. He knew too much, and his students knew too little. He had so many ideas swirling in his head that he had a hard time keeping his lectures organized—let alone explaining to a beginner how gravity bends light. When he made his teaching debut in a thermodynamics course, despite being a rising star in physics, his lackluster teaching attracted only three students. His material was often over their heads, and after he failed to draw a larger group the following semester, Einstein canceled the class. Several years

---

*This research makes a strong case for rethinking university tenure. The typical model is to require faculty to publish research and teach courses, and we're long overdue to create a second track for researchers who aren't skilled teachers—and a third for lecturers who don't do research. They're separate skills anyway: the average correlation between research productivity and teaching effectiveness is zero. The researchers could vet the curriculum for rigor and comprehensiveness, and the lecturers could inform research on effective teaching.

down the road, he was nearly denied another faculty position because the university president was underwhelmed by his teaching skills.

It's often said that those who can't do, teach. It would be more accurate to say that those who can do, can't teach the basics. A great deal of expert knowledge is tacit—it's implicit, not explicit. The further you progress toward mastery, the less conscious awareness you often have of the fundamentals. Experiments show that skilled golfers and wine aficionados have a hard time describing their putting and tasting techniques—even asking them to explain their approaches is enough to interfere with their performance, so they often stay on autopilot. When I first saw an elite diver do four and a half somersaults, I asked how he managed to spin so fast. His answer: "Just go up in a ball." Experts often have an intuitive understanding of a route, but they struggle to articulate all the steps to take. Their brain dump is partially filled with garbage.

Instead of helping you find your way, directions from expert guides can leave you stuck. Even worse, they can leave you feeling like your own limitations are preventing you from progressing. I started college torn between majoring in psychology and physics—my two favorite subjects in high school. I was thrilled to get into a class with an eminent astrophysics professor. One day he proclaimed that the universe was everything and presented evidence that it was expanding . . . but couldn't explain what it was expanding into. I went from feeling fascinated to frustrated and confident to incompetent. Although he was passionate and caring, he had learned too much—and been a novice too long ago—to relate to my ignorance. I never took another physics course.

Even if your chosen expert can walk you through their route, when you ask for directions on yours, you'll run into a second challenge. You don't share the same strengths and weaknesses—their hills and valleys aren't the same as yours. You might be heading for the same destination, but you're starting far from their position. This makes your path as unfamiliar to them as theirs is to you.

Of course, you'll get more personalized advice from a guide who knows you well. But as tempting as it is to turn to a trusted mentor for sage advice, no individual will have all the right directions. You can see this in a study of lawyers navigating the path to partner. Guidance from a single mentor didn't make a difference in promotions. There were other upsides: lawyers who had a supportive mentor were more satisfied and committed than their peers who lacked one. But when it came to getting promoted to partner, what mattered was being guided by multiple mentors. Different mentors were able to share different tidbits on how to advance. It didn't take a village, though—all it took was two or three mentors to help lawyers make the climb to partner rather than seeing their careers stall.

Just as it's unwise to seek rudimentary instruction from the most eminent experts, it's a mistake to rely on a single guide. No one else knows your exact journey. But if you collect directions from multiple guides, they can sometimes combine to reveal routes you didn't see. The more uncertain the path and the higher the peak, the greater the range of guides you'll need. The challenge is to piece the various tips together into a route that works for you.

WRITING YOUR OWN GUIDEBOOK

Learning from multiple guides is an iterative, interactive process. It's not as simple as going to people and asking, "Can I pick your brain?" *Also, the image of picking a brain is gross.* The information isn't just sitting there, waiting to be extracted. We don't live in the Matrix. Guides can't simply upload their insights for us to download.

The point of engaging guides isn't to blindly follow their leads. It's to chart possible paths to explore together. To do that, you have to make their implicit knowledge explicit. Being a sponge starts with seeking their advice—but instead of asking to pick their brain, you ask them to retrace their route.

The goal is to get your guides to drop pins—the key landmarks and turning points from their climbs. To jog their memories of paths long forgotten, you might inquire about the crossroads they faced. Those could be skills they sought out, advice they took or ignored, or changes they made. It can also help to tell them about the roads you've taken so far. As they learn about your prior paths and current location, they may begin to notice avenues for progress that they didn't think to point out originally.

The pins you gather won't form an accurate map. Some won't apply to you—one pin might lead you across a stream, and your bicycle makes for a terrible boat. Some may no longer apply at all—they'll take you to a road that's closed. You may end up doing plenty of loops before you find the right path. And your guides are likely to be unaware of bridges that have only recently been built.

PROGRESS

HOW WE WANT IT TO FEEL:
FASTBALL

HOW IT ACTUALLY FEELS:
KNUCKLEBALL

@RESEARCHDOODLES BY M. SHANDELL

When I asked R. A. Dickey how he found his way, one of the first things he mentioned was the number of guides he had to enlist. He didn't have a single ongoing mentor. When RA started his journey in 2005, Tim Wakefield was the only active knuckleballer in the majors. Few others had even tried it; there were only about a dozen retired players who had wielded the pitch successfully. There wasn't one expert who could unlock all the mysteries of the knuckleball or one coach who could give him all the directions. He had to become a sponge in finding credible sources, filtering out the tips that weren't relevant to him, and adapting his approach accordingly.

After many months of struggling solo, RA took the initiative to seek out some guides. Since it was a long and winding road, he needed a range of perspectives. He started reaching out to the handful of people alive who had become knuckleball wizards. His hope was to collect some of their pins. They didn't have a full set of ready-made solutions—they surfaced ideas for RA to test.

In 2008, before a game against Tim Wakefield's team, RA convinced him to offer some guidance. *That's how lonely the knuckleball road is: a player will hand his trade secrets to an opponent just to keep the pitch alive.* After watching him throw and asking questions, RA came away with a new path to try: he should make sure his arm went down the center of his body as he released the ball. The following year he made a pilgrimage to see Hall of Famer Phil Niekro, the greatest knuckleballer ever. Niekro noticed that he wasn't pushing his hips forward as he threw, which gave him another road to test out. And RA made multiple trips to see another retired knuckleballer, Charlie Hough, who taught him to adjust his grip and streamline his windup. To keep the ball from spinning, RA learned to picture himself standing in a doorway and executing the entire throw without letting his body touch the doorframe. It restricted his arm to the point that he felt like a *Tyrannosaurus rex*, but it became a pivotal turn.

RA also had to learn which pins to ignore. His pitching coaches kept telling him to throw the ball slower, in the 60-miles-per-hour zone Wakefield and Hough had favored. But after experimenting with different speeds, RA found that his best knuckleballs often zipped at 80 miles per hour.

Sometimes we need to discover things no guide can provide and write our own directions. Through trial and error, RA discovered that he needed to learn a new skill: the art of the manicure. To throw a good knuckleball, his fingernails had to be long enough to get traction but short enough not to break. He became a one-man nail salon.

After three years of loops, RA was no longer stuck. He was on a path forward, thanks to a guidebook he had written himself.

Even so, that path was not an easy one. His guides had warned him that the emotional journey might be as bumpy as the physical one. Since the knuckleball didn't fly like a bullet, it was impossible to aim—all he could do was let it go like a butterfly. He would have to embrace imperfection: his performance would be as erratic as the flight path of the pitch itself. "Without talking to people who walked a mile in my shoes, I would not have been able to trust that there was a turning point in the future," RA told me. "Hope is incredible fuel. I had people to help me sustain that hope."

He estimates that he threw over 30,000 knuckleballs at brick walls, cinder blocks, and nets before he had a consistent command of the mechanics. The glacial pace of progress left him wondering if he would ever make it in the big leagues. It didn't help when he tied another "worst ever" record in 2008. Maybe he was destined to go down in history as Mr. Four Wild Pitches in One Inning. As he described it to me, "When you throw yourself into something and don't see results, it's discouraging."

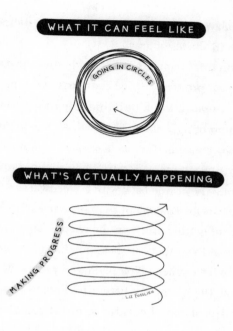

RUNNING ON EMPTY

Getting discouraged is a common obstacle after turning around. That's because going backward doesn't always lead directly to a new peak. Sometimes you end up stuck, and it's not because you're on the wrong path. It's because your path is taking you in long circles toward the top, and you can't even tell that you're gaining ground. You're not seeing enough progress to maintain your motivation.

There's a name for that feeling: it's called languishing. Languishing is a sense of stagnation and emptiness. The term was coined by a sociologist (Corey Keyes) and immortalized by a philosopher (Mariah Carey).

Languishing is the emotional experience of stalling. You may not be depressed or burned out, but you definitely feel blah. Every day starts with a case of the Mondays. You're muddling through the moments, watching your weeks go by in shades of gray.*

While writing this chapter, I struggled to find the right framework to capture nonlinear progress. I tried countless ideas that didn't work—demolishing and renovating a building, digging a tunnel, breaking through a wall, uprooting a plant. *That draft got a 4/10 from my judges—and they were being generous. They came up with a mantra: kill the plant.* I kept going back to the drawing board. When nothing resonated, I tried to revive the plant. They came back with a Weedwacker.

After several weeks, I'd gone in so many circles that I started to languish. The irony of getting stuck on the chapter about getting unstuck was not lost on me. I was meta-stuck and not at all amused. As a linear thinker and disciplined writer, I typically start my morning at the keyboard with a clear vision. Not having one was unsettling. Staring at the blinking cursor on my blank screen, I decided to investigate the origins of the term. *Is it called a cursor in homage to all the writers who've cursed it?* By dinnertime, it felt as if I'd wasted the entire day—it was exasperating. Searching for something to take my mind off the chapter, I stayed up too late eating ice cream and hanging out with my friends Monica and Chandler. *Hello, revenge bedtime procrastination.* It didn't help. My tank was near empty.†

As I've studied hidden potential, I've realized that languishing is more than the feeling of being stuck. It also keeps you stuck. Research shows that languishing disrupts your focus and dulls your motivation. It becomes a Catch-22: you know you need to do something, but you doubt

---

* I first wrote about languishing in a 2021 *New York Times* article, calling it the neglected middle child of mental health: the void between depression and flourishing. I've never seen people so excited to talk about their utter lack of excitement, although they rarely mustered more than a syllable. *Meh.*

† In case you were wondering, *cursor* derives from the Latin *currere*, "to run," and sometimes translates to "running messenger" or "errand boy." It was originally the name for a part on a slide rule—the piece that moves back and forth—and some computer pioneers borrowed it. For a while, they tried calling it a bug, but let's be honest: no one likes bugs.

whether it will do anything. That's when you need to pull off the freeway and refuel.

TAKING A DETOUR

When I ask people what it takes to achieve greater things, one of the most common answers is that you need to be laser focused and single-minded in your dedication. You need to double down and block out anything that threatens to drain your energy or divide your attention. If you want to excel at your job, spend more time at work: get in early, go home late. Put your hobbies on the back burner . . . and definitely *don't* take on a side hustle. You don't want to wind up distracted and exhausted.

But the evidence tells a different story. A digression doesn't have to be a diversion. It can be a source of energy.

In one study, when people had spent engaging evenings on their side hustles, they performed better the next day in their regular jobs. The progress they made at night put an extra spring in their step the following morning. The motivation benefits outweighed any distraction costs.

Hobbies have similar benefits. In another study, when people took on serious hobbies at home, their confidence climbed at work—but only if the hobbies were in a different area from their jobs. If you're an artist and you're languishing, doing ceramics on the side won't do much to spur a sense of mastery. But if you're feeling meh as a social worker or an accountant, a pottery project might just be a new path to progress.

Of all the factors that have been studied, the strongest known force in daily motivation is a sense of progress. You can't always find motivation by staring harder at the thing that isn't working. Sometimes you can build momentum by taking a detour to a new destination.

A detour is a route off your main road that you take to refuel. You're not taking a break; you're not sitting still, idling. You're temporarily veering off course, but you're still in motion. You're advancing toward a different goal.

Psychologists find that achieving a sense of progress doesn't require huge gains. Fuel can come from small wins. When you make headway, even if you've turned off the main road, it reminds you that forward movement is possible. Instead of feeling daunted by the long road ahead, you're ready to make the next turn.

When I was spinning my wheels on this chapter, I realized I needed to take my own message to heart. My diversion of choice was online Scrabble—a longtime hobby of mine. A few games in, I had *r-a-l-g-n-o-i*. I unscrambled it and joined it with an open *i* on the board. *Original.* The small win was the fuel I needed. I was ready to get back on the main road to work on the chapter.

My first step was to reset my expectations. I wouldn't crack the whole chapter in one sitting. Instead of waiting for the perfect map, I should just start making one small turn at a time. Kill the plant. Find a better overarching metaphor (navigation). Pick one key tool (a compass). *I'd avoided those since I have a terrible sense of direction. It's so bad that when I make a U-turn, my in-laws call it the Adam Turn.* With a few small wins, I started to gain speed. Some of the turns would take me backward, but together they'd help me move forward—much like R. A. Dickey did.

At first, RA had found his own small wins without a detour. He tracked his progress by counting how many pitches he could throw without spin. Each pitch that didn't spin was a jolt of motivation. Within a few years, he had improved from being able to throw a good knuckleball half the time to about three quarters of the time.

By the time the Mets recruited him in 2010, at age 35, RA was a solid big-league pitcher. But he still hadn't reached the top of his mountain. If his fast knuckleball didn't zig or zag enough, batters would crush it. To keep moving forward, he needed something more in his tank.

He decided to refuel by finding a new mountain to climb. Against the advice of his managers, RA meant that literally.

A HIGHER PEAK

In the winter of 2012, RA decided to climb Mount Kilimanjaro—Africa's tallest peak. It was a challenge he'd dreamed of conquering ever since he read a Hemingway story about it as a teenager. RA was doing it for charity: he'd raised over $100,000 to rescue teenagers from sex trafficking in Bombay.

The Mets tried to talk him out of it, and even sent a letter asserting their right to void his contract if he got hurt. Risking his full salary for the upcoming season, RA pressed forward. When he reached Tanzania, he spent seven days climbing over 16,000 feet with a group, battling altitude sickness, extreme exhaustion, and biting wind. Upon reaching the Kilimanjaro summit, "I somehow feel smaller than I have ever felt in my life," he wrote. "It is intoxicating."

That year, RA had the best season of his baseball career. Stretching beyond his comfort zone of the fast knuckleball, he developed one that was extremely slow, changing up speeds to leave batters guessing about when to swing as well as where. They would sometimes burst out laughing at how badly they missed the ball. He earned his nickname: the Baffler.

At the ripe age of 37, RA achieved greater things. He made his first All-Star Game. He pitched back-to-back games in which he only gave up a single hit and set a Mets record for pitching 32 straight scoreless innings. He led the entire league in strikeouts and became the first knuckleballer ever to win the Cy Young Award for best pitcher.

"Did Mt. Kilimanjaro Turn New York Mets Pitcher into an All-Star?" one reporter asked. It's a provocative question. As a social scientist, I can confidently answer this question with a definitive maybe.

The evidence on side hustles and hobbies suggests that the climb could have made a difference. But it also could've just been a matter of chance. When I asked RA about it, though, he didn't hesitate. "I don't think it's a coincidence," he said. "For me, it was very important. I enjoyed challenging myself."

The detour to Kilimanjaro may have been the final charge for RA's battery. Raising money for charity gave him a sense of contribution. Feeling small relieved the pressure to perform and refueled him to do bigger things. The successful climb gave him a burst of confidence. "It was a quest," he recounted. "I began the year on an African summit and I am ending it on a baseball summit."

To observers, the breakout season looked as if it came out of nowhere. But that couldn't be further from the truth. It took RA seven trips down to the minors and seven years of knuckleball effort to become an overnight success. What looks like a big breakthrough is usually the accumulation of small wins.*

When you get stuck on your way up a mountain, it's better to shift into reverse than to stand still. As you take U-turns and detours, you'll feel as if you're going in circles. In the short run, a straight line brings faster progress. But in the long run, loops lead to the highest peaks.

Progress is rarely noticeable at a snapshot in time—it unfolds over extended periods of time. If you focus your attention on a specific difficult moment, it's easy to feel stuck. It's only when you look at your trajectory over the course of weeks, months, or years that you appreciate the distance you've traveled.

---

* When you plant a Moso bamboo seed, you can water it for many months or even years without seeing a single sprout. It looks like nothing is happening until one day it bursts through the surface. Then, in just a few weeks, it shoots up over twenty feet. What you couldn't see is that underground, the seed was sprouting roots and storing energy. It was growing, slowly but surely, beneath the surface. *Plant resuscitated.*

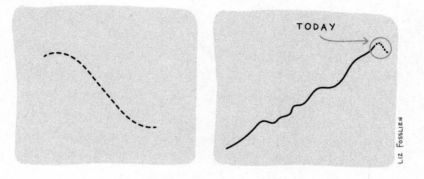

WHAT YOU SEE   WHERE YOU ARE

CHAPTER 6

Defying Gravity

The Art of Flying by Our Bootstraps

I believe in pulling yourself up by your own bootstraps.

I believe it is possible.

I saw this guy do it once in Cirque du Soleil.

—STEPHEN COLBERT

The mysterious messages came in different forms, but the recipients all felt the urgency. Jesse Arbor was in the midst of a poker game when someone told him a car was waiting downstairs and his train would leave in 35 minutes. He didn't even have time to get some of his clothes out of the washing machine. James Hair was out on a tugboat when he was sent back to shore to retrieve a big brown envelope. As he broke the red wax seal, what he found inside wasn't an invitation. It was an order to report to a location north of Chicago.

That order was delivered to sixteen men around the country. They ranged from their mid 20s to mid 30s and came from varying walks of life—the group included a mechanic, a bookbinder, a porter, a lawyer, and a sheet metal worker. It was January 1944, and they had no idea what was in store for them. In the heat of World War II, they would have a chance to make history. They were about to become the first Black men to enter officer training in the U.S. Navy.

Among the branches of the military, the Navy was known to be particularly prejudiced. Just a quarter century earlier, the Navy had banned Black citizens from enlisting altogether. When the policy finally changed, Black men were limited to servile roles as cooks and shoe shiners. Now political pressure from Eleanor Roosevelt had cracked the door open for them to join the officer ranks, but many leaders doubted whether they were smart enough to command white sailors.

When they arrived for officer training, the Black candidates were in their own cohort, segregated from the white sailors. They endured racial slurs and demeaning comments from the very instructors who were assigned to teach them. To them, the message was clear: they were expected to fail.

Some of the men had additional reasons to doubt themselves. A few had struggled academically in the past. Jesse Arbor was a C student who had failed introductory economics, and Charles Lear hadn't made it past tenth grade. And William "Syl" White had no military experience at all, having just finished his basic training at boot camp. "It was demanding," White recalled. "Officer training was kind of like fighting in the dark."

To make matters worse, with the country at war the training period was cut in half. The candidates had to complete a full semester of coursework in just ten grueling weeks. They would wake up each day at 6 a.m. to march, take eight hours of classes, and study well into the night. They were tasked with mastering seamanship, navigation, gunnery, law, naval regulations, aircraft recognition, signaling with flags and Morse code, and survival—all in record time.

In a typical Navy officer training class, only three quarters of candidates passed their exams. But that first class of Black officer candidates didn't just scrape by—all sixteen of them soared far above the bar. Leaders in Washington were immediately suspicious. To prove they hadn't cheated or benefited from grading errors, the men had to retake some of their exams. They ended up scoring even higher, finishing with a collective GPA of 3.89 out of 4.0. Years later, they would learn that they attained the highest marks in Navy history. Their potential was no longer hidden.

Thirteen of the candidates ended up being called to serve as Navy officers.* As the first group of Black men in America to wear gold stars and stripes, they're known as the Golden Thirteen. Instead of succumbing to the forces of gravity weighing them down, the Golden Thirteen managed to rise above them. As Samuel Barnes observed, "We were determined to succeed in spite of the burden that was being placed on our shoulders."

The Golden Thirteen got something right that the rest of us often get wrong. In the face of seemingly insurmountable obstacles, it can be tempting to give up. It's just too hard; the forces against us are just too strong. At times like this, we're advised to pull ourselves up by our own bootstraps. The message is that we need to look inside ourselves for hidden reserves of confidence and know-how. But it's actually in turning outward to harness resources with and for others that we discover—and develop— our hidden potential. When the odds are against us, focusing beyond ourselves is what launches us off the ground.

PERCENTAGE OF YOUR WORST DAYS YOU'VE MADE IT THROUGH

---

*It's still unknown why three of the original sixteen candidates—Augustus Alves, J. B. Pinkney, and Lewis "Mummy" Williams—weren't called up. It also remains something of a mystery why these sixteen men were chosen in the first place.

SCHOOLING EACH OTHER

When we're facing a daunting task, we need both competence and confidence. Our ability to elevate our skills and our expectations depends first on how we interpret the obstacles in front of us. Extensive evidence shows that when we view hurdles as threats, we tend to back down and give up. When we treat barriers as challenges to conquer, we rise to the occasion.

Seeing obstacles as challenges depends partly on having a growth mindset—believing in your ability to improve. But the pioneering psychologist behind this idea, Carol Dweck, has recently demonstrated that a growth mindset alone does little good without scaffolding to support it. Rigorous experiments with over 15,000 students reveal that nurturing a growth mindset among high schoolers boosts their grades only when their teachers recognize their potential and their schools have cultures of embracing challenges.

If we aren't lucky enough to have others hand us that scaffolding, we may have to assemble it ourselves. That's where bootstrapping comes in. Bootstrapping is using your existing resources to pull yourself out of a sticky situation. The term is sometimes traced to a folktale about a baron who was stuck in a swamp with his horse—and escaped by using his pigtails as a rope. Later tellings may have replaced the baron's hair with his bootstraps.

Bootstrapping is normally seen as an individual skill. You don't rely on assistance from others. *You* pull at the loop at the back of your *own* boots to lift *yourself* over obstacles. It sounds like an expression of rugged individualism—an independent act. But it's when we approach it interdependently that we gain the competence and the confidence to overcome obstacles. I saw it happen in my own classroom.

One fall, I told my students at Wharton that the final exam would be unusually difficult and sent them some sample questions. They came to class panicked about the multiple-choice section. I'd wanted to motivate them to master the material, but I'd undermined their confidence.

I reminded them that I was rooting for all of them to succeed. I even promised to curve their scores upward if the class average was low. They were still stressed and filled with doubts, so I decided to throw them a bone. For the one multiple-choice question that stumped them, they could write the name of a classmate who might know the answer. If that student got it right, they would get credit too. It was the academic equivalent of a lifeline in *Who Wants to Be a Millionaire*.

When I looked at their scores on the exam, I was in for a surprise. Compared to the past year's exam, the class average had gone up by multiple points, and it wasn't due to the lifeline. In subsequent years, the performance of each new class continued to climb. I started cycling through the list of possible explanations. The test hadn't gotten easier. The students weren't smarter than previous years. Eventually, I found out what was going on: the small lifeline had a big impact on how students prepared.

To excel on the exam, the students still had to master all the content—it wasn't as simple as dividing and conquering the material. But if they wanted the extra credit on one question, they had to find out who knew what. So instead of cramming solo, they opted to study together. They started meeting in small groups to synthesize the key concepts.

The students had created their own scaffolding. A later class took the collaboration to the next level: they created a giant map of the content from the entire semester. One student reserved a room for Saturday afternoon studying and invited the entire class to join and pool their knowledge. Others jumped in to share their own reading summaries, study guides, and practice quizzes. The students realized that the strongest bootstraps weren't the ones they created alone, but the ones they built together.

Considerable evidence shows that studying with knowledgeable colleagues is good for growth. In U.S. intelligence agencies, if you want to predict which teams will produce the best work, the most important factor to consider is how often colleagues teach and coach one another. In medical schools, students learn as much when they're taught by peers as by faculty. In the Saturday session in my class, no single student walked in an expert. They had to leverage the collective knowledge of the group. And there's reason to believe that they did some of their learning by teaching.

Teaching is a surprisingly powerful method of learning. In a meta-analysis of 16 studies, students who were randomly assigned to tutor their peers ended up earning higher scores in the material they were teaching. Students who taught reading improved in reading; those who taught math got dramatically better at math. The more time they spent tutoring, the more they learned. As one group of researchers concluded, "Like the children they helped, the tutors gained a better understanding of and developed more positive attitudes toward the subject matter covered in the tutorial program."*

Psychologists call this the tutor effect. It's even effective for novices: the best way to learn something is to teach it. You remember it better after you recall it—and you understand it better after you explain it. All it takes is embracing the discomfort of putting yourself in the instructor's seat before you've reached mastery. Even just being told you're going to teach something is enough to boost your learning.

---

*The tutor effect helps to illuminate one of the great mysteries of the mind: Why do firstborns have a cognitive edge over laterborns? Although it doesn't show up in every analysis, numerous rigorous, large-scale studies have shown that the oldest child in a family tends to slightly outperform younger children on tests of intelligence—even after accounting for family size, socioeconomic status, parental intelligence, and a host of other factors. We can rule out biological and prenatal causes: a study of over 240,000 Norwegian teenagers showed that laterborns whose older siblings die in infancy—and thus are raised like firstborns—end up with higher intelligence scores. When the oldest child has a learning advantage, it's due to nurture, not nature. A popular theory is that firstborns get more time and energy from their parents. Parental attention might be part of the story, but it doesn't explain why only children—who get the most undivided attention—test as *less* bright than firstborns with younger siblings. That's where the tutor effect comes in. If you're an only child, you don't get to turn your siblings into your students, and as with lastborns, that limits your development. If you're the firstborn in a big family, you learn through educating your little brothers and sisters. Interestingly, these benefits of tutoring start to emerge around age 12, when older siblings have more to teach and their younger siblings are more ready to learn.

This is another twist on the trope that those who can't do, teach. Those who can't do yet can learn by teaching. The historian Henry Adams became an expert in medieval history by teaching a class on it. He confessed to his students that he knew nothing at the start and progressed just one lecture ahead of them. The painter Georgia O'Keeffe honed her techniques of abstraction in charcoal and watercolor as she taught art classes. The physicist John Preskill learned quantum computing by signing up to deliver a course in it. And the Golden Thirteen aced their Navy officer exams by teaching what they wanted to learn.

UNEXPECTED POTENTIAL

At the outset of officer training, many members of the Golden Thirteen felt it would be impossible to accumulate so much knowledge in so little time. As George Cooper captured it, "Each of us . . . said, 'The hell with it, this is just too damn much.'" With few leaders supporting them, their best hope was to support one another. But they would have to do so in a notoriously cutthroat environment.

Since Navy tradition held that not everyone would make the cut, officer candidates tended to see one another as rivals, not teammates. Yet the Golden Thirteen met in their barracks and made a prosocial vow: *All for one and one for all.* "We decided early in the game that we were all going to either sink or swim together," Cooper stated. "Fortunately, at least one of us was already familiar with almost every subject we were exposed to."

To manage the overwhelming course load, the Golden Thirteen resolved to rely on one another. They would become sponges by pooling and filtering the knowledge in the room. Each member would teach his expertise to the rest of the group. When they got their textbooks, they went through the topics and waited for someone to shout out, "That's mine."

Being strong in math, Cooper, Graham Martin, and Reginald Goodwin led many of the analytical subjects along with John Reagan on technical topics. The history buffs, Samuel Barnes and Dennis Nelson, took charge on military history. What Lear lacked in formal education, he made up in leadership as well as experience with seamanship and knot-tying, so he chipped in there along with Alves. And since Arbor had advanced navigation training and experience, the group turned to him for a crash course on Morse code—he tapped on the wall and gave his peers clues as they tapped back. They were tying their bootstraps together.

The official time for lights out was 10:30 p.m. Night after night, the Golden Thirteen huddled in the bathroom with flashlights studying well past midnight. To make sure they wouldn't get caught, they hung sheets over the windows to block the light.

I learned about the Golden Thirteen thanks to a seminal book by Paul Stillwell, a Navy historian who did the great service of documenting their experiences before they passed away. As I pored over his extensive interviews for stories, quotes, and insights, the obvious explanation for their success was that they were able to learn from qualified peers. Then it occurred to me that the tutor effect was also at play: the act of sharing knowledge enhanced the competence of the men doing the teaching. They were working together to build stronger bootstraps.

When the first law question came up, everyone turned to White as the lawyer. He told them he had no knowledge of Navy law—he had to look it up. He learned Navy regulations by teaching them—and gained efficacy in subjects he had just learned in boot camp by teaching some of those too. Serving as an instructor made the lessons stick.

Drawing on his background as a machinist, Frank Sublett was responsible for mechanical, gunnery, and boilers along with Dalton Baugh. But plenty of questions came up that they couldn't answer. When the appointed teacher didn't have relevant knowledge, the Golden Thirteen went around the room for everyone to weigh in. It gave them all the chance to teach something relatively new to them. Once they'd reached a consensus about the best explanation, it was time for "drilling" and "grilling." By quizzing one another, they created more opportunities for everyone to share knowledge they'd just gained. As he saw that they each had insights to offer, Sublett realized that "the men in our group had the capacity and ability to grasp the information." Their boots were sturdy. By the time they took their exams, they each had the knowledge to pass every subject with flying colors.

HEEDING OUR OWN ADVICE

Teaching others can build our competence. But it's coaching others that elevates our confidence. When we encourage others to overcome obstacles, it can help us find our own motivation. I've seen it happen as a parent.

When I was nervous about giving my first TED talk, I decided to ask our oldest daughter for advice. At the time, Joanna was an extremely shy eight-year-old, and she told me to look for one person in the audience who was smiling and nodding. I came home excited to tell her I found encouragement from a beaming face in the front row.

A few weeks later, my wife, Allison, and I could sense that Joanna was anxious about her role in a school play. When she walked onstage, she locked eyes with us in the audience and broke out into a grin as big as ours. Instead of relying on us for advice, she had remembered her own advice and followed it. It was a turning point: we watched her expectations of herself rise afterward. It wasn't long before she was volunteering to give presentations, and her teachers were praising her poise and confidence.

I've come to think of this as the coach effect. We're more confident in our ability to surmount struggles after guiding others through them.

That's the consistent result of elegant experiments led by the psychologist Lauren Eskreis-Winkler. In one experiment, high schoolers earned higher report-card grades in multiple subjects—including math—after being randomly assigned to give advice to younger students on how to stay motivated and avoid procrastinating. In another, middle schoolers spent more time on homework after they were randomly assigned to give motivational advice to younger students—rather than receive motivational advice from expert teachers. And people who were struggling to save money, lose weight, control their tempers, and find jobs all came away more motivated after giving advice than receiving it.

This is different from the tutor effect, which highlights how we can learn through sharing the very knowledge that we want to acquire. The coach effect captures how we can marshal motivation by offering the encouragement to others that we need for ourselves. By reminding us of the tools we already possess, coaching others raises our expectations of ourselves.

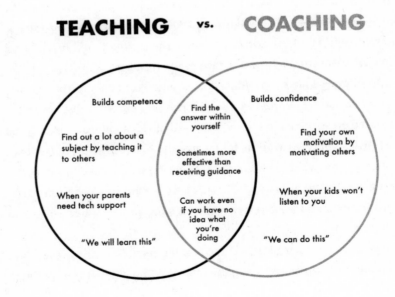

TEACHING vs. COACHING

Builds competence

Find out a lot about a subject by teaching it to others

When your parents need tech support

"We will learn this"

Find the answer within yourself

Sometimes more effective than receiving guidance

Can work even if you have no idea what you're doing

Builds confidence

Find your own motivation by motivating others

When your kids won't listen to you

"We can do this"

Coaching is the opposite of what we usually do when we need help. In trying times, our first instinct is to pick up the phone and ask for advice. We're better off pausing to reflect on the advice we've provided in the past or calling someone in a similar situation and offering them some suggestions. We should listen to the advice we give to others—it's usually the advice we need to take for ourselves.

In my research, I've found that it's more motivating to be a giver than a receiver. Receiving is passive—if you're always the one being coached, it puts you in the position of depending on others for guidance. Giving is active—coaching others reminds you that you have something to offer. It convinces you that your bootstraps are strong enough to support you. You've already seen them support others.

Throughout the winter, the Golden Thirteen leaned on one another for coaching and encouragement. To rally the group, Lear showed up early. When they struggled with learning to use a sextant for navigation, he motivated them to keep trying and guided them on techniques. It showed him—and his peers—that he had a contribution to make.

In coaching one another, the Golden Thirteen didn't just offer advice and encouragement. They also held one another accountable. "Each one of us, at one point in time or maybe more than one, got to the point where we were ready to throw in the towel," George Cooper recounted. "And the others would have to be there to say, 'Oh, no, man, we must do this.'" Graham Martin told them they had to make the grade and shot down excuses for slacking off. Others called their peers out if they got distracted and exchanged tips for staying focused. As they pulled one another up by their bootstraps, their expectations of themselves rose.

After interviewing most of the Golden Thirteen, Paul Stillwell marveled at their response: "Even their toughest instructors weren't as demanding of them as they were of themselves." The difficult task in front of them was no longer a threat—it was a challenge. Instead of doubting themselves individually, they believed in their collective capacity. As George

Cooper articulated it, "We were convinced that if one of us made it, we were all going to make it."

The Golden Thirteen found a way to fill the initial gaps in their confidence and competence. But with leaders doubting them, there would be plenty of reasons ahead for them to question themselves. When other people don't believe in your abilities, it can tie your boots to the ground or send you running in the other direction. Being disrespected presents a particular barrier to growth and requires a particular kind of scaffolding to overcome.

Recently, I came across someone who navigated that challenge. For years, I'd been hearing about her as the speaker who'd electrified the crowd before I got onstage. When I finally met her, she taught me something surprising about finding motivation in an uphill battle.

A MOUNTAIN OF DOUBT

As she gasped for air, Alison Levine wondered if she had made a mistake. It was 2002, and Alison was captaining the first expedition by a group of American women up Mount Everest—the highest peak on earth. Alison had reached the most treacherous part of the climb: the Khumbu Icefall. Above her were 2,000 vertical feet of ice, which would become increasingly unstable as the sun's heat intensified. She needed to move quickly to avoid the possibility of a crack in the ice or a sudden avalanche.

But speed was not Alison's forte. At just 5'4" and 112 pounds, she lacked the size and strength to take long, powerful steps. She was in her mid 30s, and she had only started climbing a few years earlier. As a child in the sweltering summers of Phoenix, she devoured books about Arctic explorers and watched every movie she could find about mountain climbers. It was her dream to go on polar expeditions, but physical limitations prevented her from braving the cold.

Alison was born with a hole in her heart; a career as an expeditioner was not supposed to be in the cards. She spent her teenage years sporadically passing out and getting shuttled back and forth to the emergency room. After multiple surgeries, the hole was finally closed, and she was finally cleared to climb. But she still faced a major barrier: a circulatory disorder. In frigid temperatures, her arteries would stop sending blood to her fingers and toes, leaving them numb and at severe risk of frostbite.

That hadn't kept Alison from making the trek to Everest. She'd spent months recruiting a corporate sponsor and assembling a team of women who were accomplished outdoor athletes. Now they stood together, staring at a giant hole in a glacier that they needed to cross. If they slipped, they could fall to their deaths.

As Alison put her foot on the ladder, she heard a voice behind her. "You're never going to make it to the summit at this pace," a male climber shouted. "If you can't go faster, you shouldn't be here. Maybe you should call it quits and go home." Doing her best to ignore him, she made her way, slowly but surely.

She and her team eventually cleared the Icefall. Shortly afterward, a section collapsed into an avalanche, and another climber narrowly made it out alive. That wouldn't be their only brush with death. A helicopter that transported the team through the Khumbu Valley crashed on its return to a nearby mountain, leaving no survivors. And one of the climbers they had met at base camp had later slipped and fallen to his death. Alison knew their lives were hanging in the balance of countless tiny decisions and conditions beyond their control.

After nearly two months of climbing, Alison and her teammates made it to the last stretch of the journey. It was known as the death zone—at that altitude most humans couldn't absorb enough oxygen to survive. Even with supplemental oxygen, Alison had to take five to ten breaths just to get enough oxygen to take a single step. As they pressed forward, the peak was finally in sight.

Then a storm blew in. Between heavy winds and a whiteout, it was too dangerous to proceed or even wait it out. After climbing nearly 29,000 feet, they were forced to quit . . . less than 300 feet from the top. Instead of becoming the first American women to summit Everest, they turned around. Alison led them back down the mountain.

As soon as she got home, she had to face a slew of questions from reporters. *Congratulations, you didn't make it. How did it feel to give up?* Against her better judgment, Alison read the online comments. *They weren't qualified. They didn't deserve to be there.* She met people at dinner parties who belittled her efforts. *Stop saying you climbed Everest . . . if you didn't get to the top, it doesn't count.* She felt like a failure.

Alison sank into a spiral of self-doubt and depression. She felt she'd let her team, her sponsor, and her country down. She kept hearing the voice of the climber behind her echoing in her head. *You're not fast enough.* She swore she would never set foot on Everest again.

LIGHTING A SPARK

The expectations people hold of us often become self-fulfilling prophecies. When others believe in our potential, they give us a ladder. They elevate our aspirations and enable us to reach higher peaks. Dozens of experiments show that at work, when leaders hold high expectations, employees generally work harder, learn more, and perform better. In schools, when teachers set high expectations, students get smarter and earn higher grades—especially if they start out with disadvantages.

Whereas high expectations offer support for us to climb, low expectations tend to hold us back—it feels like our boots are made of lead. It's called the Golem effect: when others underestimate us, it limits our effort and growth. These kinds of self-fulfilling prophecies are particularly pronounced among stigmatized groups, who are frequently inundated by low expectations. But groundbreaking research by my colleague Samir Nurmohamed offers a twist. There are times when you can turn others' low expectations to your advantage. They don't have to strap you in place—you can grab on to them and pull yourself forward.

In one experiment, Samir gave people a task where they had to click moving circles with their mouse. After they finished a practice round, an observer sent them a message. Some people were randomly assigned to receive high expectations: *You will blow others away in this task. . . . I think you've got what it takes to beat all of them.* Others got low expectations: *Others will blow you away in this task. . . . I don't think you've got what it takes to beat any of them.*

The impact of these expectations depended on who was setting them. High expectations led to greater effort and performance . . . if they came from someone knowledgeable about the task. But if the observer lacked credibility, being uninformed about the task, the effect reversed: people actually ended up trying harder and doing better when they were doubted rather than encouraged.

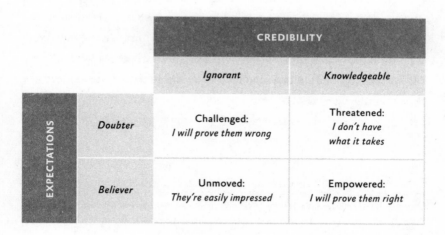

		CREDIBILITY	
		Ignorant	*Knowledgeable*
EXPECTATIONS	*Doubter*	Challenged: *I will prove them wrong*	Threatened: *I don't have* *what it takes*
	Believer	Unmoved: *They're easily impressed*	Empowered: *I will prove them right*

When you're invested in a goal, being doubted by experts is a threat. They may be credible, but since they don't recognize your potential, they're not coaches who will help you improve. Their disbelief quickly becomes your insecurity. It shatters your confidence and stifles your growth. That's a self-fulfilling prophecy.

But the research suggests that when they come from an uninformed audience, low expectations can become a self-negating prophecy. You're motivated to shatter *their* confidence that you won't succeed. Samir calls it the underdog effect.

Being doubted by novices is a challenge. It fires you up. They're clueless, so you don't internalize their low expectations—but you don't ignore them either. You become driven to defy them. *I'll show you.* The doubts that threaten to crush your confidence can become crucibles that fortify it. You feel like an underdog who can beat the odds.* Just ask Alison Levine.

After failing to reach the summit of Mount Everest in 2002, Alison couldn't get the naysayers out of her head. She was well aware that they weren't credible. The online trolls, journalists, and acquaintances didn't know anything about mountaineering. The climber on her heels had no idea what it took to scale a peak at her size and weight. "My fear of not making it again was not as strong as my desire to prove the naysayers wrong," Alison tells me. "When someone ignorant doubts you, it feels like a challenge. I didn't want to let the naysayers win. I wanted to make them eat their words."

---

*The underdog effect isn't limited to people with high self-confidence. Samir finds that low expectations from ignorant naysayers can be motivating regardless of whether you feel capable in the task. But persistent experience with low expectations can be debilitating, as Samir and his colleagues showed in a pair of experiments with job seekers. Those who had faced significant discrimination struggled more in finding employment—it was a blow to their confidence. Randomly assigning them to tell a story about a time when they'd succeeded in the face of low expectations was enough to boost their efficacy and improve their odds of landing a job. Once you've overcome adversity, reminding yourself of that history can reinforce your belief in your ability to prove others wrong. As Oscar winner Michelle Yeoh says, "Limitations set by yourself give you boundaries to respect, but limitations set by others give you boundaries to bust through."

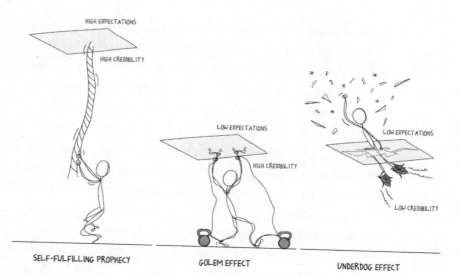

HIGH EXPECTATIONS

HIGH CREDIBILITY

LOW EXPECTATIONS

HIGH CREDIBILITY

LOW EXPECTATIONS

LOW CREDIBILITY

SELF-FULFILLING PROPHECY   GOLEM EFFECT   UNDERDOG EFFECT

@RESEARCHDOODLES BY M. SHANDELL

Our biggest challenges require scaffolding beyond the underdog effect. For Alison, the drive to put the critics in their place wasn't enough to tip her over the edge to embrace the discomfort of returning to Everest. If she pulled on her bootstraps again, they might snap. A second failed attempt could be the end of her climbing career. She might never attract another team or another sponsor. She needed a bigger reason to take the risk.

CARRYING A TORCH

The desire to prove others wrong can light a spark of motivation. Turning the spark into a flame, though, often requires more. Ignorant naysayers may give us something to fight against, but a roaring fire comes from having something to fight for.

It's easier to overcome obstacles when we're carrying a torch for people who matter to us. When others are counting on us, we find strength we didn't know we had. In one study, Marissa Shandell and I compared the performance of Olympic divers when they were competing individually versus in synchronized events with a partner. Divers were less likely to choke on the exact same difficult dives when they were doing it synchro rather than solo. You can see a similar pattern with kids in a version of the marshmallow test. In experiments in Germany and Kenya, kids had the chance to eat one cookie now or wait a few minutes to be rewarded with a second cookie. They delayed gratification longer when they knew caving in would also deprive another child of an extra cookie. Having a partner can prevent rumination about your own abilities (*Can I do this?*) and boost determination (*I won't be the reason you fail*). As Maya Angelou wrote, "I do my best because I'm counting on you counting on me."

After her failed Everest expedition, Alison Levine had someone counting on her. Her friend Meg urged her to try again. "Only if you go with me," Alison responded, knowing it was impossible. Although Meg was an elite athlete, two bouts of lymphoma had damaged her lungs.

Tragically, Meg passed away in 2009 due to a lung infection. Alison wanted to do something meaningful to honor her legacy, so she decided to climb Everest in Meg's memory. That was something worth fighting for. In a matter of months, she had carved Meg's name on her ice axe and booked a flight to Nepal to join an expedition with mountaineers she didn't know. This time, she wasn't leading a hand-picked team—she would be loosely affiliated with a group of independent climbers.

As Alison traversed the Khumbu Icefall, she thought about all the people who had doubted her. Not just the guy on her heels and the online trolls, but also the doctors who claimed her circulatory disease made it too dangerous. *All I have to do to prove all these people wrong,* she thought, *is put one foot in front of the other.* When that wasn't enough, she looked down at her axe and reminded herself, *I'm doing this for Meg.* It gave her an extra boost of confidence.

After many long weeks, Alison made it back to the point where her climb had ended eight years earlier. She was running on empty and starting to doubt herself. Then she heard someone scream her name: "Hey, Alison . . . I need you to promise me that you are going to go farther than *this.*" A guide from another expedition, Mike Horst, had stayed behind to encourage her. "I felt this weight come off my shoulders," she told me. She trusted him, because he was a knowledgeable believer: "Mike had summitted Everest multiple times. If he thought I could do it, I could do it." Along with ignorant naysayers to disprove and a beloved friend to honor, now she had a credible supporter rooting for her. She shook Mike's hand and kept going.

When she reached the top, Alison didn't just achieve her goal of summiting the tallest mountain on the planet. Scaling Everest was her last step in completing the Adventurers Grand Slam. Alison became one of only a few dozen people on earth to climb the tallest peak on all seven continents and ski to both the North and South Pole. But looking back, she says her proudest moment wasn't the last step she took to reach the summit. It was the distance she traveled back to Everest to reach the spot where she had turned around.

Making progress isn't always about moving forward. Sometimes it's about bouncing back. Progress is not only reflected in the peaks you reach—it's also visible in the valleys you cross. Resilience is a form of growth.

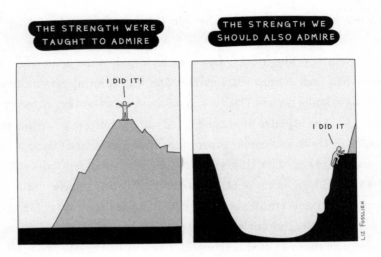

BLAZING A TRAIL

The Golden Thirteen found purpose in fighting for others—and against low expectations. They faced far worse than typical naysayers. On multiple occasions, Navy leaders had to call out instructors for prejudice. "Many of them did not want any part of it," lamented a white lieutenant, John Dille. "Officers had to be told that a certain attitude could not be displayed—that they must treat the Black recruits in the same fashion they would the whites." Even then, multiple white instructors told them they would never make it.

It was clear to the Golden Thirteen that their naysayers weren't qualified to judge them. Their lead instructor had only graduated from the Naval Academy two years earlier. He had less experience than many of them—and they felt he didn't know the first thing about their capabilities. They harnessed his doubts as motivational fuel: they decided to prove him wrong. "It was hoped by some that we would fail so there'd be an excuse to just discontinue any ideas of commissioning Black officers because they were just not competent, they were not intelligent enough,"

Samuel Barnes pointed out. "That gave us greater determination to succeed. . . . We said, 'We'll take advantage of this. . . . We're going to do this because there are those who expected us not to succeed.'" To prove their naysayers wrong, they all had to make it. And they didn't want to let one another—or their community—down.

We find our deepest reserves of resolve when an entire group is relying on us. My colleague Karren Knowlton has shown that when we feel a strong sense of belonging to a group, we feel our bootstraps are linked. We become driven to defy low expectations of our group in order to pull the entire group up. We don't just want to prove ourselves—we want to blaze a trail for others to follow.

The Golden Thirteen knew they were representing something far bigger than themselves. "We recognized that we were plowing new ground," George Cooper remarked. "If we failed, there were 120,000 men out there who wouldn't have a shot at this for a hell of a long time. . . . It was an awesome responsibility. We talked about it constantly." They were pulling future generations up by their bootstraps. In the words of Jesse Arbor, "We learned to walk so that the ones behind us could run."

They went far beyond breaking the color barrier for future Navy officers. The Golden Thirteen cleared many paths for their heirs to march on the way to achieving greater things. Dalton Baugh got a master's degree in engineering from MIT and became the Navy's first Black chief engineer. Dennis Nelson rose to lieutenant commander and ran a literacy program that educated thousands of sailors and enabled many to vote for the first time. Reginald Goodwin ran the Navy's selection office. Samuel Barnes earned his doctorate in educational administration and became the first Black officer of the NCAA. Syl White served in the Illinois governor's cabinet and became a judge. He and George Cooper advocated for women's rights and gay rights in the Navy decades before doing so was common or accepted.

It's more important to be good ancestors than dutiful descendants. Too many people spend their lives being custodians of the past instead of stewards of the future. We worry about making our parents proud when we should be focused on making our children proud. The responsibility of each generation is not to please our predecessors—it's to improve conditions for our successors.

Despite their historic achievements, the Golden Thirteen went unrecognized by the Navy for many years. When they completed officer training in 1944, there was no graduation ceremony or celebration. They were banned from the officers' club at Great Lakes.

In 1987, the surviving members of the Golden Thirteen finally returned to the place outside Chicago where it all began. The Navy's first Black admiral presided over the dedication of a building to commemorate their achievements. To this day, when new recruits arrive for basic training, they enter the Golden Thirteen Recruit In-Processing Center.

Even more than the place named in their honor, the Golden Thirteen were moved by the people they touched. When they gathered for their first reunion three decades after completing training, most of them had only ever seen a handful of Black officers together. Now an entire auditorium was filled with hundreds who had walked through the door they opened. Captain after captain came up to them to express their gratitude: "We owe it all to you."

The Golden Thirteen were doubted by many people around them. They had their share of moments of doubting themselves. But they believed in one another, and they were determined to pave the way for others.

It's possible to confront obstacles alone. Yet we reach the greatest heights when we attach our bootstraps to other people's boots. If multiple credible supporters believe in us, it's probably time to believe them. If ignorant naysayers don't believe in us, it might be time to prove them wrong. And when our faith falters, it's worth remembering what we're fighting for.

PART III

Systems of Opportunity

Opening Doors and Windows

Character skills and scaffolding can help us unlock hidden potential in ourselves and those around us. But to give more people the chance to achieve greater things, we need something bigger. Creating opportunities on a larger scale requires us to build better systems in our schools, teams, and organizations. Some powerful evidence on the impact of opportunity comes from Raj Chetty—the economist behind the research we covered earlier linking the character skills we learn in kindergarten to our future success.

Chetty and his colleagues were interested in how opportunity shapes who ends up innovating. They reasoned that some kids would grow up in environments that gave them special access to resources. When they linked federal income tax returns with patent records for more than a million Americans, they found an alarming result. People raised in the top 1 percent of family income were ten times more likely to become inventors than people from families below the median income.

If you grew up wealthy, your odds of earning a patent were 8 out of 1,000. If you grew up poor, they plummeted to 8 out of 10,000.

Family income made a difference even when comparing people at the same level of cognitive skills. If two third graders scored in the 95th percentile on math tests, one from a high-income family had more than double the odds of inventing as one from a low-income family. And to make things worse, those same math whizzes from low-income families were no more likely to become inventors than affluent kids who scored below average on the same math tests.

When we think of geniuses as people with extraordinary abilities, we neglect the importance of life circumstances in shaping them. When they had an idea, rich kids got to shoot their shot. Some of the less fortunate were lost Einsteins: they could have become great innovators, if only they'd had the opportunity.

It wasn't difficult to figure out why. Chetty's team discovered that one of the advantages kids got in wealthy families was more exposure and access to innovators in their homes and neighborhoods. They had more guides available to provide a compass and drop pins. They got to dream bigger, aim higher, and travel farther.

The effect of opportunity is more than just a correlation, and it goes beyond wealth—it lies in geography too. Some zip codes are hotbeds of invention, and landing in them has an impact. Chetty's research revealed that after families relocated to areas with higher rates of innovation, their kids were more likely to file a patent as adults. If your parents packed their bags to leave New Orleans for Austin during your childhood—taking you from the 25th to 75th percentile of inventors per capita—your probability of earning a patent would rise by 37 percent. Geography also predicted the domain of innovation. If you moved to Silicon Valley, your odds of patenting in computers went up.

Yet being in the right zip code doesn't have the same benefit for every resident. Role models do matter, and underrepresented groups often have a hard time finding them. In the data, girls only had a better chance at patenting if they grew up in an area surrounded by female inventors—which was rare. Chetty and his colleagues estimate that if girls had as much exposure to female inventors as boys do to male inventors, it would more than double women's patent rates—closing more than half the gender gap in innovation.

Good systems provide the opportunity for people to travel great distances. They open doors for people who don't grow up with means, offer windows to those who get turned away at the door, and shatter glass ceilings for those who are all too often denied a shot to break through. When we build systems to unleash the hidden potential in populations, we reduce our risk of losing Einsteins—and Carvers, Curies, Hoppers, and Lovelaces too.

If we design them the right way, admissions and hiring systems can recognize the potential in late bloomers and long shots. Team and organizational systems can recognize that good ideas don't flow only from the top down—and fill silence with voices from the bottom up. And school systems can give kids who start out behind a fighting chance to get ahead. Instead of only looking for geniuses where we expect to find them, we can reach humanity's greatest potential by cultivating the genius in everyone.

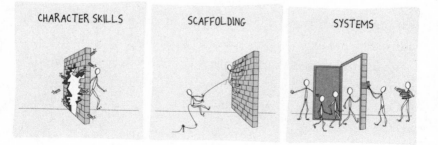

@RESEARCHDOODLES BY M. SHANDELL

CHAPTER 7

Every Child Gets Ahead

*Designing Schools to Bring Out
the Best in Students*

Just as Michelangelo thought there was an angel locked
inside every piece of marble,

I think there is a brilliant child locked inside every student.

—MARVA COLLINS

At the start of the new millennium, thousands of teenagers
represented their countries in an international competition.
Although it was about to send shock waves across the globe, it
attracted little attention. There were no arena showdowns, no cheering
crowds, and no medals awarded. There was only a small press conference
in Paris to announce the results.

For the first time in history, experts had devised a way to directly
compare the aptitudes of young people around the world. Beginning in
2000, every three years the OECD would invite 15-year-olds from dozens
of countries to take the PISA—a standardized test of their math, reading,
and science skills. Their scores would reveal which nation had the most
knowledgeable young minds—and thus the best schools.

The results weren't just for bragging rights. Nothing is more vital
to the progress of future generations than the quality of our current
education systems. The top countries would become lighthouses for the
rest of the world to build better schools and more educated societies.

The favorites in the inaugural contest of 2000 included Japan and Korea. They were renowned for having smart students with strong study habits. But when the results came in, people were stunned. The highest-performing country wasn't anywhere in Asia. It also wasn't one of the usual education superpowers in the Americas or Europe—not Canada, the United Kingdom, or Germany. It wasn't Australia or South Africa either. The winner was none other than the unheralded underdog country of Finland.

Just a generation earlier, Finland had been known as an education backwater—on par with Malaysia and Peru, and trailing behind the rest of Scandinavia. As of 1960, 89 percent of Finns didn't make it past ninth grade. By the 1980s, in international comparisons of graduation rates as well as math and science Olympiad performances, Finnish students were still mediocre.

It was rare to see a country travel such a distance in such a short time. Some observers argued it was just a fluke. Then the 2003 contest proved them wrong: Finland won the top spot again, with even higher scores. In 2006, they claimed victory for the third time in a row, outperforming the other 56 participating countries.

Of course, all tests have flaws, but Finland's educational excellence wasn't limited to the PISA—or even to high schoolers. In 2012, when the OECD gave a different aptitude test to over 165,000 adults across dozens of countries, Finland finished first among teens and twentysomethings in both math and reading.

Principals, policymakers, and journalists quickly flocked to Finland, hoping to find the secret sauce that would turn their own schools around. But international education experts warned them that the recipe couldn't be easily exported. Some of the essential ingredients were local: Finland had an affluent, culturally homogeneous population of just five million people.

Although these ingredients might have played a role in Finland's achievements, they weren't enough to explain the country's meteoric rise. Take Finland's northern neighbor, Norway, which had even lower child poverty rates and smaller classes. Strangely, during the same period that Finland ascended, Norway's test scores plummeted. And Finland consistently outperformed the rest of Scandinavia too. Something more had to be going on.

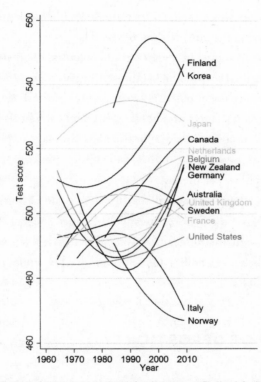

Sources: Ripley, *The Smartest Kids in the World*; Hanushek and Woessmann, *The Knowledge Capital of Nations*. For the years before the PISA was introduced, economists created a common metric to compare different tests administered in each country.

While Finland kept exceeding expectations, America was busy falling short of them. On the 2006 PISA, out of 57 countries, the United States ranked 35th in math and 29th in science—and by 2018, we weren't doing much better, landing in 25th place overall. Our schools had a lot to learn from Finland's extraordinary leap.

In search of the recipe behind the secret sauce, I went to Finland. After I spoke with a range of education experts and combed through extensive research, it was clear that Finland didn't have one magic ingredient. *Not even their signature blueberry juice, which is delicious.* But rigorous evidence suggests that some of their best ingredients can work anywhere—and there are adjustments we can make to improve them. Based on studying what Finland does differently, I believe much of their success stems from the culture they've created.

That culture is rooted in a belief in the potential of all students. Instead of singling out the best and brightest, Finnish schools are designed to give every student the opportunity to grow. On the PISA, their achievement gaps between schools and between students were the smallest in the world. Being disadvantaged was less of a disadvantage in Finland than anywhere else: along with the highest rate of high performers, they had the lowest rate of low performers.

In Finnish schools, a popular mantra is "We can't afford to waste a brain." This ethos makes their educational culture distinct. They know that the key to nurturing hidden potential is not to invest in students who show early signs of high ability. It's to invest in every student regardless of apparent ability.

THE LAND OF OPPORTUNITY

Our experiences in school can either fuel or flatten our growth. Using whatever resources they have, some schools and teachers manage to create learning environments that bring out the best in us. Around the world, evidence shows that whether children get ahead or fall behind depends in part on the cultures created in schools and classrooms.

In organizational psychology, culture has three elements: practices, values, and underlying assumptions. Practices are the daily routines that reflect and reinforce values. Values are shared principles around what's important and desirable—what should be rewarded versus what should be punished. Underlying assumptions are deeply held, often taken-for-granted beliefs about how the world works. Our assumptions shape our values, which in turn drive our practices.

The U.S. education system is built around a culture of winner take all. We assume that potential is rooted primarily in innate ability that shines through early. As a result, we value demonstrated excellence—which leads us to adopt practices geared toward identifying and investing in students who show obvious signs of brilliance. If you win the intelligence lottery, you're rewarded with special attention in gifted-and-talented programs. If you're branded as slow, you might be forced to repeat a grade and endure a lasting blow to your self-esteem. And if you win the wealth lottery, it's easier for you to attend the best schools with the best teachers; your peers from poorer families face an uphill battle. To give these disadvantaged students a fighting chance, in 2001 Congress intervened to legislate the No Child Left Behind Act. The goal was to achieve 100 percent proficiency in math and reading in every grade—and hold schools accountable for making sure their weakest students didn't fall short. Despite bipartisan support, the plan didn't work. We still have substantial achievement gaps between schools, and between richer and poorer students.

In contrast, Finland's education system has created a culture of opportunity for all. The underlying assumption is that intelligence comes in many forms and every child has the potential to excel. This assumption gives rise to a central value of educational equity—and then a set of practices designed to help every child get ahead. Success isn't just reserved for the gifted and talented; the aim is to give all students great teachers and a personalized plan for growth. If students fall behind, it's extremely unusual to hold them back to repeat a grade. To get them up to speed, schools offer early interventions with individual tutoring and extra support. And they focus on developing the individual interests of each student—not just promoting their success.

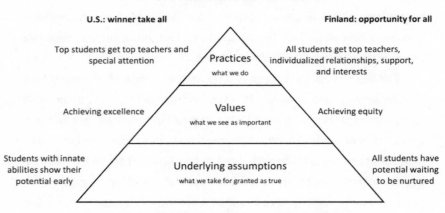

CONTRASTING EDUCATION CULTURES

U.S.: winner take all   Finland: opportunity for all

Top students get top teachers and special attention   **Practices** *what we do*   All students get top teachers, individualized relationships, support, and interests

Achieving excellence   **Values** *what we see as important*   Achieving equity

Students with innate abilities show their potential early   **Underlying assumptions** *what we take for granted as true*   All students have potential waiting to be nurtured

Inspired by Edgar Schein's iceberg model of culture

The overarching value we place on education doesn't only affect schools; it permeates societies. In the United States, if you ask people what career they respect the most, the most common answer is doctor. In Finland, the most admired profession is often teaching.

It might seem like an enviable accident that Finland's culture happens to nourish excellent education. But a country's values and assumptions about education aren't a given—they're chosen. Starting in the 1970s, Finland launched a major reform to professionalize education. As the education expert Samuel Abrams explains, they advanced a core value of "education as an instrument for nation building."

The reform began with overhauling how teachers were recruited and trained. Unlike Norway, Finland started requiring all teachers to complete master's degrees offered at top universities. That attracted highly motivated, mission-driven candidates. They got advanced training in evidence-based practices, many of which were pioneered in other countries. They also paid teachers well.

These values and practices didn't transform the culture overnight. In the early 1990s, a new leader came in and called for another set of dramatic changes to create "a new culture of education." Policymakers started engaging teachers and students in a collaborative effort to define their ideal culture. They articulated a new assumption—teachers were trusted professionals—and supported it by introducing practices that gave teachers freedom and flexibility to shape a previously rigid curriculum.

Today, Finnish teachers have a great deal of autonomy to use their judgment to help students grow. They're expected to stay up-to-date on the latest research—and to educate and coach one another on applying it. And they don't have to waste time teaching to the test.[*]

These reforms set the stage for Finnish schools to build cultures of opportunity. By placing such a premium on teaching, they instilled the assumption that everyone is teachable. As Pasi Sahlberg, the world's foremost authority on Finland's education system, put it: "A high-performing school in Finland is one where all students perform beyond expectations."

To discover and develop the potential in each of their students, teachers make a fundamental assumption that education should be tailored to individuals. Surprisingly, that doesn't require small classes; a typical Finnish teacher has around 20 students. It involves a set of practices for personalized learning. Finnish schools create cultures of opportunity by enabling students to build individualized relationships, receive individualized support, and develop individualized interests.

LET'S STAY TOGETHER

What if there was a simple practice every school could implement—with the resources they already have—that would help students achieve greater things across the board? Finland has one. It's designed to promote

---

[*] Finland tracks progress by administering standardized tests that cover the entire curriculum to very small samples of students. In contrast to their American and Norwegian peers, the vast majority of Finnish students don't take a single standardized test until the end of high school, when they're ready to apply to college. Also, if you noticed that Finnish teacher salaries appear to be lower than in the United States and Norway, that's the case in nominal rather than real terms. Since the dollar goes further in Finland and benefits are more generous, teachers have greater purchasing power.

individualized relationships. It enables teachers to get to know their students, not just their material. And it's recently been tested across the Atlantic.

When economists studied several million elementary school students in North Carolina, they found that certain fourth- and fifth-grade classrooms were more likely than others to achieve spikes in their math and reading performance. They traced these gains to about 7,000 teachers in particular. I was immediately curious about what those teachers did differently. But it turned out that the critical difference was at the level of the school systems, not the teachers.

Students who made significant progress didn't have better teachers. They just happened to have the same teacher for two years in a row.

The practice is called looping. Instead of staying in the same grade and teaching new students each year, teachers move up a grade with their students. The benefits of looping aren't specific to North Carolina. A separate team of economists replicated the study with nearly a million elementary and middle schoolers in Indiana—and found the same results.

With another year to get to know each student personally, teachers gain a deeper grasp of their strengths and challenges. They're able to tailor their instructional and emotional support to help everyone in the class reach their potential.* The nuanced, tacit knowledge they gain about each student isn't lost in the handoff to the following year's teacher.

Finland loves to loop, and I was unprepared for how far they take it. It's common for Finnish elementary schoolers to have the same teacher for multiple grades—not just two years in a row, but up to six straight

---

* Looping also had spillover benefits to other students. As long as at least 40 percent of a class had that teacher the prior year, the rest of the class was more likely to improve in math and reading too. It might be that when teachers had preexisting relationships with some students, they put extra effort into getting to know the others—and had an easier time managing the classroom and building a supportive learning environment.

years. Instead of just specializing in their subjects, teachers also get to specialize in their students. Their role evolves from instructor to coach and mentor. Along with delivering content, they're able to help students progress toward their goals and navigate social and emotional challenges.

It didn't occur to me until I read the research, but I was lucky to benefit from looping. My middle school piloted a program to keep students with the same two core teachers for all three years. When I struggled with spatial visualization in math, Mrs. Bohland didn't question my aptitude. Having seen me ace a year of algebra, she knew I was an abstract thinker and taught me to use equations to identify the dimensions of shapes before drawing them in 3D. And after multiple years of observing what fired me up in social studies and humanities, Mrs. Minninger knew my interests well. She saw a common theme underlying my passions for analyzing character development in Greek mythology and anticipating counterarguments in mock trial—and suggested doing my year-end project on psychology. *Thank you, Mama Minnie.*

Yet looping isn't the norm in American schools. In North Carolina between 1997 and 2013, 85 percent of schools didn't do any looping at all, and just 3 percent of students got the same teacher two years in a row. Critics have long worried that switching grades will prevent teachers from developing specialized skills. Parents fret about rolling the dice on the same teacher more than once. *What if my kid gets stuck in Mr. Voldemort's class?* But in the data, looping actually had the greatest upsides for less effective teachers—and lower-achieving students. Building an extended relationship did the most good for the teachers and students who were struggling. It gave them the opportunity to grow together.

But what happens when students have challenges beyond what a single teacher can address? When students are struggling, they need more than individualized relationships. That's where Finland goes above and beyond in offering practices for individualized support.

I'LL STAND BY YOU

Years ago in the Finnish city of Espoo, a sixth grader named Besart Kabashi was faltering in his classes. His Albanian parents had moved him there seeking refuge from the Kosovo war, and the Finnish language was new to him. The school principal, Kari Louhivuori, called for an unusual early intervention. He decided to hold Besart back a year and have him work with a special needs teacher. But to make sure he didn't flounder, Kari stepped up: "I took Besart on that year as my private student."

In the United States, I don't remember my school principals even setting foot in a classroom to see students learning. Yet here was a Finnish school principal who didn't hesitate to volunteer to take time out of his busy schedule to tutor one personally. Kari's love of students runs so deep that for years, his "morning exercise" was to stop by preschool classes and lift 45 kids up above his shoulders as they laughed and cheered. He didn't think twice about helping Besart. "No big fuss," he said. "This is what we do every day, prepare kids for life."

Benjamin Franklin famously observed that "an ounce of prevention is worth a pound of cure." Dozens of experiments have shown that early interventions can help students facing disadvantages and learning disabilities make leaps in math and reading. But in America, students in many under-resourced schools don't have access to the individualized support they need. The majority of states don't even comply with federal special education laws, let alone have the personnel to offer free tutoring and support to students who fall behind or face language barriers. Students like Besart can easily get lost in the shuffle here . . . and all too often do.

In Finland, every student has access to personalized help and support. It starts at the top: Finnish school leaders aren't merely administrators. They're responsible for checking in on the progress and well-being of every single student. And they're expected to spend at least part of their week teaching classes of their own.*

As principal, Kari's official job title was Head Teacher. He spent part of each week teaching a class of third-grade students. He brought Besart into his classroom for the year, helping him with reading while the third graders were doing their daily activities. He activated the tutor effect by inviting Besart to assist the younger students. Over the course of the year, that scaffolding made a real difference. Besart mastered his new language, caught up to his peers, and learned that he was capable of greater things.

The following year, Besart moved up to another school. Kari touched base with his new teacher periodically to see how he was doing. Years later, Besart showed up at Kari's Christmas party and handed him a bottle of brandy to thank him for his help. Kari beamed with pride to see that at 20, Besart was running not one but two businesses—an auto repair firm and a cleaning company.

Although support begins at the top, it doesn't end there. It's built into each level of the Finnish education system. Every school in Finland has a student welfare team. Along with each student's classroom teacher, the team typically includes a psychologist, a social worker, a nurse, a special education teacher, and the school principal. That's how Kari first learned about Besart's difficulties: the student welfare team met to discuss how they could best support him.

---

* Having leaders who are knowledgeable about the core work of an organization isn't just beneficial to schools. Research shows that when hospitals are led by physicians, they provide higher-quality cancer, digestive, and heart care—and after universities appoint presidents who are accomplished scholars, their research impact increases. A deep understanding of the work seems to make it easier for leaders to attract talented people, earn their trust, and develop effective strategies. And there's a case to be made that just as Finnish principals keep teaching, physician leaders should keep seeing patients and university presidents should keep publishing research. My colleague Sigal Barsade coined a term for it: leading by doing. She recommended that instead of just managing by walking around, leaders should spend 5 to 10 percent of their time doing the actual work of their teams. It's a powerful way to stay connected to what's happening on the ground—and signal that what people do below us is not beneath us.

This support system is like a social safety net for students. In most cases, it's an alternative to holding students back when they're struggling. Access to free tutoring gives them the opportunity to improve without being pulled off track. And it isn't only reserved for students who are in dire need. During their first nine years of school, about 30 percent of Finnish students receive extra assistance. By identifying challenges early, they're able to prevent bigger problems from brewing.

The emphasis on prevention helps to explain why Norway—Finland's Scandinavian neighbor—has fallen short. Norway's education system doesn't do nearly as much early intervention when students show initial signs of stumbling. In America, some states have started to improve in this area: Alabama and West Virginia have raised high school graduation rates by intervening early to support freshmen whose grades have suffered in the transition from middle school to high school.

In Finland, starting in the fall of kindergarten, teachers meet with parents to develop individualized learning plans for each student. You're probably wondering how teachers can possibly find the time. Finland has cracked that problem with a practice that I've come to find as appealing as blueberry juice. *Well, almost.*

What's distinctive about the Finnish school day is not the length so much as the schedule. Compared to the United States, in Finland teachers (and students) have an hour more break time. That gives teachers the space to do lesson planning, grading, and personal development during regular hours, shielding them from night and weekend work. It's also a kind of early intervention for teachers: limiting demands and providing control prevents burnout. Keeping their energy high maintains their harmonious passion for teaching—which helps them promote a love of learning in their students from their very first days in school. That love of learning flourishes in an environment designed for students to discover and develop their individual interests.

CHILD'S PLAY

I originally became curious about what Finland was doing differently in early education when a clever headline grabbed my attention. "The Joyful, Illiterate Kindergartners of Finland" was written by an American elementary school teacher, Tim Walker, who had burned out after struggling to plan lessons that could make his students light up. His wife was from Finland, so they decided to move there for a fresh start.

After arriving in Helsinki and landing a teaching job, Tim started popping into different classrooms to get a sense of how things worked. When he visited a public kindergarten, he could hardly believe his eyes. He expected to see students sitting at their desks doing worksheets to build their cognitive skills, like in the United States. Over time, American kindergarten has become more like first grade. Students spend more time on spelling, writing, and math—and less time on dinosaurs and space, arts and music, and free play. How else could they get ahead on core competencies and be ready to ace standardized tests in seven years?

But Tim saw something completely different in Finland. Kindergartners only sat at their desks for spelling, writing, and math one day a week.* Each lesson was a maximum of 45 minutes, followed by 15 minutes of recess. This is another practice backed by research: much like they do for adults, short activity breaks are known to improve children's attention and some aspects of their learning.

---

*Finnish educators aren't big on teaching reading in kindergarten. Research shows that the teenagers who achieve the strongest reading comprehension weren't necessarily the most sophisticated readers in kindergarten—they were the clearest talkers and storytellers. And by the time they finish elementary school, kids who were taught to read at seven have caught up to their peers who learned to read at five—and might even have better reading comprehension. Many kindergartners haven't yet developed the vocabulary to decode words or the broad knowledge to comprehend sentences and follow stories. The time kindergarten teachers are forced to spend drilling and testing reading might be counterproductive; at that stage, it's more useful for kids to learn to break down words by sound than by sight. But Finland doesn't ban reading in kindergarten—if students show interest and readiness, it becomes part of their individualized learning plan.

In Finnish early education, students spend most of their time in play. Mondays might be dedicated to games and field trips; Fridays may be for songs and activity stations. Tim watched kindergartners go from playing board games in the morning to building dams in the afternoon, and from singing in a circle to doing the activity of their choice. Some chose to make forts; others dove into arts and crafts.

Teachers weren't catering to kindergartners' so-called learning styles. They were giving them ample time to explore their individual interests. "Why?" some Americans might ask. Because Finnish educators assume the most important lesson to teach children is that learning is fun.

It's an assumption supported by evidence. Research in the United Kingdom reveals that students who enjoy school at age six go on to earn higher standardized test scores at sixteen—even after controlling for their intelligence and socioeconomic status. A refrain among Finnish teachers captures it nicely: "The work of a child is to play."

In the United States, play is practiced in Montessori schools. In Finland, it's mandated in the common core for all primary schools. The Finnish government insists that children play, because their policymakers understand that play fosters a love of learning. That's a value best developed early on—and one that ultimately builds both better cognitive skills and better character skills.

In the Finnish kindergarten that Tim visited, one of the most popular stations was an ice cream shop. Students used a version of Monopoly money to buy and sell imaginary ice cream. As they operated a cash register, took orders, and counted out change, they learned to be proactive and prosocial while practicing basic math and verbal skills. Sure enough, dozens of studies have found that deliberate play is more effective than direct instruction in teaching students some cognitive skills as well as character skills like discipline and determination. And we know Finnish students excelled on the PISA in part because they were among the most persistent in the world.

TROUBLE IN PARADISE

When I traveled to Finland a few years ago, I expected citizens to be proud of their education system. But the people I met—from their prime minister to education experts to parents—were generally critical of their schools. At first, I chalked it up to Nordic humility. I had learned that the first principle of a Scandinavian social code is "Don't think you're anything special."

I soon found out there was good reason for them to be disappointed and frustrated. Finland had started slipping on the fourth PISA exam in 2009. After three straight victories, for the first time, their scores had dipped on all three subjects—math, reading, and science.

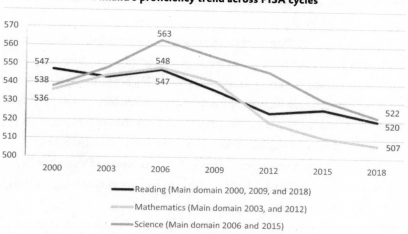

Finland's proficiency trend across PISA cycles

━━ Reading (Main domain 2000, 2009, and 2018)
━━ Mathematics (Main domain 2003, and 2012)
━━ Science (Main domain 2006 and 2015)

Those scores kept on sliding for the next three exams. By 2018, Finland hadn't just been eclipsed by several Asian countries—they were bumped down to second best in Europe. A tiny country just across the sea had leaped over them.

Estonia had climbed up the charts despite a relatively low budget and a sizeable number of students per teacher. By 2018, they were fifth in the world overall—and they also had some of the world's smallest performance gaps between schools and between rich and poor students. Estonia's policymakers had studied the Finnish recipe and imported many of their ingredients. Their primary and secondary schools had highly qualified teachers, with master's degrees required and high levels of autonomy offered. They had first-grade teachers looping with their students until third, fourth, fifth, or even sixth grade; a strong support system for assisting struggling students rather than having them repeat grades; and a curriculum of play-based education. So if it was working for Estonia, why was Finland suddenly lagging?

Let's be clear: Finland might have been falling, but they certainly weren't failing. They were still in the top ten worldwide, and they'd maintained small performance gaps between schools—and between students based on socioeconomic status. But it seemed that their students had somehow lost a step.

Experts quickly began examining the many possible reasons for the decline. They speculated about the rise of complacency and the toll of budget cuts from the 2008 financial crisis. They highlighted that efforts by other countries to import Finnish practices and teach to the test hurt Finland's standing. But there was direct evidence for another explanation: challenges with motivation among boys and high school students.

In 2018, 70 percent of students in Finland reported that they didn't try their best on the PISA.* And their declining motivation wasn't limited

---

*Even on a carefully designed assessment like the PISA, performance is influenced by motivation—not just ability. Some have argued that Americans underperform on the PISA because unlike the SAT and ACT, it's a low-stakes test. This does appear to be part of the story, but not the dominant reason for lackluster scores. Economists conducted an experiment comparing the performance of Chinese and American high schoolers on tests with and without incentives. Chinese students did equally well regardless of incentives, presumably because collectivistic cultures place strong emphasis on representing one's group even in the absence of individual rewards. American students did better when they were paid based on their performance, possibly because being raised in an individualistic culture led them to put in more effort when there was a personal return. Empirically, raising the stakes of the PISA would move Americans up significantly—but it would make up less than half the distance between the U.S. and top performers like Finland, South Korea, and China.

to the test: Finnish students had some of the world's lowest scores on the desires to persist and improve in school. Somewhere along the way, they seemed to have lost their love of learning—the very intrinsic motivation that their system was designed to cultivate. A culture of opportunity only succeeds when students are motivated to take advantage of those opportunities.

KEEPING THE LOVE

Finnish policymakers and educators didn't abandon their values in the face of a challenge. As their PISA scores dropped, they didn't rush to introduce initiatives to boost their rankings. Instead, they started running experiments on how to make school more motivating. Extensive evidence shows that the wellspring of intrinsic motivation is having the freedom of opportunity to explore our interests. Finnish policymakers tested ways to give students at all levels a sense of agency to shape their own learning experiences.

In one experiment, Finnish sixth graders got to do a major project that culminated in running their own miniature city. The students operated a local bank, managed a grocery store, and supervised a health clinic. They produced a newspaper and had a student mayor oversee the government. By the end of the project, a student mayor had held court with a pair of distinguished visitors: the actual king and queen of Sweden.

The royal couple was in town to learn from one of Finland's new programs, Me & MyCity. The initiative has won international awards for educational innovation and promoting entrepreneurial thinking. It's a powerful example of deliberate play for older students. Think of it as the middle school equivalent of running an imaginary ice cream shop. Students apply for the roles that pique their interest, and then interview with their teacher for the jobs they want.

Me & MyCity was such a hit that the majority of Finland's sixth graders now participate in it. The program is powerful because it puts students in charge of their individualized learning. They're excited to spend weeks preparing for their roles, and they have the freedom to decide how to play them. It's up to them to set their visions, manage their money, and maintain their reputations. They're paid digital salaries, and they get bank cards to buy goods and services from their classmates. Teachers don't have to pull teeth or dangle prizes to encourage students to participate; their motivation comes from within. And there's reason to believe it might stick: preliminary research suggests that along with gaining knowledge, students who participate in the program become more interested in economics.

To learn more about how Finnish schools were promoting intrinsic motivation, I went back to Kari Louhivuori. He now serves on Finland's Council for Creative Education with his daughter Nelli—a beloved elementary school teacher who advises schools worldwide on adopting Finland's educational practices. The father-daughter duo was kind enough to let me crash their family reunion.

They told me that although experiential learning programs are a start, there's another key ingredient for intrinsic motivation. "Reading is the basic skill for all subjects," Kari explained. "If you don't have the motivation to read, you can't study any other subject." Cultivating the desire to read nourishes individual interests.

A DIFFERENT KIND OF RECESS

A love of reading often begins at home. The Finnish Reading Center recently found that over half of parents felt they weren't reading enough to their kids. They started giving a free bag of books to every baby born in Finland.

Although filling our homes with books might be a start, psychologists find that it's not enough. If we want our kids to enjoy reading, we need to make books part of their lives. That involves talking about books during meals and car rides, visiting libraries or bookstores, giving books as gifts, and letting them see us read. Children pay attention to our attention: where we focus tells them what we prize.

When my daughter Elena was in kindergarten, she asked why I didn't read books. My shelves were overflowing with books. How could she think a writer wouldn't read? That's like an actor not watching movies or a painter refusing to set foot in a museum. Then I realized why she'd never seen me tear through a novel: I did my reading in bed after she was asleep. The next night, I told her it was time for us to start reading the first Harry Potter book together. Her older sister joined in, and taking turns every few pages, we read the entire book out loud. Fast-forward a few years, and our kids have created a family book club. When they discover a series they love, my wife, Allison, and I read it and talk about it with them. One night, over an hour past their bedtimes, I caught all three of our kids with their lamps on—they were sneaking extra reading time in. I could barely contain my delight.

Reading is a gateway to opportunity: it opens the door for children to keep learning. But books face increasingly stiff competition from TV, video games, and social media. Compared to 2000, in 2018 the average Finnish teen was spending 77 fewer hours a year reading for fun. This isn't unique to Finnish students; in America, students' enthusiasm about reading continues to wane year after year. By high school, they're typically somewhere between indifferent toward reading and disliking it outright.

One of the great failings of English and literature classes is forcing students to slog through the "classics" rather than giving them the opportunity to choose books that pique their interest. Research reveals that when students get to pick their own books and read in class, they become more passionate about reading. It's a virtuous cycle: the more they read for fun, the better they get and the more they like it. And the more they like it, the more they learn—and the better they perform on exams. A teacher's task is not to ensure that students have read the literary canons. It's to kindle excitement about reading.

In Finland, when Nelli Louhivuori saw her elementary schoolers languish through reading, she invented a new kind of recess. Every Monday, she took her students on a little field trip to "library recess." There wasn't a set list of books—they got to choose their own. They got to know the librarians—who in turn got to know their interests and started stopping by Nelli's classroom with teasers on relevant new releases. Once students had selected their books for the week, Nelli also gave them the choice of where they wanted to read. Soon they had a new class tradition: they took their books to a nearby forest and pored over their pages between the trees.

Throughout the year, Nelli invited students to write about the books they loved. The assignment wasn't a traditional book report, where you trudge through a summary to hand in to your teacher. "They don't get inspired that way," she told me. To make it engaging and interactive, whenever students were passionate about a book, the floor was theirs to tell their classmates about it. That became another tradition—before she knew it, Nelli had a room full of budding book critics.

This is the kind of fuel that can propel learning anywhere, for almost any kid, about almost anything. Interest is amplified when we have the opportunity to choose what we learn and share it with others. Intrinsic motivation is contagious. When students talk about the books that light up their imaginations, it crystallizes why they love them—and gives others the chance to catch that enthusiasm.

Only time will tell whether these kinds of opportunities are enough to spark and sustain a love of learning. But Finland remains a role model on what may be the most important dimension of all. As much as they value education, what impresses me most about their culture is that they don't put performance above well-being.

In too many elite education systems, students sacrifice their mental health for excellence. In America, research shows that students at high-achieving high schools are clinically depressed and anxious at rates three to seven times above national norms. In China, students topped the PISA charts in 2018 for performance but landed in the world's bottom ten countries on life satisfaction. Between the pressure to be perfect and the stress of studying for long hours, more than half of Chinese students reported feeling sometimes or always miserable, and over three quarters felt sometimes or always sad.

By contrast, in Finland, fewer than a third of high school students were miserable, and under half were sad. They pulled off high test scores while doing an average of only 2.9 hours of homework per week—less than the typical Chinese teen does in a single day. On the 2018 PISA, Finland ranked first of all 77 countries on performance per hour studying. That means they've maintained their reign on the ultimate metric for growth: learning efficiency.

Exactly how they do it remains too complex to distill into a simple recipe. Most experts believe it's a combination of high-quality teaching, intrinsic motivation fueling deeper learning, lower stress and test anxiety improving focus, and character skills developed early paying off over time. Right now, what we know is that Finland is the best in the world at helping students progress without monopolizing their time, wreaking havoc on their lives, or making them hate school. Their deepest underlying assumption may be that the tradeoff between doing well and being well is a false choice.

An education system isn't truly successful until all children—regardless of background and resources—have the opportunity to reach their potential. Building schools where students achieve greater things isn't about focusing on a select few and pushing them to excel. It's about fostering a culture that allows all students to grow intellectually and thrive emotionally.

CHAPTER 8

Mining for Gold

Unearthing Collective Intelligence in Teams

Some other eyes will look around, and find the things I've never found.

—MALVINA REYNOLDS

The second they saw the avalanche start raining down from above, a group of men raced for cover. Some of their colleagues couldn't see it yet, but the sound was unmistakable: an ominous low rumble that intensified into an earsplitting crack. A gust lifted one of them off the ground and sent another sailing through the air. They picked themselves up and started making their escape on foot.

Struggling to see or hear with rocks flying everywhere, they feared they wouldn't make it. Then they spotted a pickup truck barreling down the road. They jumped aboard and held on for dear life as the truck crashed twice. When they reached the bottom of the road, they were finally safe from the avalanche. But they weren't really safe. They were trapped 2,300 feet underground.

It was August 2010, and a gold and copper mine in the Chilean desert had just collapsed. A massive chunk of rock as tall as a 45-story building had broken free from the mountain above. The only entrance was blocked by more than 700,000 tons of rock. There were 33 men sealed inside. They were given less than a 1 percent chance of making it out alive.

Yet 69 days later, they were all reunited with their families. It was a monumental and miraculous rescue effort—this was the longest humans had ever survived after being trapped underground. As I watched the rescue capsule bring the first miner to safety, my eyes welled up with tears of joy and relief. If you were one of the billion people tuning in to the event live, yours probably did too. At the time, most of the coverage focused on how the miners made it. It wasn't until years later that I realized how much the rescue team could teach us about how groups travel great distances together.

At the outset of the rescue mission, no one knew if the miners were even still alive. And there was no easy way to determine that. The maps of the mine were unfinished and outdated, leaving the rescue team "drilling blind." It was like searching for a needle in a haystack twice the height of the Eiffel Tower. They had to estimate the location of the miners and the curved path of a massive drill. If they were off by just a few degrees at the surface, they could miss the mark by hundreds of feet in the mine.

On day seventeen, the rescue team found a glimmer of hope. As one of the drills finally reached the area where they expected the safety refuge to be, they tried to send a signal to the miners by pounding the drill with a hammer. It sounded like something was banging back. Sure enough, when they spun the drill in reverse to bring it to the surface, they found the end covered in orange paint, with pieces of paper attached to it. The trapped miners had written notes announcing that they had all survived. Just in case the notes got shredded or detached, they'd spray-painted the drill as proof of life.

By that point, however, the miners were in dire straits. Their supplies had dwindled. They were down to contaminated water and a single bite of tuna fish every three days. The rescue team was able to buy them some time by drilling tiny holes that wouldn't risk another collapse of the mine—one for food and water, another for oxygen and electricity. But now they had to figure out how to drill a hole wide enough for humans . . . half a mile deep . . . through rock harder than granite . . . without burying the miners alive. A rescue like this had never been attempted before, let alone successfully.

When we face complex and pressing problems, we know we can't solve them alone. We assume our most important decision is to assemble the most knowledgeable people. Once we've found the right experts, we put our future in their hands.

But that's not what the leaders of the Chilean mine rescue did. Instead of merely relying on an exclusive group of established experts, they built a system to bring a broader and deeper pool of ideas and intelligence to the surface. When they made their first voice contact with the miners, it was thanks to a $10 innovation from a small-time entrepreneur. The eventual rescue was made possible by a series of suggestions from a 24-year-old engineer who wasn't even part of the core team.

Maximizing group intelligence is about more than enlisting individual experts—and it involves more than merely bringing people together to solve a problem. Unlocking the hidden potential in groups requires leadership practices, team processes, and systems that harness the capabilities and contributions of all their members. The best teams aren't the ones with the best thinkers. They're the teams that unearth and use the best thinking from everyone.

ANY TEAM WON'T DO

I first started wondering how groups come together to achieve greater things when I was a junior in college. It happened in the class that hooked me on organizational psychology, affectionately known as Psych 8:30 a.m. Rumor had it that the professor taught it so early in the morning in the hopes of attracting only the most motivated students.

When I showed up early for the opening lecture, the room was already packed, but the professor wasn't there. Then I looked through the window and saw a disheveled giant of a man outside, tall enough to be an NBA forward. He paced back and forth, holding a pipe in one hand and scanning a stack of notes in the other. When he lumbered into the classroom, he didn't walk us through the syllabus. He announced that he had failed our country.

It was September 13, 2001.

The professor's name was Richard Hackman, and he was the world's leading expert on teams. He'd spent nearly half a century studying teams in every field imaginable—from airline cockpit crews to hospital units to symphony orchestras. He'd found that in most cases, teamwork failed to make the dream work. *It was more likely to be a nightmare . . . as anyone who ever did a group project in school can attest.* Most teams were less than the sum of their parts.

For several years, Richard had been studying how to improve collaboration within the major U.S. intelligence agencies. He told us that although analysts had tried to sound the alarm about the threat of airplanes being hijacked as weapons, the intelligence community had failed to heed their warnings. If his research had produced the needed results sooner, they might have been able to prevent the 9/11 attacks.

Richard spent the next few years working with one of his star protégés, Anita Woolley, to study how to make teams smarter. Eventually, Anita and her collaborators made a breakthrough. They revealed something vital to making teams more than the sum of their parts.

Anita was interested in collective intelligence—a group's capacity to solve problems together. In a series of pioneering studies, she and her colleagues tracked how well various teams performed on a wide range of analytical and creative tasks. It was basically an IQ test for groups. I expected collective intelligence to depend on how well the task matched the abilities of individuals in the group. I thought teams of verbal virtuosos would dominate word scrambles, teams of math whizzes would win out at geometry problems, and teams of proactive people would have the edge in planning and execution situations. I was wrong.

Surprisingly, certain groups consistently excelled, regardless of the type of task they were doing. No matter what kind of challenge Anita and her colleagues threw at them, they managed to outperform the others. My assumption was that they were lucky to have a bunch of geniuses. But in the data, collective intelligence had little to do with individual IQs. It turned out that the smartest teams weren't composed of the smartest individuals.

Since these initial studies, scientific interest in collective intelligence has exploded, shedding light on what propels teams to achieve greater things. In a meta-analysis of 22 studies, Anita and her colleagues discovered that collective intelligence depends less on people's cognitive skills than their prosocial skills. The best teams have the most team players—people who excel at collaborating with others.

Being a team player is not about singing "Kumbaya." It's not about getting along all the time and ensuring everyone's cooperation. It's about figuring out what the group needs and enlisting everyone's contribution. Although it's nice to have a savant or two on the team, they do little good if no one else sees their value and people pursue their own agendas. It's well documented that a single bad apple can spoil the barrel: when even one individual fails to act prosocially, it's enough to make a team dumb and dumber.

You can see the bad-apple problem in a study of NBA basketball teams—a setting where players who lack prosocial skills stand out as self-centered and narcissistic. Psychologists coded players' narcissism from their Twitter profiles. *Yes, I'm flexing, and no, I couldn't find a shirt. When I look in the mirror, all I see staring back is greatness. My biggest regret is that I'll never be able to watch myself play live.* If teams had many narcissists or even one extreme narcissist, they completed fewer assists and won fewer games. They also failed to improve over the season—especially if their point guard (the primary passer and play caller) scored high on narcissism. Narcissists are ball hogs, and the most undervalued players are the ones who help their teammates score.

When they have prosocial skills, team members are able to bring out the best in one another. Collective intelligence rises as team members recognize one another's strengths, develop strategies for leveraging them, and motivate one another to align their efforts in pursuit of a shared purpose. Unleashing hidden potential is about more than having the best pieces—it's about having the best glue.

IT'S NOT ALL ABOUT ME

Prosocial skills are the glue that transforms groups into teams. Instead of operating as lone wolves, people become part of a cohesive pack. We normally think about cohesion in terms of interpersonal connection, but team building and bonding exercises are overrated. Yes, icebreakers and ropes courses can breed camaraderie, but meta-analyses suggest that they don't necessarily improve team performance. What really makes a difference is whether people recognize that they need one another to succeed on an important mission. That's what enables them to bond around a common identity and stick together to achieve their collective goals.

This kind of cohesion is what the Golden Thirteen built to ace Navy officer training together. And it's what Richard Hackman eventually found was missing in too many intelligence units. In his research, most analysts were assigned to specific units, but that's all it really was—an assignment. They shared a boss and a water cooler, but not much else. They didn't spend enough time exchanging ideas, coaching one another, or learning together. When they sent reports to one another, it was mostly a formality. They were just checking a box.

Putting people in a group doesn't automatically make them a team. Richard showed that the best groups of intelligence analysts gelled into real teams. They were evaluated on a collective outcome. They aligned around a common goal and carved out a unique role for each member. They knew their results depended on everyone's input, so they shared their knowledge and coached one another on a regular basis. That made it possible for them to become one big sponge—they were able to absorb, filter, and adapt to information as it emerged and evolved.

Leaders play an important role in establishing cohesion. They have the authority to turn independent individuals into an interdependent team. But all too often, when it comes time to decide who takes the helm, we fail to consider the glue factor.

When we select leaders, we don't usually pick the person with the strongest leadership skills. We frequently choose the person who talks the most. It's called the babble effect. Research shows that groups promote the people who command the most airtime—regardless of their aptitude and expertise. We mistake confidence for competence, certainty for credibility, and quantity for quality. We get stuck following people who dominate the discussion instead of those who elevate it.

It's not just the loudest voices who rise to lead even if they aren't qualified. The worst babblers are the ball hogs. In many cases, the people with the poorest prosocial skills and the biggest egos end up assuming the mantle—at a great cost to teams and organizations. In a meta-analysis, highly narcissistic people were more likely to rise into leadership roles, but they were less effective in those roles.* They made self-serving decisions and instilled a zero-sum view of success, provoking cutthroat behavior and undermining cohesion and collaboration.

---

*Sadly, the gravitation toward narcissistic leaders starts early: psychologists find that narcissistic kids get more peer nominations as leaders and claim to be better leaders, even though they aren't. In 22 out of 23 Dutch primary and secondary school classrooms, the most leadership nominations went to the students most likely to agree with statements like "Kids like me deserve something extra." When they grow up, those narcissists often wreak havoc on their teams.

Collective intelligence is best served by a different kind of leader. The people to promote are the ones with the prosocial skills to put the mission above their ego—and team cohesion above personal glory. They know that the goal isn't to be the smartest person in the room; it's to make the entire room smarter.

GLUED TOGETHER WE STAND

After the mine collapsed in Chile, the first few days of the rescue effort were sheer chaos. There were multiple police units on the scene along with mining professionals, firefighters, rescue workers, and rock climbers. There were geologists and engineers analyzing the technical possibilities. There were mining convoys working haphazardly to deploy six different types of drills. It was a group of capable people, not a cohesive team capable of collective intelligence. Four days in, Chile's president summoned a leader.

The order came so suddenly that André Sougarret would later say it felt as if he'd been kidnapped. After more than two decades as a mining engineer in Chile, André was managing the world's largest underground mine. He was working there, about 600 miles south of the accident, when he got an urgent request to report to the presidential palace. He was still wearing his miner's helmet as he boarded the presidential jet and received his directive in midair: lead the mission to rescue the 33 men trapped in the Copiapó mine.

It was a race against the clock—every second counted. Facing that level of pressure with lives hanging in the balance, many of us would rely on drill sergeants to whip the group into shape and establish order. But when people are already determined, we don't need a leader to bark commands. Research demonstrates that when organizations have cultures that prize results above relationships, if they have a leader who puts people first, they actually achieve greater performance gains. When everyone is scrambling to make a rapid rescue, you want someone in charge who cares about everyone.

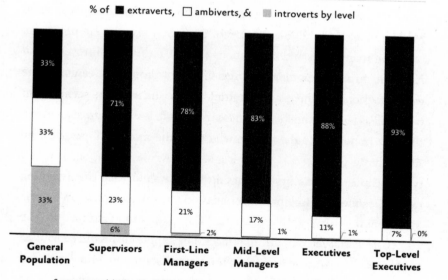

It's Very Extraverted at the Top

% of ■ extraverts, ☐ ambiverts, & ▨ introverts by level

Source: research by Stephan Dilchert and Deniz Ones with over 4,000 U.S. leaders and managers

Competence matters, but it isn't enough. André was certainly respected for his technical knowledge, but so were many other candidates. What set him apart was his reputation for prosocial skills. He was selected based on his ability to bring out the best in teams. "He has a lot of patience," an executive who recommended him observed, and "an exceptional ability to listen and reach conclusions after listening to all sides."

We don't normally think of listening skills as vital to leadership. Around the world, great leaders are stereotyped as outgoing and assertive. In the United States, the vast majority of leaders and managers score above the midpoint on extraversion. The higher you look up the hierarchy, the more extraverts you find. Even in more traditionally introverted countries like China, extraverts are seen as the prototypical leaders. But one of my research projects examined whether extraverts are actually more effective leaders than introverts, and revealed a more nuanced picture of the ideal leadership style. What made for effective leadership depended on how proactive a team was.

When teams were relatively reactive, waiting for direction from above, extraverts drove the best results. They asserted their visions and motivated teams to follow their lead. But when teams were proactive, bringing many ideas and suggestions to the table, it was introverts who led them to achieve greater things. The more reserved leaders came across as more receptive to input from below, which gave them access to better ideas and left their teams more motivated. With a team of sponges, the best leader is not the person who talks the most, but the one who listens best.

In Chile, André's first leadership move was to wield his listening skills. Despite the time pressure, he didn't rush into action. When he arrived at the mine, aptly nicknamed Campamento Esperanza (Camp Hope), he was greeted by familiar faces. His support team of 32 included people he already knew well from years of collaboration—they included mine superintendents he'd trained with and a crisis communication psychologist he'd worked with. The shared mission was clear: to find the miners and save them as quickly as possible.

What was missing was a cohesive strategy. André began interviewing the experts on-site to find out what they knew. As he listened, he learned that his original plan of entering the mine through the tunnels wasn't an option. He quickly shifted his attention to drilling and set out to appoint the right leaders to coordinate the efforts.

André intentionally didn't hand the reins to the most experienced drillers or the most assertive managers. Instead, he put the people with the strongest prosocial skills in charge. The mine superintendent who ended up spearheading the collaboration between the drillers was known for his consultative leadership style. He went out of his way to seek the team's input on strategy and walk them through his reasoning as he made each and every decision.

Due to the collapse, the mine was increasingly unstable, with the ground shifting as the team worked. To maximize the chances of a rescue, André and his colleagues made a critical decision. Instead of committing to one drilling plan, they would pursue multiple plans simultaneously.

André needed ideas—fast. He started holding daily meetings with the full rescue team. As he put it later, he knew there would be "no super leader who had all the answers." It was time to build a team process and an organizational system to unlock collective intelligence.

MANY BRAINS MAKE LIGHT WORK

When we're confronting a vexing problem, we often gather a group to brainstorm. We're looking to get the best ideas as quickly as possible. I love seeing it happen . . . except for one tiny wrinkle. Brainstorming usually backfires.

In brainstorming meetings, many good ideas are lost—and few are gained. Extensive evidence shows that when we generate ideas together, we fail to maximize collective intelligence. Brainstorming groups fall so far short of their potential that we get more ideas—and better ideas—if we all work alone. As the humorist Dave Barry quipped, "If you had to identify, in one word, the reason why the human race has not achieved, and never will achieve, its full potential, that word would be: 'meetings.'"

The problem isn't meetings themselves—it's how we run them. Think about the brainstorming sessions you've attended. You've probably seen people bite their tongues due to ego threat (I don't want to look stupid), noise (we can't all talk at once), and conformity pressure (let's all jump on the boss's bandwagon!). *Goodbye diversity of thought, hello groupthink.* These challenges are amplified for people who lack power or status: the most junior person in the room, the sole woman of color in a team of bearded white dudes, the introvert drowning in a sea of extraverts.

MEETINGS
NONE OF US IS AS DUMB AS ALL OF US.

To unearth the hidden potential in teams, instead of brainstorming, we're better off shifting to a process called brainwriting. The initial steps are solo. You start by asking everyone to generate ideas separately. Next, you pool them and share them anonymously among the group. To preserve independent judgment, each member evaluates them on their own. Only then does the team come together to select and refine the most promising options. By developing and assessing ideas individually before choosing and elaborating them, teams can surface and advance possibilities that might not get attention otherwise.

Research by Anita Woolley and her colleagues helps to explain why this method works. They find that another key to collective intelligence is balanced participation.* In brainstorming meetings, it's too easy for participation to become lopsided in favor of the biggest egos, the loudest voices, and the most powerful people. The brainwriting process makes sure that all ideas are brought to the table and all voices are brought into the conversation. Sure enough, there's evidence that brainwriting is especially effective in groups that struggle to achieve collective intelligence.

Collective intelligence begins with individual creativity. But it doesn't end there. Individuals produce a greater volume and variety of novel ideas when they work alone. That means that they come up with more brilliant ideas than groups—but also more terrible ideas than groups. It takes collective judgment to find the signal in the noise.

---

* Interestingly, smarter teams also tend to have higher proportions of women. The key reason is that on average, women outperform men in tests of reading other people's thoughts and feelings. It's not clear whether they're more capable or more motivated to use prosocial skills, but there's a case to be made that women tend to instill these skills in their teams. Both economists and psychologists find that good team players motivate the rest of the group to contribute more. And when a law professor studied corporate boardroom dynamics, he found that as women joined Norwegian boards, they were more likely to actually read the materials before the meeting. Not wanting to be unprepared and outdone, men picked up the norm and started doing their homework too.

@RESEARCHDOODLES BY M. SHANDELL

In Chile, André Sougarret didn't get the best ideas by gathering his team for long brainstorming sessions. Instead, he and his colleagues established a global brainwriting system to crowdsource search and rescue proposals from a diverse network of contacts. To shield the process from the havoc at the mine, they set up a separate team to gather and vet ideas off-site, hundreds of miles south in Santiago.

That team gathered submissions from around the world via Chile's Ministry of Mining website. They also invited ideas from sources as varied as UPS, NASA, the Chilean Navy, an Australian company that specialized in 3D mapping software, and a group of American drilling experts who had been stationed in Afghanistan. They ranked the proposals on feasibility and then interviewed the people with the most promising submissions.

Hundreds of ideas poured in, and some were far-fetched. One contributor suggested strapping panic buttons to a thousand mice and letting them loose in the mine, hoping the miners would find them. Another had spent two weeks inventing a miniature yellow plastic telephone to send down a hole to the miners. It looked as if it had arrived straight from 1986 and gave the engineers on-site a much-needed laugh. As usual, brainwriting yielded variance as well as volume.

Thankfully, some of the submissions provided more than entertainment value. An independent mining engineer pitched the idea of transporting food and water via 3.5-inch tubes. The team adopted his suggestion, and it ended up becoming a lifeline for the miners. Along with providing sustenance, it became their conduit for communicating with the rescuers.

The rescue team sent a high-tech camera down to the miners. For the first time, they could see one another. But the audio didn't work. The engineers tried a number of solutions, but all of them failed. Finally, they swallowed their pride and called for the tiny yellow phone. After attaching it to a fiber-optic cable, the plastic device that cost $10 to make became the sole means of speaking with the miners. The solo entrepreneur who built it, Pedro Gallo, talked with the trapped men every day.

LETTING A THOUSAND FLOWERS BLOOM

Having located the miners and opened communication lines, the rescue team moved full speed ahead on extracting them. Plan A was to use a massive drill to bore a hole. The problem was that it was expected to take four months, and there was no guarantee that the mine would remain intact through the process. And no one could predict whether the miners would face medical emergencies or mental breakdowns before then.

The most extensive analysis of the collaboration lessons from the rescue team was led by my colleague Amy Edmondson. She started her career as an engineer, became a disciple of Richard Hackman's, and is now among the world's foremost experts on teams. After interviewing many of the key players in the rescue effort, Amy encouraged me to dig into one story in particular, assuring me it was worth its weight in gold.

One day, a young engineer named Igor Proestakis was on-site delivering drilling equipment when he bumped into the geologists overseeing the drilling. He told them about an idea he had to access the miners faster. It was a bold alternative to plan A: Instead of slowly drilling a new hole, what if they rapidly expanded one of the existing holes? Igor thought they might be able to do it with a tool called a cluster hammer—a special drill designed to smash right through rock.

Igor didn't expect his suggestion to go anywhere. He was one of the youngest, least experienced engineers at the site. His role was to advise drill operators on how to use his company's equipment effectively, not to propose new strategies and technologies. But when he mentioned his idea to the geologists, they asked him to share it with André Sougarret. Could he have his presentation ready in two hours? "You want me to do *what?*" Igor remembers thinking. He didn't know why anyone would listen to him. "I was just a 24-year-old, giving my opinion."

Igor immediately got to work. He wasn't sure whether the right tools even existed, so he called the owner of an American company that manufactured cluster hammers, and they hatched a plan. They predicted that it would only take a month and a half—but with that speed came higher risk. The technology had never been tried in Chile, and it had never been used to drill holes this wide anywhere near this deep. They would also have to custom-design a drill to do it, and they wouldn't have time to test it before they used it.

Later that day, when Igor presented the idea, André didn't shut him down. He wasn't looking for an excuse to say no—he was listening carefully for reasons to say yes. "This was probably the most important job of his life," Igor recalls, "and despite my experience and age, he listened to me, asked questions, gave it a chance." André asked him to put together a pitch for Chile's mining minister. Soon, the idea was approved: it was now plan B, and the two plans would operate in parallel.

In many organizations, Igor wouldn't have had the chance to pitch his idea in the first place, let alone have it adopted. "In a normal organization, he would never have spoken up," Amy Edmondson told me. "But in this setting, the climate had been created where he felt he could—and he did."

We normally call that a climate for voice and psychological safety. There's evidence that just being looked at by the leader is enough to encourage people who lack status to speak up. But as I dug into Amy's research, something caught my eye. The rescue leaders hadn't just established a climate—they had built an unconventional system for making sure that ideas were carefully considered rather than dismissed. And it's a system that I've seen unlock collective intelligence in all kinds of settings.

BARBARIANS AGAINST THE GATEKEEPERS

In most workplaces, opportunity exists on a ladder. The person immediately above you is in charge of decisions about your growth. Your direct boss sets your job description, vets your suggestions, and determines your readiness for promotion. If you can't get your boss to hear you out, your proposal is toast. The system is simple. But it's also stupid—it gives one individual far too much power to shut creativity down and shut people up. A single no is enough to kill an idea—or even stall a career.

It's easy for managers to find reasons to say no. Your idea might be a threat to their ego (if it's good) or their image (if it's bad). They might question your motives or your reasoning. My research shows that when you bring a suggestion to managers, if you don't have a reputation for being prosocial and levelheaded, that can be enough to turn the tide against you.

In many cases, unproven ideas carry too much risk and uncertainty.

Managers know that if they bet on a bad idea, it might be a career-limiting move, but if they pass on a good idea, it's unlikely anyone will ever find out. And even if managers are supportive of an idea, if they perceive leaders above them as opposed to it, they tend to see it as a losing proposition. All it takes is one gatekeeper to close off a new frontier.

That kind of hierarchy is set up to reject ideas with hidden potential. You can see it clearly in the tech world. Xerox programmers pioneered the personal computer but struggled to get managers to commercialize it. An engineer at Kodak invented the first digital camera but couldn't persuade management to prioritize it.

Organizations can solve this problem with a different kind of hierarchy. A powerful alternative to a corporate ladder is a lattice. A physical lattice is a crisscrossing structure that looks like a checkerboard. In organizations, a lattice is an organizational chart with channels across levels and between teams. Rather than one path of reporting and responsibility from you to the people above you in the hierarchy, a lattice offers multiple paths to the top.

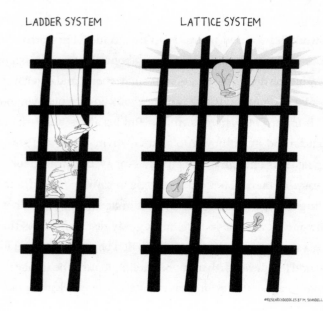

LADDER SYSTEM   LATTICE SYSTEM

#RESEARCHDOODLES BY M. SHANDELL

A lattice system isn't a matrix organization. You're not stuck with eight different bosses breathing down your neck like in *Office Space*. You don't have multiple managers holding you back and shooting you down. The goal is to give you access to multiple leaders who are willing and able to help move you forward and lift you up.

The best example I've seen of a lattice system is at W. L. Gore, the company known for making waterproof Gore-Tex gloves and jackets. Back in the mid-1990s, a rank-and-file medical device engineer at Gore named Dave Myers figured out that coating the gear cables on his mountain bike with Gore-Tex protected them from grit. It dawned on him that Gore-Tex might also be useful for repelling the grit from human hands that leads guitar strings to lose their tone over time.

Even though it wasn't part of his day job, Dave took the initiative to mock up a prototype. He brought it to some senior people, but they didn't think it was worth pursuing. They had technical objections. *You can't coat a vibrating string with fluoropolymer—you'll ruin the sound!* They had strategic concerns too. *We're not in the music business—why would we make guitar strings?*

In a typical organization, those protests would have been enough to squash the idea. But Gore has a lattice system. Whenever you have an idea, you're granted the freedom to go to a range of different senior people. To get your project off the ground, all you need is one leader who's willing to sponsor it. So Dave kept socializing his idea. Eventually he found a sponsor, Richie Snyder, who connected him with an engineer named John Spencer.

For the next year, Dave and John dedicated part of every work week to their unproven idea. Instead of seeing those kinds of side projects as diverting or disobedient, Gore encouraged them—they gave people "dabble time" to tinker. To make headway on the guitar strings, Dave and John didn't need Richie's formal approval. They just gave him regular updates as they developed and tested prototypes with thousands of musicians.

A lattice system rejects two unwritten rules that dominate ladder hierarchies: don't go behind your boss's back or above your boss's head. Amy Edmondson's research suggests that these implicit rules stop many people from speaking up and being heard. The purpose of a lattice system is to remove the punishment for going around and above the boss.

At Gore, Dave and John weren't shy about going above Richie when they needed ideas and support. They took advantage of the leeway to contact anyone at any time. At one point, they even had the chairman-CEO himself dropping into their meetings and giving advice.

It took Dave, John, and their makeshift team 18 months to develop and launch the product. Just 15 months later, their Elixir strings became the market leader in strings for acoustic guitars. It's not every day that an idea hatched in a medical products division makes a dent in the music industry. But it did, thanks to the lattice system.

Even when organizational charts look like ladders, it's possible to design ad hoc lattice systems to surface and propel fledgling ideas. I see these systems often in innovation tournaments—contests to generate novel solutions to problems. Dow Chemical once issued an internal call for proposals to save energy and reduce waste, offering to sponsor the most promising ideas from employees that cost no more than $200,000 and had the potential to pay for themselves within a year. Over the next decade, they bet on 575 ideas, which saved the company an average of $110 million a year.

In this kind of innovation tournament, decisions aren't up to individual gatekeepers. A lattice system engages people at different levels to do peer reviews of the submissions. This prevents entries from being shut down prematurely or unfairly, ensuring that every idea gets due consideration.

Weak leaders silence voice and shoot the messenger. Strong leaders welcome voice and thank the messenger. Great leaders build systems to amplify voice and elevate the messenger.

LIGHT AT THE BOTTOM OF THE TUNNEL

When I first learned about how Igor Proestakis pitched his plan B, I immediately recognized the hallmarks of a lattice system. It was why he was able to bring his idea to the geologists supervising the drilling—and why they took him straight to the top despite his youth and inexperience. But the benefits of the lattice system became even more visible about a month into the rescue initiative.

Plan A was moving even slower than anticipated, and plan B was looking better and better. Igor had been right about the cluster hammer: it was smashing swiftly and smoothly through the rock. It had a clear advantage . . . until it stopped working altogether. A third of the way down, it kept spinning but stopped cutting.

It turned out that they'd hit a series of iron rods that were in place to reinforce the mine, which had shattered the hammer's drill bit into pieces. One of those pieces—a hunk of metal the size of a basketball—was now blocking the hole they were expanding to reach the miners. The team tried to bash the metal out and pull it out with magnets, but it wouldn't budge. They were ready to give up on Igor's plan B.

The next day, Igor had another idea. He remembered an extraction tool he'd read about in school—an industrial version of an arcade claw machine. *My wife, Allison, is the master of that machine, but we had no idea it served a purpose higher than winning plush teddy bears.* It was exactly the kind of approach they needed. If they could lower a metal jaw and clamp its teeth around the obstructing piece of metal, they could extract it and clear the hole.

When Igor first suggested the claw machine to a few people on-site, they didn't listen. But due to the lattice system, he knew he had other routes to getting his idea heard. After two days of having his idea ignored at lower levels, Igor managed to get an audience with the Chilean mining minister himself, who gave it the green light right away. For the next five days, they tried and failed until it finally captured the broken drill bit, lifted it out, and opened the hole. *Best claw prize ever.* To everyone's relief, plan B was back on track.

Late one evening the following month, a rescue worker went down through that hole in a capsule. Shortly before midnight, the capsule came back up carrying the first miner. And less than 24 hours later, the rescue capsule carried the foreman—the last of the 33 miners—out through the hole.

Igor's claw idea saved his plan B—and his idea for plan B helped save 33 lives. There's no question that we should applaud the creative, heroic efforts from him and so many others. But let's not forget the unsung heroes of this story: the leadership practices, team processes, and systems of opportunity that made it possible for people to speak up and be heard.

If we listen only to the smartest person in the room, we miss out on discovering the smarts that the rest of the room has to offer. Our greatest potential isn't always hidden inside us—sometimes it sparks between us, and sometimes it comes from outside our team altogether.

CHAPTER 9

Diamonds in the Rough

Discovering Uncut Gems in Job Interviews and College Admissions

Success is to be measured not so much by the position that one has reached in life

as by the obstacles . . . overcome while trying to succeed.

—BOOKER T. WASHINGTON

On a historic evening in 1972, ten-year-old José Hernandez kneeled in front of an old black-and-white television. He gripped the rabbit ears of the antenna, using his body to boost the signal. As the fuzzy image on the screen became clearer, José watched the last Apollo astronauts bound across the surface of the moon.

José was mesmerized by the moonwalk, but he yearned for an even better view. He unglued his eyes from the screen, raced outside to look at the moon, and ran back in time to see one of the astronauts take his final giant leap. José hoped that one day, he could etch his own footsteps alongside theirs in the lunar dirt.

Many kids go through an astronaut phase, but José was committed to making his dream a reality. Since his strongest subjects were math and science, he decided engineering would be his ride to space. Over the next two decades, he earned a bachelor's and master's degree in electrical engineering and landed a job as an engineer at a federal research facility. He wanted to make his application as strong as possible for NASA.

In 1989, José was ready to throw his hat in the ring. He carefully filled out the 47 sections of the astronaut application, enclosed his resume and transcripts, and shipped his packet off to Houston. Soon he was checking his mailbox daily, eagerly awaiting an envelope from NASA. After ten long months, it finally arrived. He ripped it open and read the letter from the head of the astronaut selection office. *Not selected.*

José wasn't fazed. His aspirations were high, but his expectations were modest—he knew the odds were long. He took the initiative to call NASA for feedback, and followed up with a letter asking how he could improve:

I would like to increase my chances during the next selection process by correcting or improving any deficiencies that I may be unaware of but were discovered in my application package. I would therefore deeply appreciate any feedback you can provide regarding the status of my application, the level of consideration it was given and any comments, if possible, made by reviewers concerning my application.

A special thank you for taking time off your schedule to fulfill one of what must be thousands of requests.

NASA got back to him with disappointing news. Since he hadn't made it past the initial screening, they didn't have notes or advice for him to absorb. Undeterred, he applied again . . . and was rejected again.

José didn't give up hope. He kept putting himself back in the ring— revising his resume, highlighting his strengths, updating his references as he reapplied—only to be met with rejection after rejection. He couldn't even get his foot in the door for an interview.

National Aeronautics and
Space Administration

Lyndon B. Johnson Space Center
Houston, Texas
77058

NASA

January 26, 1990

AHX

Mr. Jose M. Hernandez

Dear Mr. Hernandez:

This letter is in response to your application for the Astronaut
Candidate Program.

I regret to inform you that you were not selected for the
Astronaut Candidate Program. The Johnson Space Center received
more than 2,400 applications for the 16 mission specialist and
7 pilot positions filled. The large number of well-qualified
applicants available made the selection process a difficult one.
Regrettably, we were able to select only a small number of those
with the potential to make a contribution to this nation's space
program.

We intend to select a small number of Astronaut Candidates every
2 years as our needs dictate. We will continue to accept updates
and applications for consideration for the next selection
process.

We appreciate having had the opportunity to consider you for the
Astronaut Candidate Program and wish you success in your future
endeavors.

Sincerely,

Duane L. Ross
Manager, Astronaut
Selection Office

AHX   April 7, 1992

Dear Mr. Hernandez:

Thank you for applying for the Astronaut Candidate Program.

I regret to inform you that you were not selected for the
Astronaut Candidate Program during the recent selection process.
The Johnson Space Center received more than 2,200 applications
for the 15 mission specialist and 4 pilot positions filled.

AHX   December 20, 1994

Dear Mr. Hernandez:

Thank you for applying for the Astronaut Candidate Program.

I regret to inform you that you were not selected for the
Astronaut Candidate Program during the recent selection
process. The Johnson Space Center received more than 2,900
applications for the 9 mission specialist and 10 pilot
positions filled.

AHX   May 9, 1996

Dear Mr. Hernandez:

Thank you for applying for the Astronaut Candidate Program.

I regret to inform you that you were not selected for the
Astronaut Candidate Program during the recent selection
process. The Johnson Space Center received more than 2,400
applications for the 25 mission specialist and 10 pilot
positions filled.

In 1996, the last rejection broke his spirit. José had the sinking feeling that he would never be enough for NASA. He crumpled the letter into a ball and threw it at the garbage can. He was so disappointed that when it missed, he just left it on the floor.

In life, there are few things more consequential than the judgments people make of our potential. When colleges evaluate students for admission and employers interview applicants for jobs, they're making forecasts about future success. These predictions can become gateways to opportunity. Whether the door swings open or slams shut hangs in the balance of their assessments.

What José didn't know was that none of his applications even registered a blip on NASA's radar. They were looking for people with operational experience making decisions in high-stress environments. They expected to see noteworthy accomplishments by engineers. They took notice of applicants who graduated at the top of their class. NASA was focused on finding people who had already achieved great things, and by their standards, that wasn't José. But what NASA's process failed to capture—

as so many organizations do—was a candidate's potential for doing greater things.

In the time between application cycles, José had developed and demonstrated the unusual combination of technical, physical, and character skills that NASA supposedly prized. With a mentor at work, he won a government grant and developed a digital cancer detection technology that helped save many lives. In his spare time, he ran seven marathons with a personal best under three hours—26.2 miles at a pace under seven minutes per mile. Along with being disciplined and determined, he was prosocial: he volunteered to tutor high school students in math, started a chapter of a professional society for Mexican American scientists and engineers, and served his community in a series of local and national leadership roles. Each time he reapplied to be an astronaut, he highlighted new accomplishments, but they didn't make a dent.

NASA missed the markers of José's potential because their selection process wasn't designed to detect them. They had information about work experience and past performance, not life experience and background. They didn't know that José was raised in a family of migrant farmworkers. They didn't know that when he started kindergarten in California, he didn't speak English, and it wasn't until he turned twelve that he finally felt fluent. They didn't know that he had traveled a great distance just to make it to college and become an engineer. The lack of accomplishments in his early applications seemed to reveal the absence of ability, but it actually indicated the presence of adversity.

It's a mistake to judge people solely by the heights they've reached. By favoring applicants who have already excelled, selection systems underestimate and overlook candidates who are capable of greater things. When we confuse past performance with future potential, we miss out on people whose achievements have involved overcoming major obstacles. We need to consider how steep their slope was, how far they've climbed, and how they've grown along the way. The test of a diamond in the rough is not whether it shines from the start, but how it responds to heat or pressure.

THE SORTING HAT IS OUT OF SORTS

For much of human history, opportunity was a privilege of birthright. If you had noble blood, the world was your oyster. If you weren't from the right background, your lot was already cast and your options were limited. Across centuries in many cultures, this dynamic has transformed as people have challenged monarchies, aristocracies, and caste systems. In Confucian China, successive dynasties began opening government posts to anyone who could pass a difficult civil service exam. *They still had a long way to go, because women and people with disabilities were prohibited from taking the exam.* In ancient Greece, Socrates and Plato proposed that societies should be ruled by philosopher kings who earned their wisdom by studying. Their intent was not merely to reimagine how people are chosen to lead; it was to pave the way for new social orders that rewarded individuals for agency and ability.

Today, opening doors to anyone qualified is a high priority for universities and employers. In principle, application processes invite people from a wide range of backgrounds to show what they're capable of. But in practice, our systems for judging qualifications are flawed.

In schools and workplaces, selection systems are usually designed to detect excellence. That means people who are on their way to excellence rarely make the cut. We don't pay enough attention to these people and their paths—which are often filled with speed bumps and roadblocks. When we fail to see hidden potential, along with shattering people's dreams, we lose out on their contributions.

Our errors in identifying potential come at multiple stages of the assessment process as we struggle to contend with limited time and large applicant pools. During an initial screen, it's impossible to really get to know every candidate. There isn't an algorithm for spotting diamonds in the rough, and there aren't enough hours in the day to do a deep dive into each person's life history. Evaluators end up making life-altering decisions for candidates who have been reduced to thin slices of information.

In the first stages of hiring, employers try to address this challenge by relying on credentials. The assumption is that the best colleges admit and produce the best candidates. Yet pedigrees aren't all they're cracked up to be. In a study of over 28,000 students, those who attended higher-ranking universities performed only slightly better than their peers on consulting projects. If you look at the quality of their work and their contributions as collaborators, a Yale student was just 1.9 percent better than a Cleveland State student. And if you require a bachelor's degree, you lose out on over half the American workforce. This systematically disadvantages candidates who acquire skills through alternative routes— at trade schools or two-year community colleges, through apprenticeships or military service, or by teaching themselves or learning on the job.

Beyond college degrees, many managers turn to prior experience to get an initial sense of candidates' qualifications. But it turns out that the amount of experience is also borderline irrelevant. In a meta-analysis of 44 studies with over 11,000 people across a wide range of jobs, prior work experience had virtually no bearing on performance. A candidate with 20 years of experience on a resume may have just repeated the same year of experience 20 times. So, you need experience to get a job, but you need a job to get experience . . . and that experience reveals little about your potential.[*] The key question is not how long people have done a job. It's how well they can learn to do a job.

---

[*] An exception was in extremely complex jobs, where experience became a relevant predictor of performance. That list doesn't just include cognitively demanding fields like surgery and rocket science. As you know from the prologue—and from Finland—it also includes socially and emotionally challenging occupations like teaching kindergarten, where experience does matter.

EXPERIENCE REQUIRED

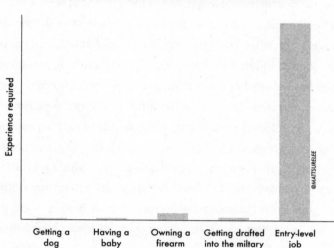

To decide which candidates to advance to the next round, many employers look at prior performance. Compared to credentials and prior work experience, this is a better clue to potential. How well someone has performed in the past can give us a sense of their ability in the present. But this metric also has drawbacks that lead us to overlook the potential in too many people.

Past performance is only helpful if the new job requires similar skills to the old one. In a study of over 38,000 salespeople, economists found that the most successful salespeople were more likely to be promoted to manager. But sales skills aren't the same as managerial skills—the candidates who were better at closing deals were worse at managing people. It turned out that the managers who elevated a team's performance weren't the biggest rainmakers, but the most prosocial members—as indicated by how often they'd made collaborative sales with their colleagues.

This is an example of a phenomenon known as the Peter Principle. It's the idea that people at work tend to get promoted to their "level of incompetence"—they keep advancing based on their success in previous jobs until they get trapped in a new role that's beyond their abilities. In this case, the best salespeople went on to become incompetent managers, and the best potential managers got stuck as mediocre salespeople.*

Even if a candidate's past performance is relevant to the current role, this metric is designed to detect polished diamonds, not uncut gems. Take Tom Brady: whether you love him or hate him, he's widely regarded as the greatest quarterback in football history. But when he entered the NFL, he wasn't drafted until the 199th pick. Based on his performance in college and in the draft combine, scouts had serious doubts about whether Brady's arm was strong enough to zip a spiral and hurl a Hail Mary. It was unlikely that he would be fast enough to escape a blitz.

The problem is that scouts were focusing on Brady's body, not his mind. They were right about his physical limitations: despite weighing only 211 pounds, Brady was outrun by 25 different linemen who tipped the scales at 300+ pounds. But scouts didn't account for what journalists would later call his "nerves of steel." They "didn't open up his chest and look at his heart," one coach lamented. It's often said that talent sets the floor, but character sets the ceiling. Brady went on to break through the assumed ceilings: the year he turned 40, he beat his 40-yard dash time from when he was 20. *Of course, when you're as slow as Tom Brady, the floor is pretty low.*

If natural talent determines where people start, learned character affects how far they go. But character skills aren't always immediately apparent. If we don't look beyond the surface, we risk missing the potential for brilliance beneath.

---

*The best solution I've seen to this problem is dual promotion tracks: one for leadership and one for individual contributors, with similar pay and prestige. This approach expands advancement opportunities for candidates who lack the motivation or skill to manage people—and creates more avenues for people with strong managerial potential to rise. We need to be careful about how we assess that potential, though. When candidates don't match our stereotypes for the job, biases creep in. Economists find that despite receiving higher performance ratings than men, women are less likely to be promoted, because they're rated as having lower potential. That accounts for nearly half the gender gap in promotions—even though women who get promoted outperform men and are more likely to stay.

UNCUT GEMS

When I wanted to find out how to identify hidden potential, I knew NASA was an ideal organization to study. The stakes are sky-high: picking the wrong astronaut could jeopardize a mission and cost crews their lives. That left the agency much more concerned about false positives (accepting bad candidates) than false negatives (rejecting good ones).

To understand why we miss potential and how we can spot it, I reached out to Duane Ross. He led astronaut selection at NASA for four decades, signing the rejection letters personally by hand—including each of José's. I wanted to learn about the process of sifting through the dreams of thousands of applicants to put the future of space exploration in the hands of a select few.

Duane and his colleague Teresa Gomez were hunting for the rare candidates with the right stuff. With between 2,400 and 3,100 applications for only 11 to 35 spots, they had to quickly size up who had potential and who didn't. From what they could see, José Hernandez didn't have it.

NASA had no idea that José was raised in poverty by undocumented immigrants. To make ends meet, the entire family took a long road trip from central Mexico to Northern California each winter. They stopped at farms along the way to pick everything from strawberries and grapes to tomatoes and cucumbers. Come fall, they headed back down to Mexico for a few months and then started the routine again. The journey forced José to miss several months of school and scrape by during the rest of the year in three different districts. After José started second grade, his father began cobbling together day jobs so they could stay in one place, but José still had to work weekends in the fields to help support his family. That left him with limited time for homework, and he couldn't rely on his parents for assistance—they only had third-grade educations.

That history was invisible to NASA. In their search for the right stuff, they didn't have access to the right stuff. "What should figure into the process is how hard it was for them to get there," Duane Ross told me recently, having retired after half a century at NASA. "Early on, we developed our own application forms so we could ask about that. Then the government decided that all applications had to be exactly the same, so we lost a lot of that." With thousands of candidates, they could only check references on 400 and interview the top 120.

For the initial screen, the federally regulated application process focused on work experience, education, special skills, and honors and awards. The form didn't ask for unconventional skills like picking grapes. It didn't signal that gaining a command of the English language would qualify as an honor. The awards section wasn't a place to mention passing physics while working in the fields. The system wasn't designed to identify and weigh the adversity candidates had overcome.

This reinforced José's belief that his background should stay underground. The last section of the application asked for other experience in pertinent activities, like flying. When I asked José why he didn't volunteer his history as a migrant farmworker, he said, "I didn't think it had any relevance. I even thought it might hurt me in a world where I was trying to assimilate as a professional." If NASA had been aware of his past difficulties, they might have caught a glimpse of his future potential.

QUANTIFYING THE UNQUANTIFIABLE

We all know that performance depends on more than ability—it's also a function of degree of difficulty. How capable you appear to be is often a reflection of how hard your task is. The same *Jeopardy!* contestant will look smarter on the $200 questions than the $1,000 stumpers. The same comedian will seem funnier in front of a tipsy crowd at a nightclub than with a bunch of bankers in the morning.

Yet when we judge potential, we often focus on execution and ignore degree of difficulty. We inadvertently favor candidates who aced easy tasks and dismiss those who passed taxing trials. We don't see the skills they've developed to overcome obstacles—especially the skills that don't show up on a resume.

Many systems aren't designed to surface and measure degree of difficulty . . . because doing that is, well, difficult. Some have tried—and failed miserably. In 2019, the SAT introduced an adversity score, awarding students up to 100 points for the hardships they faced in their families, neighborhoods, and schools. The backlash was so fervent that it didn't even last the year. There was little consensus on the types of adversity to count, let alone how to score them.

Social scientists have long found that people can have dramatically different reactions to the same event. One person's trauma may be another's setback; one person's roadblock is another's hurdle. We can calculate the degree of difficulty in a dive, but there isn't a formula to quantify the degree of difficulty in a life.

This is a problem that has long plagued affirmative action efforts. Creating policies that favor underrepresented groups is a politically charged issue. Liberals and conservatives have heated debates about whether it levels the playing field by compensating for historical injustice or perpetuates injustice by introducing reverse discrimination. Wherever you stand ideologically, as a social scientist, it's my job to look to the best evidence. It turns out that affirmative action is often a double-edged sword—even for the people it's designed to serve.

In a meta-analysis of 45 studies, when their organizations had affirmative action, members of disadvantaged groups struggled more with their tasks and got poorer performance reviews. The mere presence of an affirmative action policy was enough to raise questions about their competence in the eyes of observers (did they really deserve that promotion?) and in their own minds (did I get in on my own merit?). This effect even held in experiments establishing that women and racial minorities were highly qualified.

Many groups are still restrained by cultural and structural shackles. It's important to find systematic ways to open doors for people who have been deprived of opportunity. But it's unfortunate that these well-meaning efforts are implemented in ways that leave the intended beneficiaries— and others—wondering whether they earned their place. Even if we could solve that problem, policies that address group hardship don't capture all the difficulties individuals have endured.

When professional orchestras finally started making concerted efforts to hire women, a popular solution was to have candidates audition from behind a screen. Being unable to identify the gender of musicians forced evaluators to focus on their skill. Although that improved the odds for women, it didn't entirely close the gender gap. Since women didn't have access to the same professional training, affirmative action advocates might argue for gender quotas—or for temporarily lowering skill requirements for women based on the disadvantages they'd faced as a group. But doing so runs the risk of casting doubt on the competence of female musicians. Accounting for their individual degree of difficulty points to a more helpful solution: adjusting skill expectations by access to opportunity. For example, orchestra auditions would have different standards for candidates who were self-taught than those who trained at Juilliard.

The goal of measuring degree of difficulty at the individual level isn't to advantage people who face adversity. It's to make sure we don't disadvantage people for navigating adversity. It seems that personal essays would give us a window into college applicants' challenges, but students who have experienced extreme suffering are understandably distraught at the thought of advertising their trauma and marketing their pain. Meanwhile, those who have been lucky enough to avoid significant setbacks often feel pressure to exaggerate their own struggles. Ultimately, the key indicator of potential isn't the severity of adversity people encounter—it's how they react to it. That's what a better selection system would assess.

MAKING THE INVISIBLE VISIBLE

Too often, our selection systems fail to weigh achievements in the context of degree of difficulty. Research shows that when students apply to graduate school, admissions officers pay surprisingly little attention to the difficulty of their courses and majors. Acing easy classes might give you higher odds of acceptance than doing reasonably well in hard classes.

Think about how unfair that is. If admissions officers were Olympic figure skating judges, they might have a skater who gets 6s on a quadruple axel losing to one who gets 8s on a simple loop. If they were choosing a financial advisor, they'd pick one who earned great returns in a bull market over one who achieved good returns in a bear market.

I don't blame admissions officers—or hiring managers. Many don't know their proxy measures are poor, and few have been trained to look for better signs of potential. I've been serving on Ivy League admissions committees and making hiring decisions for two decades, and it didn't occur to me until now to look at applicants' grades relative to the difficulty of their majors. Without being able to compare one curriculum to another, I was ill-equipped to compare one applicant's accomplishments to another's. I should've known better.

Selection systems need to put performance in context. It's like having wrestlers compete in their own weight class. A promising approach is to create metrics that objectively compare students to their peer group. Along with each student's grades, transcripts should display the grade point averages and ranges for their schools and majors.

Displaying the difficulty of the task is only one way of contextualizing performance. We can also adjust for difficulty outside the classroom by comparing students to peers in similar circumstances. Some schools have taken the promising step of expanding transcripts to show students' grades relative to their neighborhood. Experiments show that this can help admissions officers spot the potential in lower-income students without reducing their enthusiasm about students from families with greater means. In the United Kingdom, universities and employers are starting to weigh discrete signs of economic hardship—like holding a work-study job and receiving free meals. I asked Duane Ross about this idea, and he told me that if this kind of information had appeared on José's application, NASA would have given him a closer look. "If a candidate was a migrant farmer, we'd better notice that—particularly if he went on and did something so positive."

Although this approach can help us identify some uncut gems, many difficulties are more subjective and harder to measure than tough grading and financial hardship. We need a way to assess the distance people have traveled to overcome the unique obstacles on their path. The good news is that schools and employers already have access to some valuable data—if only they knew where to look.

What we see

1st
2nd
3rd

What we don't see

DESIRE · PASSION · FOCUS
DOUBT · EFFORT · TRAINING · FAILURE · HARD WORK
TESTS · GOALS · PAIN · INJURY · EARLY MORNINGS · LATE NIGHTS · BLOOD, SWEAT & TEARS
ANGST · SPIRIT · ELATION · LISTENING · SACRIFICE · IMPROVEMENT
WORK · GRIT · JOY · FEAR · INNOVATION · DISCIPLINE · FEEDBACK · PATIENCE
PREP · GUTS · TIME · BRAVERY · LONELINESS · REJECTION · PERSEVERANCE · COURAGE
DIET · SUPPORT · REST · MOTIVATION · STRATEGY · LEARNING · SADNESS · PLANNING
PAIN · DRIVE · HOPE · SLEEP · COMMITMENT · SADNESS · VISION
AIMS · ZEAL · LOSS · HONESTY · PAIN · TRY · TEAM · WILL · TACTICS
DARING · TEAM · ATTITUDE

officeguycartoons.com
© GUY DOWNES

RISE OVER RUN

In a startling study, economist George Bulman analyzed a massive dataset containing every high school graduate in Florida from 1999 to 2002. The goal was to investigate whether their grades would predict their future success—measured in terms of college graduation rates and income earned a decade later.

Freshman year grades revealed nothing about students' potential for future success. Sophomore and junior year grades did matter—every GPA point higher was worth 5 percent more income later. And senior year grades were twice as important: every GPA point was worth 10 percent higher income.

But what really foreshadowed earning potential was whether students improved over time. Unfortunately, colleges typically erased that trajectory by collapsing it into a single score. They sorted students based on their average grades over four years, neglecting to consider whether they got better or worse.

Similar patterns held for the odds of finishing college. Students whose grades improved from freshman to junior year of high school were significantly more likely to graduate from college—and less likely to drop out—than those whose grades declined over the same period. But admissions officers didn't take that delta into account.

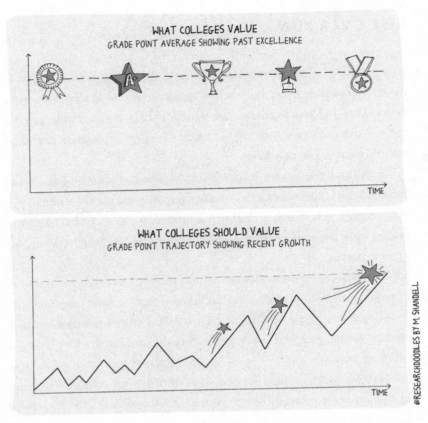

It's hard to overstate how ridiculous that is. Schools judge you as much for your performance three years ago as for three months ago—and they don't even bother to look at the most recent and relevant data at all. We penalize people who rise after rocky starts when we should be rewarding them for the distance they've traveled.

It's time for universities and employers to add another metric. Along with GPA, I think they should be assessing GPT: grade point trajectory. They can calculate the rate of improvement over time with basic division: rise over run. Early failure followed by later success is a mark of hidden potential.

On the basis of GPA alone, compared to the other engineers applying to become astronauts, José didn't stand out. In college, he had gotten Cs in chemistry, calculus, and programming. His lackluster performance raised questions about whether he had the technical aptitude required to be a flight engineer or mission specialist. To their credit, NASA didn't have strict grade cutoffs. But they did favor candidates who excelled academically. And they didn't know why José's grades had suffered—or why they improved over time.

To afford tuition, José worked the graveyard shift at a fruit and vegetable cannery, arriving at 10 p.m. and finishing at 6 a.m. It was a strain to stay alert in class, let alone master the material. When the fruit season ended, he worked nights and weekends as a restaurant busboy. Between demanding classes and a grueling schedule, he finished his first semester with a C average.

As he struggled academically, José started to feel like an outsider and question his abilities. Extensive evidence has identified a social class achievement gap: first-generation college students tend to underperform academically due to a series of invisible disadvantages. The expectation to pave their own paths discourages them from seeking help. The pressure to pay their own way, the presence of self-doubt, and the absence of belonging all interfere with their ability to focus.

The first semester of college was a particularly bumpy period for José. Things improved as he found work with more reasonable hours, established a more sustainable routine, and took the initiative to seek tutoring to fill the gaps in his knowledge. With each semester, his grades climbed. His GPA rose from 2.41 to 2.9 from his freshman fall to spring, and then up again to 3.33 and 3.56 for the fall and spring of his sophomore year. He went on to earn many As and graduate with cum laude honors. He won a full scholarship to a master's program in engineering at the University of California, Santa Barbara. Although he didn't have a perfect GPA, he aced grade point trajectory.

One caveat when using improvement as a mark of potential: it's important to set reasonable expectations. In an initial screen, upward trajectories are hints that candidates have overcome adversity. But we can't always expect a sharp rise. When people face major setbacks, the slopes they have to climb get steeper, and maintaining steady performance can be an achievement in itself.

No single measure of improvement should be our sole metric. Trajectories are a valuable start, but they don't paint a full picture of potential. To gauge the distance people are capable of traveling on steep slopes, it's also critical to take a closer look at the skills and abilities they've gained so far. Instead of looking at past experience or past performance, we should find out what they've learned and how well they can learn. And to do that, we need to rethink how we interview people. The most fascinating approach I've seen is at a call center in Israel.

INTERVIEW WITHOUT A VAMPIRE

Several decades ago, a therapist in training named Gil Winch became frustrated with clinical psychology. It wasn't enough to help one client at a time—he wanted to solve problems on a larger scale. One day, when talking with a neighbor who was paralyzed, Gil learned that worldwide, people with disabilities were struggling to find work. People with impairments in their hearing, vision, movement, memory, learning, and communication shared a common experience. Whether they had a physical disability or a psychological disorder, they knew from a lifetime of stigma and rejection that they were likely to be underestimated and overlooked.

Gil noticed that job interviews put people with disabilities at a disadvantage. A typical interview is set up like an interrogation. Evaluators grill you on your shortcomings: What are your greatest weaknesses? *Here's a list of every mistake I've ever made, in order.* They ask you impossible questions about your future: Where do you see yourself in five years? *Taking your job and asking better interview questions.* Some even try to stump you with brainteasers: How many golf balls can you fit in a jumbo jet? *Why would anyone fill a jet with golf balls?* * Even for candidates who aren't facing a disability, this approach amplifies anxiety and awkwardness.

The stress created in interviews prevents us from seeing people's full potential. That stress tends to be especially pronounced for people who have been underestimated in the past. Just knowing that there's a stereotype about your group is enough to undermine your performance under pressure. The fear of confirming negative stereotypes has been shown to disrupt focus and drain working memory, obscuring the abilities of women on math tests, immigrants on verbal tests, Black students on the SAT, older adults on cognitive tests, and students with physical and learning disabilities on a range of tests. They're set up to fail.

Gil wanted to showcase the abilities of people with disabilities. To make sure their differences didn't stop them from traveling great distances, he did something radical: he launched a call center staffed entirely by people with disabilities. He named it Call Yachol, which is Hebrew for "able to do anything." To set job candidates up for success, he reversed the standard interview process. The system he created is filled with surprises.

Before you show up, you fill out a questionnaire about your passions— from cherished books to beloved music to favorite hobbies. For support, you're invited to bring a partner or a pet to the interview. As soon as you arrive, you discover that the interviewers are the opposite of interrogators: they're hosts. They give you a tour, offer you coffee or tea, and treat you like a guest in their home. They direct you to what looks like a living room, with big, comfy chairs, and ask you about some of your passions.

---

* Brainteasers don't actually reveal anything useful about candidates, but they do tell us something about the interviewers who wield them. In one study, the interviewers most likely to pose brainteasers were narcissists and sadists. Unless you're a proud owner of those traits, watching an applicant squirm doesn't make you feel smart—it makes you feel like a jerk.

The goal isn't just to help you relax; it's also a chance for them to see you light up about what you love.

Next, you get to showcase your strengths. Instead of bombarding you with intimidating riddles and unfamiliar problems, Gil handcrafted a series of challenges that give you the opportunity to exhibit your skills in familiar situations. Keen to display your determination in the face of obstacles? Get ready to meet a difficult neighbor who objects to all your ideas for renovating your building. Excited to display your attention to detail? It's time for Don't Kill Granny. She's allergic to peanuts, and your task is to pick out the safe items for her from a long grocery list. Want to prove you excel at persuasion and negotiation? Tell us how you'd convince a teenager not to look at his phone during dinner.

In the science of interviewing, there's a name for these kinds of demonstrations. They're called work samples. A work sample is a snapshot of an applicant's skills. Sometimes you can provide one by submitting a portfolio of your past work. Many colleges have those built into their admissions processes, inviting students to submit their creative portfolios. You can send in recordings if you're a musician, scripts if you're a screenwriter or playwright, and videos if you're an actor, dancer, or magician.

But past work samples have similar limitations to past performance. They leave us comparing apples and oranges—with no way to account for the different difficulties candidates have endured to date. A powerful alternative is to create real-time work samples: give everyone the same problem to solve in the present. There's a wealth of evidence that these kinds of live work samples can fill gaps in interviews by illuminating candidates' capabilities. Instead of relying solely on what people say, you get to observe what they can do—which applicants appreciate.

I first stumbled onto work samples early in my career, when I didn't know they had a name. A colleague and I were hiring a team of salespeople, and we decided to ask them to sell us a rotten apple. One applicant's pitch was unforgettable: "This may look like a rotten apple, but it's actually an aged, antique apple. They say an apple a day keeps the doctor away, and the longer they age, the more nutrients they gain! And you can plant the seeds in your backyard." *After resolving some honesty concerns, that particular candidate ended up being the best salesperson I ever hired.* Since then, I've seen a range of creative approaches to real-time work samples across industries. My favorites include schools that evaluate the proactivity of teaching applicants by asking them to prepare a live class, and manufacturing firms that assess the prosocial skills of aircraft mechanic candidates by asking them to build a Lego helicopter together.

Work samples are often one-and-done. But your first effort is rarely your best effort. That's another stumbling block the system at Call Yachol removes. Their work samples are designed to give people second chances to succeed. If you get stuck when you're trying not to kill Granny, you can call a timeout and ask for some help. At the end of the interview, instead of being judged, you get to be the judge. You're asked to rate your interview experience—how welcome the interviewer made you feel, and whether you performed at your best. If you're not happy with how it went, you get a do-over. They ask you what *they* can do differently to get to know *you* better.

When a man named Harvey showed up at Call Yachol for his second interview, it was clear that he was struggling to concentrate. The interviewer paused and asked him how he was feeling. Harvey was on the autism spectrum, and he explained that when his shoes felt uncomfortable that morning, he spilled coffee on his shirt while trying to fix them and missed his bus. He was flustered after scrambling to arrive on time, and his shoes still didn't feel right. The interviewer called a break and gave him an hour to reset. Harvey aced the redo and got the job.

Collecting work samples takes time. But many work samples can now be gathered online—it's easier than ever to create digital problem-solving tasks. Even if we run them in person, it's no more time-consuming than conducting an interview. We invest that time because we know how much it matters to be thoughtful about who we let in the door. And despite all the developments in artificial intelligence, I have yet to meet an algorithm that would spot the potential in Harvey.* He has a difficult cold-calling job, where rudeness and rejection are the norm. Most people quit in the first few years, but Harvey has been a paragon of grit and resilience. He's been a star for eight years, consistently reaching his monthly goals and receiving an award in front of the whole call center as the employee of the quarter.

Industry insiders were skeptical that Gil's hiring model would work—especially for a call center. They didn't expect people with disabilities to thrive in a fast-paced, high-pressure environment. It took Gil a full year to recruit his first client. When it finally happened in 2009, he hired 15 people with a range of disabilities and disorders. In one case, he had a manager who was legally blind supervising an employee with hearing loss. It didn't sound like a recipe for success, but Gil was confident it would work. Having seen their strengths up close, he knew the distance the team was capable of traveling. They didn't just meet expectations—they shattered them. Since then, as Call Yachol has grown, many of their teams have exceeded industry benchmarks for hourly leads and time on the phone with clients, and some have outperformed teams without disabilities.

To Gil, that was only the beginning. He knew that people with dis-

---

*This isn't to say that algorithms can't be useful. In selection decisions, algorithms generally outperform humans at predicting applicants' future grades, job performance, and promotion rates. Algorithms have an edge at systematically aggregating and weighing different sources of information, and as some experts have pointed out, it's easier to fix a biased algorithm than a biased human. In college application essays, a machine learning algorithm trained to score character skills and values—from perseverance and prosocial purpose to mastery orientation, leadership, and teamwork—predicts graduation rates over and above grades and test scores. But algorithms have some fundamental limitations: they rely on data from the past to predict future potential, and there will always be important information that they overlook. For example, if you're about to pick an athlete in the draft, your algorithm probably won't account for the fact that last night, your frontrunner broke his leg in a car accident and got arrested for drunk driving. An algorithm is an input to human judgment—not a substitute for it.

abilities were only one group of people whose potential had been ignored. He expanded his hiring model to create opportunities for other disadvantaged groups—from immigrants to the formerly incarcerated. In 2018, the team was invited to Israel's parliament to receive an award honoring the good they'd done for individuals and society.

An interview model like Call Yachol's is not just a compelling way to open the door to underdogs. I think it's a way to recognize the potential in everyone—it enables each candidate's skills to shine through. Interrogations make all of us anxious, and anyone can run into mishaps on the way to a job interview. Skills are best gauged by what people can do, not what they say or what they've done before. Instead of trying to trip people up, we should give them the chance to put their best foot forward. How they respond in a do-over is a more meaningful window into their character than how they handle the first try.

A WINDOW OF OPPORTUNITY

Since NASA invited candidates to update their applications every year, José got an annual do-over. By 1996, after a string of rejections, he was on the verge of quitting when his wife, Adela, encouraged him not to throw away his dream. "Let NASA be the one to disqualify you," she urged. "Don't disqualify yourself."

José realized there was more he could do to qualify himself: he would "become a sponge." He learned that most astronauts were pilots and scuba divers, so he took a year to earn his pilot's license and spent another year driving to scuba diving training every weekend until he got his basic, advanced, and master certifications. And when his federal lab presented him with an unconventional opportunity to work on curtailing nuclear proliferation in Siberia, José took it on one condition: he would get to learn to speak Russian as part of the deal. He hoped it would help him stand out in NASA's next cycle.

Москва. Вид на Кремль с Москвы-реки.
Moscow. View of the Kremlin from the Moscow-River.
Moskau. Blick auf den Kreml uber die Moskwa.
Moscou. Le Kremlin vue de la Moskova.

MOSCOW

Hello Duane,
Just on my way back home from Siberia. Things don't seem as bad here as the press leads us to indicate. Thanks again for meeting with me and hope to hear from you and Teresa in the near future!
—José

Duane Ross
NASA - LBJ Space Center
Astronaut Selection Office
MAIL CODE AHX
Houston, TX 77058
77058
U.S.A.

In 1998, when José was 36, he sent off another astronaut application. And at long last, there was encouraging news. Of over 2,500 applicants, he was one of 120 finalists.

José finally had the opportunity to provide a complete, live work sample. He went through a full week of physical and psychological assessment at Johnson Space Center. Former astronauts queried him on engineering and flying technicalities and teamwork and communication skills. He took tests that required him to rotate objects in his mind and solve problems under pressure. Out of a possible 99 points, the astronaut selection board gave José a score of 91.

The interviewers didn't ask him about hardship directly. They gave him an hour to talk about his background. For the first time, feeling confident that he had proven his technical skills, José opened up and told NASA he'd started out as a migrant farmer. "If you could accomplish all that by coming from someplace like José did," Duane Ross says, "to overcome all that and get to the same place other people got, then you have a lot of desire and capability."

After the interview, José got a personal call from Duane. Unfortunately, they were rejecting him again. But this time, there was a silver lining. They were offering him a job . . . not as an astronaut, but as an engineer.

José had been adapting every year. Now he would have to adapt again. Although he might not be going up himself, he could be part of the mission to send humans to space. The experience taught him a lesson: "There is more than one star in the sky and more than one goal and purpose in life."

———

After a number of years working as a NASA engineer, in 2004, José heard his phone ring. The voice on the other end of the line asked if he was replaceable. José said he was happy to train someone to take his place. "Good," the manager said. "How would you like to come work for the astronaut office?"

After 15 years of applying, José was selected to go to space. "The second I heard the good news," he recalls, "my whole body went numb." He raced home to break the news to his wife, children, and parents, who celebrated by hugging and dancing.

National Aeronautics and
Space Administration
Lyndon B. Johnson Space Center
2101 NASA Parkway
Houston, Texas 77058-3696

April 20, 2004

AHX

Mr. Jose M. Hernandez

Dear Jose:

Congratulations, and welcome to our team! Get ready to begin one of the most exciting periods of your life. The Astronaut Candidate Training Program is designed to prepare you for mission-specific training. You will be actively challenged during this program, and you will be expected to demonstrate an acceptable level of performance in order to be considered for conversion to astronaut status.

In August 2009, a few weeks after turning 47, José stepped into the space shuttle. He sat down, buckled in, and braced himself for takeoff.

Just before midnight, he heard the countdown and watched the engines light up. Eight and a half minutes after blasting into the sky, the engine shut off, and José couldn't believe his eyes. To convince himself it was real, he tossed a piece of equipment up. Watching it hover, he marveled, "I guess we are in space!"

José had gone from picking strawberries in fields to floating among the stars. Over the course of two weeks in space, he flew over five million miles. It was a short hop compared to the distance he had traveled for the chance to wear a space suit.

As exciting as it is to see a candidate like José succeed, it isn't enough. His success shows us what we're missing in so many others. He had to break the mold to make it through a broken system. He's the exception, but he should be the rule.

When we evaluate people, there's nothing more rewarding than finding a diamond in the rough. Our job isn't to apply the pressure that brings out their brilliance. It's to make sure we don't overlook those who have already faced that pressure—and recognize their potential to shine.

Epilogue

Going the Distance

Hold fast to dreams
For if dreams die
Life is a broken-winged bird
That cannot fly.

—LANGSTON HUGHES

When I started telling people I was writing a book on potential, I kept getting questions about dreams. *Is it about reaching our dreams? Are you going to encourage readers to dream big?* I didn't want to go there. It sounded too Pollyanna, too juvenile. It's the sort of lofty language peddled by self-help gurus, not studied by serious social scientists.

If you have the vision, gravitas, and moral high ground of Martin Luther King Jr., you might get away with it. *Though even King's advisors feared the dream language would sound "hackneyed and trite."* For the rest of us, I figured dreams were best left behind in childhood.

Then I came across new evidence that people with bigger dreams go on to achieve greater things. When economists tracked thousands of people from birth until age 55, the aspirations they formed as adolescents foreshadowed how their adult lives would unfold. Young people with grander dreams went further in school and climbed higher at work.

Even after accounting for a host of other factors—their cognitive skills, character skills, family income, and parents' education, occupations, and aspirations—their own dreams made a unique contribution to how they progressed and who they became.

I realized that if it weren't for my dreams and the people who helped make them a reality, this book wouldn't exist.

At the start of my senior year of high school, I was planning to stay in Michigan for college. But one night in September, I went to sleep and dreamed that I went to Harvard. It wasn't an option I'd ever entertained before. I knew it was a long shot—I wasn't sure if I was qualified, and my family couldn't afford out-of-state tuition. But having recently seen *Good Will Hunting*, I couldn't get the idea out of my head.

In my hometown in the suburbs of Detroit, people earned status based on shallow qualities like wealth and beauty. The popular kids at my school were mostly rich or hot. In my vision of Cambridge, it was cool to be smart. My dorm would be filled with fellow nerds. My classes would allow me to soak up knowledge from the world's brightest minds.

Later that fall, I put on my only suit for an interview with a Harvard alum at a nearby law office. Just as I was leaving home, a thought crossed my mind. I ran back inside, grabbed a small box from a drawer, and stuck it in my jacket pocket.

When I arrived, I was shaking—I'd never been interviewed before, and I'd never met a Harvard grad either. What if I didn't understand a word he said?

The interview was scheduled for an hour, but it lasted for three. I had no clue what to make of that. Every day afterward, when I got off the bus after school, I checked the mailbox nervously. In December, I found an envelope from Harvard.

It was an acceptance letter, and it came with some financial aid—though I would still have to work my way through school. I was so overjoyed that I broke my no-dancing rule and did a touchdown dance. *Only later did I learn that whenever I did something stupid, I would forever hear people say, "YOU went to Harvard?!"*

In the spring, as I met my future classmates at events and online, I saw a pattern. Harvard seemed to attract two extremes of students: those who were sure they were a gift to the world, and those who feared they were the one mistake. I was in the latter camp. I'd somehow made the cut, but I didn't know if I was smart enough to cut it there.

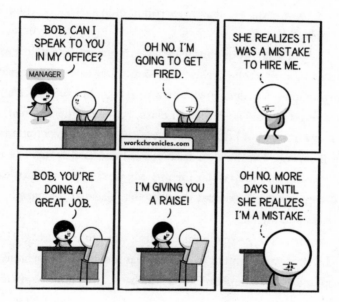

In my first week on campus, I would get the chance to find out if I was smart enough.

Before classes started, every new student had to take a mandatory writing exam. It would determine our placement in a freshman writing seminar. If we passed, we'd have a semester of writing and be done. If we failed, we'd have to start the year with an extra semester of remedial writing. A sophomore told me not to worry about it—remedial writing was for jocks and international students who spoke English as a fifth language.

I don't remember the writing prompt, but I remember what I wrote: an analysis of the characters in *Good Will Hunting*. A few days later, the envelope arrived under my door. I had failed the writing test.

I did not like them apples.

It was the first time Harvard was judging my intellect, and the jury came back with a devastating verdict. *On the charge of not being smart enough: guilty.* Forget impostor syndrome; I was an actual fraud. Meanwhile, my roommate—a heavily recruited quarterback on the football team—passed.

To find out what my options were, I set up a meeting with the experts at the writing center who graded my exam. They said that ultimately, it was up to students to decide which class to take, but they were strongly advising me to take the remedial class. After failing the test, when students went straight into the regular class, they'd never gotten better than a B minus. The writing experts confided that from reading my essay, it would be even riskier for me. My writing was so unclear and unstructured that if I skipped the remedial class, I'd probably get a C. But it was up to me.

I was torn. On the one hand, I didn't want to ruin my GPA, and I enjoyed writing and wanted to get better at it. On the other hand, I was embarrassed at the thought of being held back, and I didn't want to waste an elective.

To make the decision, I needed a guide. But the people who knew me best didn't know Harvard . . . and the people at Harvard didn't really know me at all. Then I thought of my alumni interviewer, a lawyer named John Gierak. He'd been involved in Harvard admissions for decades, and he'd invested a lot of time getting to know me.

A few months earlier, I'd seen John at a welcome reception for admitted students and asked him why I got in. He responded that he wasn't on the committee, so he didn't know for sure. But there was something he'd highlighted in his interview report to Harvard that wasn't visible in my application.

———————

The previous fall, when I arrived at his law office for my interview, John opened by asking me about my interests and hobbies. "I see you've performed as a magician," he said. "What's your favorite trick?"

I reached into my pocket and pulled out the small box I'd grabbed on my way out the door: a deck of cards. "Actually, can I show you?"

John smiled. I started shuffling the cards and told a story with the entire deck. Each time I named a card, it would magically appear at the top—even after I let him cut the pack.

At the end, audiences usually asked how I did it. But John wanted to know how I'd learned it. I told him I'd seen a magician do it on TV when I was twelve and figured out a way to do my own version.

John asked if I could perform with someone else's cards. He went hunting through his law office and came back a few minutes later with a deck. I did a few more tricks—some that I found in books, and others that I'd made up myself.

At the welcome reception, John told me it wasn't the magic that helped me stand out. It was the initiative I'd taken in teaching myself— and the courage I'd shown in doing an impromptu performance for him. *It was my first interview—I didn't know we were just supposed to talk, and it was only after becoming an organizational psychologist that I realized I'd given him a work sample.*

By sharing what stood out in my interview, John had given me a crash course in the importance of character skills. My success wouldn't depend on my initial ability. It would depend on my ability and motivation to learn.

When I failed Harvard's writing test, they hadn't declared me a failure as a writer. They'd failed a tiny snapshot of my writing. They didn't know me, so I set out to prove them wrong. I was determined to go from failing the test to acing the class.

I skipped the remedial writing seminar and signed up for the regular one. I became a sponge, embracing the discomfort of seeking endless rounds of constructive criticism from the professor and anyone else who would read my writing. Instead of going home for Thanksgiving, I stayed on campus to write and rewrite and rewrite an essay. By the end of the semester, I'd traveled a great distance. The professor congratulated me on earning the only A in the class.

I loved them apples.

Impostor syndrome says, "I don't know what I'm doing. It's only a matter of time until everyone finds out."

Growth mindset says, "I don't know what I'm doing yet. It's only a matter of time until I figure it out."

Scaffolding gives you the support you need to figure it out.

I haven't seen John Gierak in two decades. But the insight he gave me about the power of character skills was a critical bit of scaffolding. It became my compass, and it guided my progress for years afterward.

Looking back, if I hadn't challenged myself to take the regular seminar, I might never have become a writer—or a psychologist. The writing seminars covered a range of topics, and for my seminar that fall I was able to pick social influence. One of the assigned readings happened to be a book by a psychologist, Robert Cialdini. It was filled with surprising evidence, and I found it so riveting that when it was assigned for one of my other classes, I read it a second time. It was the first time I considered becoming a psychologist. I started dreaming of writing a book like that one day.

For the next decade, that dream faded into the background. As a professor, I had to figure out how to teach. Even after I got my anxiety under control, I was still fairly robotic until a mentor, Jane Dutton, dropped a pin. She advised me to unleash my inner magician.

I started introducing surprise endings with counterintuitive studies and unexpected twists in experiential learning. I was focused on teaching memorable classes and doing worthwhile research. Then I got tenure at Wharton. Having made it to the top of that mountain, I wanted to do more to help others climb theirs. I felt a responsibility to share what I was learning beyond the classroom and academic journals—with an audience broader than students and researchers.

A few weeks later, a mentor reached out to tell me he was starting his next book. It was on incentives, and since I studied motivation, he wondered if I wanted to coauthor it with him. He was one of my role models, and I told my students how honored and excited I was that he was bringing me on board. They revolted. *If you're going to write a book, start with your own ideas! Have you forgotten what you taught us? The worst kind of success is achieving other people's goals. Don't live someone else's dream.* They were right. I decided to pursue a book of my own.

Several colleagues raved about a literary agent, Richard Pine, who took me under his wing. In June, after many weeks of independent brainwriting, Richard announced that it was time to draft a proposal to share with potential publishers. I'd been studying the topic for years, so the ideas came pouring out. In August, I sent him 103,914 words. In two months, I'd written a draft of the whole book.

I couldn't wait to hear Richard's reaction. Gently, he explained that it was too academic. That was an understatement—it was boring. *In other words: not a page-turner.* I was so deep in the weeds of the research that even my academic colleagues would lose interest. He encouraged me to reflect on the bigger picture and start over from scratch.

Hello, languishing.

I was stuck. I didn't know where to begin, let alone if I could do it. Impostor syndrome came back with a vengeance. Who was I to write a book? Why would anyone want to read what I had to say? Richard shifted from judge to coach and told me to stop doubting myself. "Of course you can do it! Just write like you teach, not like you write for academic journals."

I trusted him. He wasn't just a credible believer; he was a guide pointing me in a better direction. I threw out 102,000 words—there were about four pages worth salvaging—and wrote what became my first book. Writing like I teach has been my compass ever since. It's what guided me to write books that you were actually interested in reading. *Well, at least one . . . I hope you don't regret it.*

IMPOSTOR SYNDROME

Not long ago, it dawned on me that impostor syndrome is a paradox:

- Others believe in you
- You don't believe in yourself
- Yet you believe yourself instead of them

If you doubt yourself, shouldn't you also doubt your low opinion of yourself?

I now believe that impostor syndrome is a sign of hidden potential. It feels like other people are overestimating you, but it's more likely that you're underestimating yourself. They've recognized a capacity for growth that you can't see yet. When multiple people believe in you, it might be time to believe them.

Many people dream of achieving goals. They measure their progress by the status they acquire and the accolades they collect. But the gains that count the most are the hardest to count. The most meaningful growth is not building our careers—it's building our character.

Success is more than reaching our goals—it's living our values. There's no higher value than aspiring to be better tomorrow than we are today. There's no greater accomplishment than unleashing our hidden potential.

ACTIONS FOR IMPACT

To take a quiz about your hidden potential, visit www.adamgrant.net.

The learning process isn't finished when we acquire knowledge. It's complete when we consistently apply that knowledge. Here are my top forty practical takeaways for unlocking hidden potential and achieving greater things.

I. BUILD CHARACTER SKILLS

1. *Unleash hidden potential through character skills.* The people who grow the most aren't the smartest people in the room. They're the ones who strive to make themselves and others smarter. When opportunity doesn't knock, look for ways to build a door—or climb through a window.

A. Become a creature of discomfort

2. *Don't be afraid to try a new style.* Instead of focusing on the way you like to learn, embrace the discomfort of matching the method to the task. Reading and writing are usually best for critical thinking. Listening is

ideal for understanding emotions, and doing is better for remembering information.

3. *Use it or never gain it at all.* Put yourself in the ring before you feel ready. You don't need to get comfortable before you can practice your skills— your comfort grows *as* you practice your skills. As polyglots show us, even experts have to start from day one.

4. *Seek discomfort.* Instead of just striving to learn, aim to feel uncomfortable. Pursuing discomfort sets you on a faster path to growth. If you want to get it right, it has to first feel wrong.

5. *Set a mistake budget.* To encourage trial and error, set a goal for the minimum number of mistakes you want to make per day or per week. When you expect to stumble, you ruminate about it less—and improve more.

B. Become a sponge

6. *Increase your absorptive capacity.* Seek out new knowledge, skills, and perspectives to fuel your growth—not feed your ego. Progress hinges on the quality of the information you take in, not on the quantity of information you seek out.

7. *Ask for advice, not feedback.* Feedback is backward-looking—it leads people to criticize you or cheer for you. Advice is forward-looking—it leads people to coach you. You can get your critics and cheerleaders to act more like coaches by asking a simple question: "What's one thing I can do better next time?"

8. *Figure out which sources to trust.* Decide what information is worth absorbing—and which should be filtered out. Listen to the coaches who have relevant expertise (credibility), know you well (familiarity), and want what's best for you (care).

9. *Be the coach you hope to have.* Demonstrate that honesty is the highest expression of loyalty. Model effective coaching by being forthcoming in what you say and respectful in how you say it. Show people how easy

it is to hear a hard truth from someone who believes in their potential and cares about their success.

C. Become an imperfectionist

10. *Strive for excellence, not perfection.* Progress comes from maintaining high standards, not eliminating every flaw. Practice wabi sabi, the art of honoring beauty in imperfection, by identifying some shortcomings that you can accept. Consider where you truly need the best and where you can settle for good enough. Mark your growth with Eric Best's questions: Did you make yourself better today? Did you make someone else better today?

11. *Enlist judges to gauge your progress.* To figure out whether you've created a minimum lovable product, ask a few people to independently rate your work on a scale of 0 to 10. Whatever score you receive, ask them how you can get closer to 10. Be sure to set an acceptable as well as aspirational result—and don't forget that to get high scores on your top priorities, you may have to be satisfied with lower scores on the others.

12. *Be your own last judge.* It's better to disappoint others than to disappoint yourself. Before you release something into the world, assess whether it represents you well. If this was the only work people saw of yours, would you be proud of it?

13. *Engage in mental time travel.* When you're struggling to appreciate your progress, consider how your past self would view your current achievements. If you knew five years ago what you'd accomplish now, how proud would you have been?

II. SET UP SCAFFOLDING TO OVERCOME OBSTACLES

14. *Look outward for the right support at the right time.* Every challenge requires its own support. The support you need isn't permanent—it's

a temporary structure that gives you a foothold or a lift so you can keep climbing on your own.

A. Turn practice into play

15. *Turn the daily grind into a source of daily joy.* To maintain harmonious passion, design practice around deliberate play. Set up fun skill-building challenges—like Evelyn Glennie learning to play a Bach piece on a snare drum, Steph Curry trying to score twenty-one points in a minute, or medical residents honing their nonverbal communication skills by using nonsense words in improv comedy games.

16. *Compete against yourself.* Measure your progress over time, not against an opponent. The risk of competing against others is that you can win without getting better. When you compete against yourself, the only way to win is to grow.

17. *Don't hold yourself hostage to a fixed routine.* It's possible to avoid burnout and boreout by introducing novelty and variety into your practice. You can alternate between different skills you're practicing or switch up the tools and methods you use to learn those skills. Even small tweaks can make a big difference.

18. *Be proactive about rest and recovery.* Don't wait until you're burned out or bored out to take breaks—build them into your schedule. Taking time off helps to sustain harmonious passion, unlock fresh ideas, and deepen learning. Relaxing is not a waste of time; it's an investment in well-being.

B. Take the roundabout path to progress

19. *When you're stuck, back up to move forward.* When you hit a dead end, it might be time to turn around and find a new path. It feels like regressing, but it's often the only way to find a route to progress.

20. *Find a compass.* You don't need a map to start on a new route—you just need a compass to gauge whether you're heading in the right direction. A good compass is a credible source that signals when you're going off course.

21. *Seek multiple guides.* Instead of relying on a single expert or mentor, remember that the best directions come from multiple guides. Ask them about the landmarks and turning points from their own journeys— and tell them about the roads you've taken so far. As they drop pins, you can piece them together into a route that works for you.

22. *Find a side gig.* When you find yourself languishing, you can build momentum by taking a detour to a new destination. When you make progress in a side project or hobby, you rack up small wins, which remind you that forward movement is possible.

C. Fly by your own bootstraps

23. *Teach what you want to learn.* The best way to learn something is to teach it. You understand it better after you explain it—and you remember it better after you take the time to recall it. Like the Golden Thirteen, you can do this in groups, with each member teaching a distinct skill or slice of information.

24. *Build confidence by coaching others.* When you're doubting your ability to overcome an obstacle, instead of seeking advice, try giving advice. Guiding others through a challenge reminds you that you have the resources you need to tackle it. The advice you give is usually the advice you need to take.

25. *Harness both high and low expectations as motivation.* If ignorant naysayers doubt you, take it as a challenge. Instead of letting them crush your confidence, recognize it as an opportunity to prove them wrong. And when credible believers are behind you, rise to the occasion and prove them right.

26. *Be a good ancestor.* When your faith falters, recall who you're fighting for. Our deepest reserves of resilience come from knowing that other people are counting on us.

III. BUILD SYSTEMS OF OPPORTUNITY

27. *Open doors for people who are underrated and overlooked.* Create systems that invest in and create opportunities for all—not just gifted students and high-potential employees. A good system gives underdogs and late bloomers the chance to show how far they've come.

A. Design schools to bring out the best in all students

28. *Don't waste a brain.* Recognize that intelligence comes in many forms, and every child has the potential to excel. Cultivate a growth mindset in teachers, not only in students. Gauge success by the progress of every student, not just those at the top.
29. *Professionalize education.* Following Finland's example, train and treat teachers as trusted professionals. When teachers are equipped and encouraged to stay up-to-date on the latest evidence, coach one another, and shape the curriculum, the next generation can achieve greater things.
30. *Keep students with the same teachers for multiple years.* Looping allows teachers to specialize in their students, not just their subjects. With more time to get to know each student personally, teachers can become coaches and mentors, tailoring their instructional and emotional support to help all students reach their potential.
31. *Give students the freedom to explore and share their individual interests.* The most important lesson to teach students is that learning is fun. When students get to select the activity stations, books, and projects that interest them, they're more likely to develop intrinsic motivation. When

they present on the topics they love, it reinforces their enthusiasm—
and gives their classmates the chance to catch it.

B. Unearth collective intelligence in teams

32. ***Transform groups into teams.*** Collective intelligence depends on
cohesion—aligning a team around shared responsibility for a meaningful mission. When people believe they need one another to succeed
in reaching an important goal, they become more than the sum of
their parts.

33. ***Choose leaders based on prosocial skills.*** Instead of promoting babblers
and ball hogs, elevate people who put the mission above their ego—
and prioritize team cohesion over personal glory. When teams are
eager to contribute, the most effective leader is not the loudest talker,
but the best listener.

34. ***Shift from brainstorming to brainwriting.*** For more balanced participation
and better solutions, before you meet as a group, have people generate
and evaluate ideas independently. Once all the ideas are on the table and
all the voices are in the room, have the group select and refine the most
promising possibilities.

35. ***Replace the corporate ladder with a lattice system.*** Instead of leaving it up
to a single boss to shoot down suggestions, give people multiple paths
to speak up. If people can go to more than one leader, a single no can't
kill an idea—and a single yes can be enough to save it.

C. Discover uncut gems in job interviews and college applications

36. ***Eliminate requirements for credentials and experience.*** When evaluating
others, beware of mistaking past accomplishments and experience for
future potential. Background and talent determine where people start,
but character skills shape how far they can climb.

37. *Account for degree of difficulty.* Struggles don't necessarily reflect the absence of ability—often they reveal the presence of adversity. To account for the obstacles candidates have faced, put their performance in context by comparing them to peers in their school, major, and neighborhood.

38. *Use trajectories in evaluations.* It's not enough to look at recent or average performance—the trajectory of performance over time matters more. An upward slope is a clue that candidates have overcome adversity.

39. *Reimagine interviews to set candidates up to succeed.* Instead of designing interviews to maximize stress, create opportunities for candidates to shine. Invite applicants to share what they love and showcase their strengths. Afterward, ask if they thought their performance represented them well—and if not, give them a do-over.

40. *Redefine success.* The most meaningful form of performance is progress. The ultimate mark of potential is not the height of the peak you've reached, but the distance you've traveled—and helped others travel.

ACKNOWLEDGMENTS

This book would have fallen far short of its potential without the initiative of super-agent Richard Pine and crackerjack editor Rick Kot. Richard spurred me to think bigger and bolder from the first page to the last. Rick massaged drivel into prose and turned around drafts in record time. Together, the two of them guided me to turn around when I got stuck and made it a joy to explore new routes.

Writing a book can be a lonely journey, but I had the great fortune of collaborating with the ultimate dynamic duo of judging and coaching. Marissa Shandell and Karren Knowlton immeasurably enriched every page of this book. Whenever they found a half-baked idea, they rapidly tore it down and expertly built it into something stronger. They poured their ingenuity into shaping each story, their intellect into sharpening each sentence, and their energy into elevating each illustration and takeaway. Marissa introduced solutions to problems I didn't see, dropped pins I didn't realize were missing, and brought structure to chaos. Karren blazed the trails for building up bootstrapping, rethinking the essential order of ideas, and braiding the themes across chapters. I have never seen a pair of people improve a creative project so dramatically.

A crew of perceptive readers made invaluable contributions to the book. Quality-control guru Paul Durbin painstakingly fact-checked every page of this book, delving deep into the studies and stories to ensure the accuracy of all the details. Any errors are mine alone. Queen of signposting Grace Rubenstein clarified key insights, finessed clunky transitions, and pushed me to put the thesis in context. Master idea crafter Reb Rebele led the charge to amplify the big "aha!" and increase conceptual cohesion. Book detective Stacey Kalish hunted down stories and provided meta-scaffolding. She also observed a fascinating paradox at the intersection of the tutor effect and the curse of knowledge: you can learn by teaching, but once you've learned them well, it can become harder to teach them.

BlackBerry advocate Malcolm Gladwell encouraged me to let the big ideas and stories breathe, create more connective tissue between sections, and vary the narrative arc along the way. Overqualified professional editor Sheryl Sandberg helped me accentuate the fundamental contrast between nature and nurture. Perfectionist-in-a-good-way Susan Grant flagged formulaic stories and fixed grammatical mistakes and typos. And education maven Sam Abrams corrected misconceptions about classroom hours, teacher pay, standardized testing, school spending, and the PISA. He also taught me that education isn't the only place Finland loops; their renowned hockey programs typically have young players stay with one coach until they turn 15, and then work with the same professional coaches until age 20.

Liz Fosslien, Matt Shirley, and Marissa iterated creatively and cheerfully on a series of custom illustrations. Dan Pink, Lindsay and Allie Miller, Justin Berg, and the 238 Society rescued me from a litany of bad titles. And a number of people were kind enough to open doors for interviews. Shout-outs to Kelly Stoetzel for assuring Maurice Ashley I wasn't a stalker, Bjarke Ingels for the lead on Tadao Ando, Shane Battier for the introduction to Brandon Payne (and Danny Southwick for sharing the original story about him), Paul Stillwell and Janis Jorgensen for the trea-sure trove of information about the Golden Thirteen, David Epstein and Jon Wertheim for helping me pitch R. A. Dickey, Cady Coleman for the connection to José Hernandez, and Bozoma Saint John for texting the GOAT. I thank them all.

Working on this book was a bed of roses due to the support of the star-studded teams at InkWell (I'm looking at you, Alexis Hurley, Nathaniel Jacks, Eliza Rothstein) and Viking. If you've never written a book, it's a strange thing to sell: "Hi there! Please invest your precious time in a voyage through my mind. You'll love it . . . I promise." The publicity efforts of Carolyn Coleburn, Whitney Peeling, Lindsay Prevette, and Julia Falkner made it easy and fun, and the creative marketing initiatives of Kate Stark, Molly Fessenden, and Chantal Canales opened up new ways to reach audiences. Lydia Hirt grew that audience by migrating my Granted newsletter to Substack (and still owes me a pickleball game). I'm especially grateful to Jason Ramirez for his artistic genius, Camille LeBlanc for chasing down loose ends, Tricia Conley and Eric Wechter for their editorial and production excellence, Daniel Lagin for his elegant book design, Claire Vaccaro for art direction, Julie Wilson and Lauren Klein for making the audio sing even though I can't, and Brian Tart and Andrea Schulz for seeing the potential in this book and believing in some bald guy.

Our kids reminded me every day that potential is hiding in plain sight all around us. I loved seeing them model character skills. As he went through third grade, Henry surprised me with his insights on embracing discomfort (roller coasters exist for three reasons: to have fun, to face your fears, and to challenge yourself) and his cognitive dexterity (in line for a roller coaster: I regret this!). As she finished elementary school, Elena absorbed ideas for new pranks to play on her teacher (I'm bringing a fake rat to scare my teacher) and then adapted to anticipated obstacles (in case she says no to Harrison, I have a backup rat!). And as she started high school, Joanna embraced imperfections (Hidden Potential might sound a little boring, but at least it describes the book) and once again helped bring the cover concept to life.

For the past two decades, Allison Sweet Grant has nurtured my potential as a writer and a person. She's the first to see promise in a new direction—and the first to point out when I'm on the wrong path. This book was no exception: she found invisible gems, polished choppy paragraphs, and cut irrelevant details from descriptions. She convinced me it was better to have no title than a bad one (good riddance, Leaps and Bounds and Freaks of Nurture). There are no words to express my appreciation for her brilliant mind, caring heart, and endless patience with my ongoing inability to correctly pronounce the word *mayonnaise.*

NOTES

PROLOGUE

1 **Did you hear about the rose:** Tupac Shakur, *The Rose That Grew from Concrete* (New York: Pocket Books, 2002), 3.

2 **The Raging Rooks:** personal interviews with Maurice Ashley, January 10, 2022, and Francis Idehen, December 20, 2021, January 10, 2022, and February 23, 2022; Maurice Ashley, *Chess for Success* (New York: Broadway Books, 2007); Henry Louis Gates Jr., *America Behind the Color Line* (New York: Grand Central, 2007); Franz Lidz, "The Harlem Gambit," *Sports Illustrated*, November 11, 1991, and "Master Mind," *Sports Illustrated*, May 30, 1994; Steve Fishman, "Day for Knight," *New York*, June 22, 1998; Charlotte Wilder, "How Maurice Ashley, the First Black Chess Grandmaster, Uses the Game to Change Inner-City Kids' Lives," *USA Today*, May 19, 2016; Dave Von Drehle, "Chess Players Destroy Nerd, Black Stereotypes," *The Seattle Times*, June 2, 1991; The Tim Ferris Show, "Grandmaster Maurice Ashley—The Path and Strategies of World-Class Mastery," July 30, 2020; John Tierney, "Harlem Teen-Agers Checkmate a Stereotype," *The New York Times*, April 26, 1991; "Maurice Ashley 2.1.2008," City Club of Cleveland, YouTube, August 13, 2015, youtu.be /riiQ0BkMhf0; Joe Lemire, "A Star of the 'Raging Rooks,' He Helped Changed the Face of N.Y.C. Chess," *The New York Times*, November 6, 2020; Philippe Boulet-Gercourt, "The Incredible Story of the 8 'Kids,' Harlem Chess Players," Chess in the Schools, December, 26, 2020.

4 **roots of exceptional talent:** Benjamin Bloom, *Developing Talent in Young People* (New York: Ballantine Books, 1985).

5 **improved at the same rate:** Kenneth R. Koedinger, Paulo F. Carvalho, Ran Liu, and Elizabeth A. McLaughlin, "An Astonishing Regularity in Student Learning Rate," *PNAS* 120, no. 13 (2023): e2221311120.

6 **obsessed with innate talent:** Chia-Jung Tsay and Mahzarin R. Banaji, "Naturals and Strivers: Preferences and Beliefs about Sources of Achievement," *Journal of Experimental Social Psychology* 47, no. 2 (2011): 460–65.

7 **ambition is the outcome:** Agnes Callard, *Aspiration: The Agency of Becoming* (New York: Oxford University Press, 2018).

8 **more experienced kindergarten teachers:** Raj Chetty, John N. Friedman, Nathaniel Hilger, Emmanuel Saez, Diane Whitmore Schanzenbach, and Danny Yagan, "How Does Your Kindergarten Classroom Affect Your Earnings? Evidence From Project Star," *The Quarterly Journal of Economics* 126, no. 4 (2011): 1593–1660 and "$320,000 Kindergarten Teachers," *Kappan*, November 2010.

8 **added more value:** Raj Chetty, John N. Friedman, and Jonah E. Rockoff, "Measuring the Impacts of Teachers II: Teacher Value-Added and Student Outcomes in Adulthood," *American Economic Review* 104, no. 9 (2014): 2633–79.

10 **virtues of character:** Aristotle, *Aristotle's Nicomachean Ethics*, trans. Robert C. Bartlett and Susan D. Collins (Chicago: University of Chicago Press, 2012).

12 **intelligence becomes nearly irrelevant:** Alexander P. Burgoyne, Giovanni Sala, Fernand Gobet, Brooke N. Macnamara, Guillermo Campitelli, and David Z. Hambrick, "The Relationship between Cognitive Ability and Chess Skill: A Comprehensive Meta-Analysis," *Intelligence* 59 (2016): 72–83.

12 **over 20,000 hours of practice:** Guillermo Campitelli and Fernand Gobet, "Deliberate Practice: Necessary but Not Sufficient," *Current Directions in Psychological Science* 20, no. 5 (2011): 280–85.

12 **review of the research:** James J. Heckman and Tim Kautz, "Hard Evidence on Soft Skills," *Labour Economics* 19, no. 4 (2012): 45164; Tim Kautz, James J. Heckman, Ron Diris, Bas ter Weel, and Lex Borgans, "Fostering and Measuring Skills: Improving Cognitive and Non-Cognitive Skills to Promote Lifetime Success," NBER Working Paper 20749, December 2014.

13 **Psychologists call it scaffolding:** Laura E. Berk and Adam Winsler, *Scaffolding Children's Learning: Vygotsky and Early Childhood Education* (Washington, DC: National Association for the Education of Young Children, 1995).

15 **character skills matter more:** Zainab Faatimah Haider and Sophie von Stumm, "Predicting Educational and Social-Emotional Outcomes in Emerging Adulthood from Intelligence, Personality, and Socioeconomic Status," *Journal of Personality and Social Psychology* 123, no. 6 (2022): 1386–1406.

17 **no reason to believe the magic is limited:** Giovanni Sala and Fernand Gobet, "Do the Benefits of Chess Instruction Transfer to Academic and Cognitive Skills? A Meta-Analysis," *Educational Research Review* 18 (2016): 46–57; Michael Rosholm, Mai Bjørnskov Mikkelsen, and Kamilla Gumede, "Your Move: The Effect of Chess on Mathematics Test Scores," *PLoS ONE* 12 (2017): e0177257; William M. Bart, "On the Effect of Chess Training on Scholastic Achievement," *Frontiers in Pscyhology* 5 (2014): 762; John Jerrim, Lindsey Macmillan, John Micklewright, Mary Sawtell, and Meg Wiggins, "Does Teaching Children How to Play Cognitively Demanding Games Improve Their Educational Attainment?," *Journal of Human Resources* 53, no. 4 (2018): 993–1021; Fernand Gobet and Guillermo Campitelli, "Educational Benefits of Chess Instruction: A Critical Review," in *Chess and Education: Selected Essays from the Koltanowski Conference*, ed. Tim Redman (Dallas: University of Texas, 2006).

PART I

19 **"character has set like plaster":** William James, *The Principles of Psychology*, vol. 2 (New York: Holt, 1890).

20 **Character skills training had a dramatic impact:** Francisco Campos, Michael Frese, Markus Goldstein, Leonardo Iacovone, Hillary C. Johnson, David McKenzie, and Mona Mensmann, "Teaching Personal Initiative Beats Traditional Training in Boosting Small Business in West Africa," *Science* 357, no. 6357 (2017): 1287–90.

21 **dismissed as "soft skills":** Paul G. Whitmore, John P. Fry, "Soft Skills: Definition, Behavioral Model Analysis, Training Procedures," ERIC Clearinghouse Professional Paper 3-74 (1974).

CHAPTER 1

23 **"Character cannot be developed in ease and quiet":** Hellen Keller, *Helen Keller's Journal* (New York: Doubleday, 1938).

23 **Sara Maria Hasbun:** personal interview, February 14, 2022; "Interview with Sara Maria Hasbun," International Association of Hyperpolyglots, 2022, polyglotassociation.org/members/sara-maria-hasbun; John Fotheringham, "Polyglot & Miss Linguistic Founder Sara Maria Hasbun on How to Learn a Language Like a Linguist," *Language Mastery*, May 3, 2019; Sara Maria Hasbun, "I've Learned 9 Languages, All After the Age of 21," MissLinguistic, August 21, 2018, misslinguistic.com/i-learned-nine-languages; "Interview with Sara Maria Hasbun," Glossika, YouTube, November 21, 2019, youtu.be/isErps6IuoA.

24 **engineer named Benny Lewis:** personal communication, April 2, 2023; Martin Williams, "Natural-Born Linguists: What Drives Multi-Language Speakers?," *The Guardian*, September 5, 2013; Andreas Laimboeck, "How Far Did Benny Lewis Get to Learn Fluent Mandarin in Three Months?," LTL Language School, February 28, 2023; Benny Lewis, *Fluent in 3 Months: How Anyone at Any Age Can Learn to Speak Any Language from Anywhere in the World* (New York: HarperOne, 2014) and fluentin3months.com.

26 **decline in the rate of language learning:** Kenji Hakuta, Ellen Bialystok, and Edward Wiley, "Critical Evidence: A Test of the Critical-Period Hypothesis for Second-Language Acquisition," *Psychological Science* 14, no. 1 (2003): 31–38; Frans van der Slik, Job Schepens, Theo Bongaerts, and Roeland van Hout, "Critical Period Claim Revisited: Reanalysis of Hartshorne, Tenenbaum, and Pinker (2018) Suggests Steady Decline and Learner-Type Differences," *Language Learning* 72, no. 1 (2022): 87–112.

27 **teachers believe in matching:** Philip M. Newton and Atharva Salvi, "How Common Is Belief in the Learning Styles Neuromyth, and Does It Matter? A Pragmatic Systematic Review," *Frontiers in Education* 5 (2020): 602451.

27 **found and alarming lack:** Harold Pashler, Mark McDaniel, Doug Rohrer, and Robert Bjork, "Learning Styles: Concepts and Evidence," *Psychological Science in the Public Interest* 9, no. 3 (2008): 105–19.

28 **controlled experiments with specific lessons:** Laura J. Massa and Richard E. Mayer, "Testing the ATI Hypothesis: Should Multimedia Instruction Accommodate Verbalizer-Visualizer Cognitive Style?," *Learning and Individual Differences* 16, no. 4 (2006): 321–35.

28 **longitudinal studies over the course of a semester:** Polly R. Husmann and Valerie Dean O'Loughlin, "Another Nail in the Coffin for Learning Styles? Disparities among Undergraduate Anatomy Students' Study Strategies, Class Performance, and Reported VARK Learning Styles," *Anatomical Sciences Education* 12, no. 1 (2019): 6–19.

28 **deprives you of the opportunity to improve:** Donggun An and Martha Carr, "Learning Styles Theory Fails to Explain Learning and Achievement: Recommendations for Alternative Approaches," *Personality and Individual Differences* 116, no. 1 (2017): 410–16.

28 **When Steve Martin first started doing stand-up:** Steve Martin, *Born Standing Up: A Comic's Life* (New York: Scribner, 2007), *Cruel Shoes* (New York: G. P. Putnam's Sons, 1979), and *Pure Drivel* (New York: Hyperion, 1998); Harry Shearer and Steve Martin, "Not Wild but Witty Repartee with Martin, Shearer," *Los Angeles Times*, December 9, 1998; Catherine Clinch, "No Art Comes from the Conscious Mind," *Creative Screenwriting*, March 8, 2016; Steven Gimbel, *Isn't That Clever: A Philosophical Account of Humor and Comedy* (New York: Taylor & Francis, 2017).

29 **daily writing sessions:** Robert Boice, *Professors as Writers: A Self-Help Guide to Productive Writing* (Oklahoma: New Forums, 1990).

29 **shifting effort from rough drafting:** Shakked Noy and Whitney Zhang, "Experimental Evidence on the Productivity Effects of Generative Artificial Intelligence," SSRN, March 1, 2023.

29 **instant gratification monkey:** Tim Urban, "Why Procrastinators Procrastinate," Wait But Why, October 30, 2013.

29 **procrastination is not a time management problem:** Fuschia M. Sirois, *Procrastination: What It Is, Why It's a Problem, and What You Can Do About It* (Washington, DC: APA LifeTools, 2022); Adam Grant, "The Real Reason You Procrastinate," *WorkLife*, March 10, 2020.

30 **"I didn't know how to write":** Adam Grant, "Steve Martin on Finding Your Authentic Voice," *Re:Thinking*, May 4, 2023.

30 **"The word they didn't change":** Steve Martin, host, *The 75th Annual Academy Awards*, March 23, 2003.

31 **"If you're comfortable, you're doin' it wrong":** *Ted Lasso*, "Pilot," August 14, 2020.

31 **listeners enjoyed the lesson more:** David B. Daniel and William Douglas Woody, "They Hear, but Do Not Listen: Retention for Podcasted Material in a Classroom Context," *Teaching of Psychology* 37, no. 3 (2010): 199–203.

31 **activates more analytical processing:** Janet Geipel and Boaz Keysar, "Listening Speaks to Our Intuition while Reading Promotes Analytic Thought," *Journal of Experimental Psychology: General* (2023).

32 **With print, you naturally slow down:** Daniel T. Willingham, "Is Listening to a Book the Same Thing as Reading It?," *The New York Times*, December 8, 2018.

32 **closing your eyes doesn't make you any less accurate:** Michael W. Kraus, "Voice-Only Communication Enhances Empathic Accuracy," *American Psychologist* 72, no. 7 (2017): 644–54.

32 **verbal clues are more reliable than nonverbal:** Aldert Vrij, Pär Anders Granhag, and Stephen Porter, "Pitfalls and Opportunities in Nonverbal and Verbal Lie Detection," *Psychological Science in the Public Interest* 11, no. 3 (2010): 89–121.

33 **taught to produce it:** Natsuko Shintani, "The Effectiveness of Processing Instruction and Production-Based Instruction on L2 Grammar Acquisition: A Meta-Analysis," *Applied Linguistics* 36, no. 3 (2015): 306–25; Natsuko Shintani, Shaofeng Li, and Rod Ellis, "Comprehension-Based versus Production-Based Grammar Instruction: A Meta-Analysis of Comparative Studies," *Language Learning* 63, no. 2 (2013): 296–329.

33 **"flipped classrooms":** Joseph P. Vitta and Ali H. Al-Hoorie, "The Flipped Classroom in Second Language Learning: A Meta-Analysis," *Language Teaching Research* (2020): 1–25.

34 **discomfort as a mark of growth:** Kaitlin Woolley and Ayelet Fishbach, "Motivating Personal Growth by Seeking Discomfort," *Psychological Science* 33, no. 4 (2022): 510–23.

34 **"convert affective pains into cognitive gains":** Katherine W. Phillips, Katie A. Liljenquist, and Margaret A. Neale, "Is the Pain Worth the Gain? The Advantages and Liabilities of Agreeing with Socially Distinct Newcomers," *Personality and Social Psychology Bulletin* 35, no. 3 (2009): 336–50; see also Samuel R. Sommers, "On Racial Diversity and Group Decision Making: Identifying Multiple Effects of Racial Composition on Jury Deliberations," *Journal of Personality and Social Psychology* 90, no. 4 (2006): 597–612; Denise Lewin Loyd, Cynthia S. Wang, Katherine W. Phillips, and Robert B. Lount Jr., "Social Category Diversity Promotes Premeeting Elaboration: The Role of Relationship Focus," *Organization Science* 24, no. 3 (2013): 757–72; Katherine W. Phillips and Robert B. Lount, "The Affective Consequences of Diversity and Homogeneity in Groups," in *Research on Managing Groups and Teams*, vol. 10, ed. Elizabeth A. Mannix and Margaret A. Neale (Bingley, UK: Emerald, 2007).

36 **kids tend to absorb foreign languages faster:** Patricia J. Brooks and Vera Kempe, "More Is More in Language Learning: Reconsidering the Less-Is-More Hypothesis," *Language Learning* 69, no. S1 (2019): 13–41; Lindsay Patterson, "Do Children Soak Up Language Like Sponges?," *The New York Times*, April 16, 2020.

37 **Systematic desensitization starts:** Kate B. Wolitzky-Taylor, Jonathan D. Horowitz, Mark B. Powers, and Michael J. Telch, "Psychological Approaches in the Treatment of Specific Phobias: A Meta-Analysis," *Clinical Psychology Review* 28, no. 6 (2008): 1021–37.

37 **Flooding is the opposite:** Lori A. Zoellner, Jonathan S. Abramowitz, Sally A. Moore, and David M. Slagle, "Flooding," in *Cognitive Behavior Therapy: Applying Empirically Supported Techniques in Your Practice*, ed. William T. O'Donohue and Jane E. Fisher (New York: Wiley, 2008).

38 **element of surprise is critical:** Annemarie Landman, Eric L. Groen, M. M. (René) van Paassen, Adelbert W. Bronkhorst, and Max Mulder, "The Influence of Surprise on Upset Recovery Performance in Airline Pilots," *The International Journal of Aerospace Psychology* 27, no. 1–2 (2017): 2–14; Stephen M. Casner, Richard W. Geven, and Kent T. Williams, "The Effectiveness of Airline Pilot Training for Abnormal Events," *Human Factors* 55, no. 3 (2013): 477–85.

39 **randomly assigned to guess wrong:** Janet Metcalfe, "Learning from Errors," *Annual Review of Psychology* 68 (2017): 465–89.

39 **deep talk is surprisingly enjoyable:** Michael Kardas, Amit Kumar, and Nicholas Epley, "Overly Shallow? Miscalibrated Expectations Create a Barrier to Deeper Conversation," *Journal of Personality and Social Psychology* 122, no. 3 (2022): 367–98.

40 **secondary reward properties:** Robert Eisenberger, "Learned Industriousness," *Psychological Review* 99, no. 2 (1992): 248–67.

CHAPTER 2

43 **"the species that survives":** "It Is Not the Strongest of the Species That Survives but the Most Adaptable," Quote Investigator, May 4, 2014, quoteinvestigator.com/2014/05/04/adapt/.

43 **oxygen levels plunged:** David P. G. Bond and Stephen E. Grasby, "Late Ordovician Mass Extinction Caused by Volcanism, Warming, and Anoxia, Not Cooling and Glaciation," *Geology* 48, no. 8 (2020): 777–81; Jack Longman, Benjamin J. W. Mills, Hayley R. Manners, Thomas M. Gernon, and Martin R. Palmer, "Late Ordovician Climate Change and Extinctions Driven by Elevated Volcanic Nutrient Supply," *Nature Geoscience* 14, no. 12 (2021): 924–29; Xianqing Jing, Zhenyu Yang, Ross N. Mitchell, Yabo Tong, Min Zhu, and Bo Wan, "Ordovician–Silurian True Polar Wander as a Mechanism for Severe Glaciation and Mass Extinction," *Nature Communications* 13 (2022): 7941; Cody Cottier, "The Ordovician Extinction: Our Planet's First Brush with Death," *Discover*, January 16, 2021.

43 **sponges ruled the oceans:** Joseph P. Botting, Lucy A. Muir, Yuandong Zhang, Xuan Ma, Junye Ma, Longwu Wang, Jianfang Zhang, Yanyan Song, and Xiang Fang, "Flourishing Sponge-Based Ecosystems after the End-Ordovician Mass Extinction," *Current Biology* 27, no. 4 (2017): 556–62.

43 **one of the earth's oldest animals:** Frankie Schembri, "Earth's First Animals May Have Been Sea Sponges," *Science*, October 17, 2018.

44 **adept at filtering:** Sally P. Leys and Amanda S. Kahn, "Oxygen and the Energetic Requirements of the First Multicellular Animals," *Integrative and Comparative Biology* 58, no. 4 (2018): 666–76.

44 **sneeze out mucus:** Niklas A. Kornder, Yuki Esser, Daniel Stoupin, Sally P. Leys, Benjamin Mueller, Mark J. A. Vermeij, Jef Huisman, and Jasper M. de Goeij, "Sponges Sneeze

Mucus to Shed Particle Waste from Their Seawater Inlet Pores," *Current Biology* 32, no. 17 (2022): P3855–61.

44 **can live more than 2,000 years:** Steven E. Mcmurray, James E. Blum, and Joseph R. Pawlik, "Redwood of the Reef: Growth and Age of the Giant Barrel Sponge *Xestospongia muta* in the Florida Keys," *Marine Biology* 155 (2008): 159–71.

44 **strong and durable:** Sabrina Imbler, "A Swirling Vortex Is No Match for This Deep-Sea Sponge," *The New York Times*, September 9, 2021.

44 **via survival pods:** Carmel Mothersil and Brian Austin, *Aquatic Inverteberate Cell Culture* (London: Springer-Verlag, 2000).

44 **Mellody Hobson had a stressful childhood:** personal interview, November 17, 2021; Adam Grant, "Mellody Hobson on Taking Tough Feedback," *Re:Thinking*, June 15, 2021.

45 **Protestant work ethic:** Max Weber, *The Protestant Ethic and the Spirit of Capitalism* (New York: Routledge, 1992).

45 **transformed into a calling:** Amy Wrzesniewski, Clark McCauley, Paul Rozin, and Barry Schwartz, "Jobs, Careers, and Callings: People's Relations to Their Work," *Journal of Research in Personality* 31, no. 1 (1997): 21–33.

45 **moral obligation to serve society:** J. Stuart Bunderson and Jeffery A. Thompson, "The Call of the Wild: Zookeepers, Callings, and the Double-Edged Sword of Deeply Meaningful Work," *Administrative Science Quarterly* 54, no. 1 (2009): 32–57.

45 **entire countries had higher economic:** Sascha O. Becker and Ludger Woessmann, "Was Weber Wrong? A Human Capital Theory of Protestant Economic History," *The Quarterly Journal of Economics* 124, no. 2 (2009): 531–96.

48 **Although debate continues:** Sascha O. Becker, Steven Pfaff, and Jared Rubin, "Causes and Consequences of the Protestant Reformation," *Explorations in Economic History* 62 (2016): 1–25; Felix Kersting, Iris Wohnsiedler, and Nikolaus Wolf, "Weber Revisited: The Protestant Ethic and the Spirit of Nationalism," *The Journal of Economic History* 80, no. 3 (2020): 710–45; Federico Mantovanelli, "The Protestant Legacy: Missions and Literacy in India," CEPR Discussion Paper No. 913309, November 2018; Davide Cantoni, "The Economic Effects of the Protestant Reformation: Testing the Weber Hypothesis in the German Lands," *Journal of the European Economic Association* 13, no. 4 (2015): 561–98.

48 **towns built libraries:** Ezra Karger, "The Long-Run Effect of Public Libraries on Children: Evidence from the Early 1900s," *SocArXiv* (2021): e8k7p.

48 **following through to build a library paid dividends:** Enrico Berkes and Peter Nencka, "Knowledge Access: The Effects of Carnegie Libraries on Innovation," *SSRN*, December 22, 2021.

49 **Absorptive capacity is the ability:** Wesley M. Cohen and Daniel A. Levinthal, "Absorptive Capacity: A New Perspective on Learning and Innovation," *Administrative Science Quarterly* 35, no. 1 (1990): 128–52.

49 **are you proactive:** Adam M. Grant and Susan J. Ashford, "The Dynamics of Proactivity at Work," *Research in Organizational Behavior* 28 (2008): 3–34.

49 **feeding your ego or fueling your growth:** Susan J. Ashford, Ruth Blatt, and Don Vande Walle, "Reflections on the Looking Glass: A Review of Research on Feedback-Seeking Behavior in Organizations," *Journal of Management* 29 (2003): 773–99; Adam M. Grant, Sharon Parker, and Catherine Collins, "Getting Credit for Proactive Behavior: Supervisor Reactions Depend on What You Value and How You Feel," *Personnel Psychology* 62, no. 1 (2009): 31–55; Lukasz Stasielowicz, "Goal Orientation and Performance Adaptation: A Meta-Analysis," *Journal of Research in Personality* 82 (2019): 103847.

50 **Julius Yego enjoyed competing:** personal communications, September 19, 2022, and March 8, 2023; Erin C.J. Robertson, "Get to Know Julius Yego, Kenya's Self-Taught Olym-

pic Javelin-Thrower Dubbed 'The Youtube Man,'" *OkayAfrica*, okayafrica.com/get-know
-julius-yego-kenyas-self-taught-olympic-javelin-thrower-dubbed-youtube-man; "Julius
Yego—The YouTube Man," GoPro, YouTube, May 19, 2016, youtu.be/lO1fzo1aCHU; Roy
Tomizawa, "No Coach, No Problem: Silver Medalist Javelin Thrower Julius Yego and the
YouTube Generation," *The Olympians*, September 5, 2016; David Cox, "How Kenyan Javelin Thrower Julius Yego Mastered His Sport By Watching YouTube Videos," *Vice*, August
16, 2016.

51 **Ihab Abdelrahman was raised:** Mike Rowbottom, "Ihab Abdelrahman El Sayed, Almost
the Pharoah of Throwing," World Athletics, September 16, 2015; "Throw Like an Egyptian,"
World Athletics, January 12, 2015.

55 **better off asking for advice:** Jackie Gnepp, Joshua Klayman, Ian O. Williamson, and Sema
Barlas, "The Future of Feedback: Motivating Performance Improvement through Future-
Focused Feedback," *PLoS ONE* 15, no. 6 (2020): e0234444; Hayley Blunden, Jaewon Yoon,
Ariella S. Kristal, and Ashley Whillans, "Soliciting Advice Rather Than Feedback Yields
More Developmental, Critical, and Actionable Input," Harvard Business School Working
Paper No. 20-021, August 2019 (revised April 2021).

55 **people judge you as more capable:** Katie A. Liljenquist, "Resolving the Impression
Management Dilemma: The Strategic Benefits of Soliciting Advice," Northwestern
University ProQuest Dissertations Publishing (2010): 3402210.

56 **opposite is true for experts:** Stacey R. Finkelstein and Ayelet Fishbach, "Tell Me What
I Did Wrong: Experts Seek and Respond to Negative Feedback," *Journal of Consumer
Research* 39, no. 1 (2012): 22–38; Ayelet Fishbach, Tal Eyal, and Stacey R. Finkelstein, "How
Positive and Negative Feedback Motivate Goal Pursuit," *Social and Personality Psychology
Compass* 48, no. 10 (2010): 517–30; Ayelet Fishbach, Minjung Koo, and Stacey R. Finkelstein,
"Motivation Resulting from Completed and Missing Actions," *Advances in Experimental
Social Psychology* 50 (2014): 257–307.

56 **Source Be with You:** C. Neil Macrae, Galen V. Bodenhausen, and Guglielmo Calvini,
"Contexts of Cryptomnesia: May the Source Be with You," *Social Cognition* 17, no. 3 (1999):
273–97.

59 **sea sponges branched off:** Emily S. Wong, Dawei Zheng, Siew Z. Tan, Neil I. Bower,
Victoria Garside, Gilles Vanwalleghem, Federico Gaiti, Ethan Scott, Benjamin M. Hogan,
Kazu Kikuchi, Edwina McGlinn, Mathias Francois, and Bernard M. Degnan, "Deep
Conservation of the Enhancer Regulatory Code in Animals," *Science* 370, no. 6517 (2020):
eaax8137; Riya Baibhawi, "Sea Sponge Unravels 700-Million-Year-Old Mystery of Human
Evolution," *Republic World*, November 21, 2020.

59 **produce biochemicals that protect and promote life:** Danielle Hall, "Sea Sponges: Pharmacies
of the Sea," *Smithsonian*, November 2019.

59 **greatest life-giving impact:** Carl Zimmer, "Take a Breath and Thank a Sponge," *The New
York Times*, March 13, 2014; Megan Gannon, "Sponges May Have Breathed Life into An-
cient Oceans," *LiveScience*, March 11, 2014; Michael Tatzel, Friedhelm von Blanckenburg,
Marcus Oelze, Julien Bouchez, and Dorothee Hippler, "Late Neoproterozoic Seawater
Oxygenation by Siliceous Sponges," *Nature Communications* 8 (2017): 621.

CHAPTER 3

61 **"There is a crack":** Leonard Cohen, "Anthem," *The Future* (Columbia, 1992).

61 **Tadao Ando was halfway across:** Tadao Ando, *Tadao Ando: Endeavors* (New York: Flam-
marion, 2019); Michael Auping, *Seven Interviews with Tadao Ando* (London: Third Millennium, 2002); Kanae Hasegawa, "Tadao Ando Interview," *Frame*, December 6, 2014; Sharon

Waxman, "A Natural Designer," *Chicago Tribune*, May 28, 1995; Jocelyn Lippert, "Japanese Architect Ando Speaks at TD Master's Tea," *Yale Daily News*, October 12, 2001; "CNN Talk Asia Program—Japanese Architect, Tadao Ando," Daniel J. Stone, YouTube, January 13, 2010, youtu.be/dZuSoBCR-_I; Walter Mariotti, "Tadao Ando: The World Must Change," *Domus*, December 3, 2020; Bianca Bosker, "Haute Concrete," *The Atlantic*, April 2017; Julie V. Iovine, "Building a Bad Reputation," *The New York Times*, August 8, 2004; "Artist Talk: Tadao Ando," Art Institute of Chicago, YouTube, November 27, 2018, youtu.be /cV0hiUcFFG8.

65 **perfectionism takes expectations:** Adam Grant, "What Straight-A Students Get Wrong," *The New York Times*, December 8, 2018.

66 **perfectionism has been rising:** Thomas Curran and Andrew P. Hill, "Perfectionism Is Increasing Over Time: A Meta-Analysis of Birth Cohort Differences from 1989 to 2016," *Psychological Bulletin* 145, no. 4 (2019): 410–29.

66 **growing pressure from parents:** Thomas Curran and Andrew P. Hill, "Young People's Perceptions of Their Parents' Expectations and Criticism Are Increasing Over Time: Implications for Perfectionism," *Psychological Bulletin* 148, no. 1–2 (2022): 10728.

66 **Every flaw is a blow:** Andrew P. Hill and Thomas Curran, "Multidimensional Perfectionism and Burnout: A Meta-Analysis," *Personality and Social Psychology Review* 20, no. 3 (2016): 269–88.

67 **perfectionists were no better than their peers:** Dana Harari, Brian W. Swider, Laurens Bujold Steed, and Amy P. Breidenthal, "Is Perfect Good? A Meta-Analysis of Perfectionism in the Workplace," *Journal of Applied Psychology* 103, no. 10 (2018): 1121–44.

67 **graduated high school with Bs and Cs:** Kathryn D. Sloane and Lauren A. Sosniak, "The Development of Accomplished Sculptors," in Benjamin Bloom, *Developing Talent in Young People* (New York: Ballantine Books, 1985).

67 **great architects had rarely been great students:** Donald W. Mackinnon, "The Nature and Nurture of Creative Talent," *American Psychologist* 17 (1962): 484–95.

67 **perfectionists tend to get three things wrong:** Adam Grant, "Breaking Up with Perfectionism," *WorkLife*, May 3, 2022.

69 **beauty in imperfection:** Leonard Koren, *Wabi-Sabi for Artists, Designers, Poets & Philosophers* (Point Reyes, CA: Imperfect Publishing, 2008).

72 **mental block is more common among perfectionists:** Jenn Bennett, Michael Rotherham, Kate Hays, Peter Olusoga, and Ian Maynard, "Yips and Lost Move Syndrome: Assessing Impact and Exploring Levels of Perfectionism, Rumination, and Reinvestment," *Sport and Exercise Psychology Review* 12, no. 1 (2016): 14–27; Melissa Catherine Day, Joanna Thatcher, Iain Greenlees, and Bernadette Woods, "The Causes of and Psychological Responses to Lost Move Syndrome in National Level Trampolinists," *Journal of Applied Sport Psychology* 18 (2006): 151–66; Jenn Bennett and Ian Maynard, "Performance Blocks in Sport: Recommendations for Treatment and Implications for Sport Psychology Practitioners," *Journal of Sport Psychology in Action* 8, no. 1 (2017): 60–68.

73 **high personal standards:** Ivana Osenk, Paul Williamson, and Tracey D. Wade, "Does Perfectionism or Pursuit of Excellence Contribute to Successful Learning? A Meta-Analytic Review," *Psychological Assessment* 32, no. 10 (2020): 972–83.

73 **goals that are specific and difficult:** Edwin A. Locke and Gary P. Latham, "Building a Practically Useful Theory of Goal Setting and Task Motivation: A 35-Year Odyssey," *American Psychologist* 57, no. 9 (2002): 705–17, and "Work Motivation and Satisfaction: Light at the End of the Tunnel," *Psychological Science* 1 (1990): 240–46; Gerard Seijts, Gary P. Latham, Kevin Tasa, and Brandon W. Latham, "Goal Setting and Goal Orientation: An Integration

of Two Different Yet Related Literatures," *Academy of Management Journal* 47, no. 2 (2004): 227–39.

74 **mental time travel:** Thomas Suddendorf, Donna Rose Addis, and Michael C. Corballis, "Mental Time Travel and the Shaping of the Human Mind," in *Predictions in the Brain: Using Our Past to Generate a Future,* ed. Mohse Bar (New York: Oxford, 2011).

75 **Perfectionists often worry:** Daniel J. Madigan, "A Meta-Analysis of Perfectionism and Academic Achievement," *Educational Psychology Review* 31 (2019): 967–89.

75 **don't judge your competence based on one performance:** Alice Moon, Muping Gan, and Clayton Critcher, "The Overblown Implications Effect," *Journal of Personality and Social Psychology* 118, no. 4 (2020): 720–42.

75 **more weight on your peaks:** Glenn D. Reader and Marilynn B. Brewer, "A Schematic Model of Dispositional Attribution in Interpersonal Perception," *Psychological Review* 86, no. 1 (1979): 61–79.

76 **brainchild of Twyla Tharp:** Twyla Tharp, *The Creative Habit: Learn It and Use It for Life* (New York: Simon & Schuster, 2009); Robin Pogrebin, "Movin' Out beyond Missteps; How Twyla Tharp Turned a Problem in Chicago into a Hit on Broadway," *The New York Times,* December 12, 2002; Michael Phillips, "In Chaotic 'Movin Out,' Dancing Off to the Vietnam War," *Los Angeles Times,* July 22, 2022, and "Tharp Reshapes 'Movin Out' before It Goes to Broadway," *Chicago Tribune,* August 22, 2022; Tim Harford, "Bless the Coal-Black Hearts of the Broadway Critics," *Cautionary Tales,* May 20, 2022.

77 **look for convergence:** Richard P. Larrick, Albert E. Mannes, and Jack B. Soll, "The Social Psychology of the Wisdom of Crowds," in *Social Judgment and Decision Making,* ed. Joachim I. Kruger (New York: Psychology Press, 2012).

79 **set two targets:** Leigh Thompson, "The Impact of Minimum Goals and Aspirations on Judgments of Success in Negotiations," *Group Decision and Negotiation* 4 (1995): 513–24.

79 **define excellence on other people's terms:** Andrew P. Hill, Howard K. Hall, and Paul R. Appleton, "The Relationship between Multidimensional Perfectionism and Contingencies of Self-Worth," *Personality and Individual Differences* 50, no. 2 (2011): 238–42.

79 **risk factor for depression:** Karina Limburg, Hunna J. Watson, Martin S. Hagger, and Sarah J. Egan, "The Relationship between Perfectionism and Psychopathology: A Meta-Analysis," *Journal of Clinical Psychology* 73, no. 10 (2017): 1301–26.

79 **across 105 studies:** Emma L. Bradshaw, James H. Conigrave, Ben A. Steward, Kelly A. Ferber, Philip D. Parker, and Richard M. Ryan, "A Meta-Analysis of the Dark Side of the American Dream: Evidence for the Universal Wellness Costs of Prioritizing Extrinsic over Intrinsic Goals," *Journal of Personality and Social Psychology* 124, no. 4 (2023): 873–99.

80 **Seeking validation is a bottomless pit:** Jennifer Crocker and Lora E. Park, "The Costly Pursuit of Self-Esteem," *Psychological Bulletin* 130, no. 3 (2004): 392–414.

PART II

84 **cuts their flashbacks in half:** Emily A. Holmes, Ella L. James, Thomas Coode-Bate, and Catherine Deeprose, "Can Playing the Computer Game 'Tetris' Reduce the Build-Up of Flashbacks for Trauma? A Proposal from Cognitive Science," *PLoS ONE* 4 (2009): e4153; Emily A. Holmes, Ella L. James, Emma J. Kilford, and Catherine Deeprose, "Key Steps in Developing a Cognitive Vaccine against Traumatic Flashbacks: Visuospatial Tetris versus Verbal Pub Quiz," *PLoS ONE* 7 (2012): 10.1371.

84 **effect has been replicated:** Amalia Badawi, David Berle, Kris Rogers, and Zachary Steel, "Do Cognitive Tasks Reduce Intrusive-Memory Frequency after Exposure to Analogue

Trauma? An Experimental Replication," *Clinical Psychological Science* 8, no. 3 (2020): 569–83.

85 **Brain scans suggest that Tetris blocks intrusive images:** Thomas Agren, Johanna M. Hoppe, Laura Singh, Emily A. Holmes, and Jörgen Rosén, "The Neural Basis of Tetris Gameplay: Implicating the Role of Visuospatial Processing," *Current Psychology* (2021); Rebecca B. Price, Ben Paul, Walt Schneider, and Greg J. Siegle, "Neural Correlates of Three Neurocognitive Intervention Strategies: A Preliminary Step Towards Personalized Treatment for Psychological Disorders," *Cognitive Therapy and Research* 37, no. 4 (2013): 657–72.

85 **doesn't do any good to play Tetris before:** Ella L. James, Alex Lau-Zhu, Hannah Tickle, Antje Horsch, and Emily A. Holmes, "Playing the Computer Game Tetris Prior to Viewing Traumatic Film Material and Subsequent Intrusive Memories: Examining Proactive Interference," *Journal of Behavior Therapy and Experimental Psychiatry* 53 (2016): 25–33.

85 **critical period seems to be the next 24 hours:** Ella L. James, Michael B. Bonsall, Laura Hoppitt, Elizabeth M. Tunbridge, John R. Geddes, Amy L. Milton, and Emily L. Holmes, "Computer Game Play Reduces Intrusive Memories of Experimental Trauma via Reconsolidation-Update Mechanisms," *Psychological Science* 26, no. 8 (2015): 1201–1215.

CHAPTER 4

87 **"It is the dance between":** Bernard De Koven, *The Well-Played Game: A Player's Philosophy* (Cambridge, MA: MIT Press, 2013).

87 **Evelyn Glennie felt butterflies:** personal interview, August 8, 2022; Evelyn Glennie, *Good Vibrations: My Autobiography* (London: Hutchinson, 1990), *Listen World!* (London: Balestier Press, 2019), and "How to Truly Listen," TED talk, 2003, ted.com/talks/evelyn_glennie_how _to_truly_listen; Sofia Pasternack, "Evelyn Glennie on the Olympics Opening Ceremony," *Tom Tom*, February 2013.

90 **deliberate practice is particularly valuable:** Brooke N. Macnamara, David Z. Hambrick, and Frederick L. Oswald, "Deliberate Practice and Performance in Music, Games, Sports, Education, and Professions: A Meta-Analysis," *Psychological Science* 25, no. 8 (2014): 1608–18.

90 **Mozart's violinist father:** Maynard Solomon, *Mozart: A Life* (New York: HarperCollins, 2005).

90 **"my fingers are aching":** Wolfgang Amadeus Mozart, *The Letters of Mozart and His Family*, ed. Stanley Sadie and Fiona Smart (London: Macmillan, 1985).

90 **"so much performing":** Robert Spaethling, *Mozart's Letters, Mozart's Life* (New York: Norton, 2000).

90 **longer hours yet fail to perform any better:** Malissa A. Clark, Jesse S. Michel, Ludmila Zhdanova, Shuang Y. Pui, and Boris B. Baltes, "All Work and No Play? A Meta-Analytic Examination of the Correlates and Outcomes of Workaholism," *Journal of Management* 42, no. 7 (2016): 1836–73.

90 **boreout is the emotional deadening:** Erin C. Westgate and Timothy D. Wilson, "Boring Thoughts and Bored Minds: The MAC Model of Boredom and Cognitive Engagement," *Psychological Review* 125, no. 5 (2018): 689–713; A. Mohammed Abubakar, Hamed Reza-pouraghdam, Elaheh Behravesh, and Huda A. Megeirhi, "Burnout or Boreout: A Meta-Analytic Review and Synthesis of Burnout and Boreout Literature in Hospitality and Tourism," *Journal of Hospitality Marketing & Management* 31, no. 8 (2022): 458–503.

91 **"They practiced because they were interested":** Lauren A. Sosniak, "Learning to Be a Concert

Pianist," in Benjamin Bloom, *Developing Talent in Young People* (New York: Ballantine Books, 1985).

91 **psychologists call harmonious passion:** Arielle Bonneville-Roussy, Geneviève L. Lavigne, and Robert J. Vallerand, "When Passion Leads to Excellence: The Case of Musicians," *Psychology of Music* 39 (2011): 123–38.

91 **when passion was present:** Jon M. Jachimowicz, Andreas Wihler, Erica R. Bailey, and Adam D. Galinsky, "Why Grit Requires Perseverance and Passion to Positively Predict Performance," *PNAS* 115, no. 40 (2018): 9980–85.

91 **depends on how you feel about them:** Lieke L. Ten Brummelhuis, Nancy P. Rothbard, and Benjamin Uhrich, "Beyond Nine to Five: Is Working to Excess Bad for Health?," *Academy of Management Discoveries* 3, no. 3 (2017): 262–83.

91 **obsession predicts greater conflict:** Robert J. Vallerand, Yvan Paquet, Frederick L. Phillipe, and Julie Charest, "On the Role of Passion for Work in Burnout: A Process Model," *Journal of Personality* 78, no. 1 (2010): 289–312.

92 **Deliberate play is a structured activity:** Jean Côté, "The Influence of the Family in the Development of Talent in Sport," *The Sport Psychologist* 13, no. 4 (1999): 395–417.

92 **blends elements of deliberate practice and free play:** Jean Côté, Joseph Baker, and Bruce Abernethy, "Practice and Play in the Development of Sport Expertise," in *Handbook of Sport Psychology*, ed. Gershon Tenenbaum and Robert C. Eklund (New York: Wiley, 2007); Jackie Lordo, "The Development of Music Expertise: Applications of the Theories of Deliberate Practice and Deliberate Play," *Update: Applications of Research in Music Education* 39, no. 3 (2021): 56–66.

92 **deliberate play into their most stressful tasks:** Adam M. Grant, Justin M. Berg, and Daniel M. Cable, "Job Titles as Identity Badges: How Self-Reflective Titles Can Reduce Emotional Exhaustion," *Academy of Management Journal* 57, no. 4 (2014): 1201–25.

93 **levity into the challenge of learning to interpret nonverbal cues:** Katie Watson and Belinda Fu, "Medical Improv: A Novel Approach to Teaching Communication and Professionalism Skills," *Annals of Internal Medicine* 165, no. 8 (2016): 591–92.

93 **deliberate play makes them better doctors:** Katie Watson, "Serious Play: Teaching Medical Skills with Improvisational Theater Techniques," *Academic Medicine* 86, no. 10 (2011): 1260–65.

93 **students performed better on patient examinations:** Kevin P. Boesen, Richard N. Herrier, David A. Apgar, and Rebekah M. Jackowski, "Improvisational Exercises to Improve Pharmacy Students' Professional Communication Skills," *American Journal of Pharmaceutical Education* 73, no. 2 (2009): 35.

93 **learn through playing the role of salesperson:** Richard A. Rocco and D. Joel Whalen, "Teaching *Yes, and* . . . Improv in Sales Classes: Enhancing Student Adaptive Selling Skills, Sales Performance, and Teaching Evaluations," *Journal of Marketing Education* 36, no. 2 (2014): 197–208.

93 **peak quickly and then flame out:** Arne Güllich, Brooke N. Macnamara, David Z. Hambrick, "What Makes a Champion? Early Multidisciplinary Practice, Not Early Specialization, Predicts World-Class Performance," *Perspectives on Psychological Science* 17, no. 1 (2022): 6–29.

93 **Pounding the pavement:** Shelby Waldron, J.D. DeFreese, Brian Pietrosimone, Johna Register-Mihalik, and Nikki Barczak, "Exploring Early Sport Specialization: Associations with Psychosocial Outcomes," *Journal of Clinical Sport Psychology* 14 (2019): 182–202.

93 **In sports, deliberate play:** Daniel Memmert, *Teaching Tactical Creativity in Sport: Research and Practice* (London: Routledge, 2015).

94 **compared deliberate play and deliberate practice:** Pablo Greco, Daniel Memmert, and Juan C. P. Morales, "The Effect of Deliberate Play on Tactical Performance in Basketball," *Perceptual and Motor Skills* 110, no. 3 (2010): 849–56.

94 **treadmills were invented as torture devices:** Conor Heffernan, "The Treadmill's Dark and Twisted Past," TEDEd, ted.com/talks/conor_heffernan_the_treadmill_s_dark_and_twisted _past.

95 **Brandon Payne's philosophy:** personal interview, July 22, 2022; Seerat Sohi, "Meet the Coaches Who Scrutinize the World's Greatest Shot," Yahoo! Sports, January 29, 2021; Tom Haberstroh, "The Story of Luka Doncic's Undercover Steph Curry Workout," NBC Sports, January 24, 2019.

96 **Passion for one task can lead us to neglect:** Jihae Shin and Adam M. Grant, "Bored by Interest: Intrinsic Motivation in One Task Can Reduce Performance in Other Tasks," *Academy of Management Journal* 62 (2019): 1–22.

97 **His name is Stephen Curry:** Nick Greene, "8 Early Criticisms of Stephen Curry That Sound Absurd in Retrospect," *Mental Floss*, May 17, 2016; "How Stephen Curry Went from Ignored College Recruit to NBA MVP," Yahoo! Sports, April 23, 2015; Hanif Abdurraqib, "The Second Coming of Stephen Curry," *GQ*, January 10, 2022; Lee Tran, "Muggsy Bogues on Stephen Curry as a Child," *Fadeaway World*, January 17, 2021; Mark Medina, "'He's in Love with Getting Better': How Stephen Curry Has Maintained Peak Conditioning," NBA.com, June 13, 2022, and "After Offseason Focused on Perfection, Stephen Curry Could Be Even More Unstoppable," NBA.com, October 22, 2021.

98 **change the situation to make it less strenuous:** Brian M. Galla and Angela L. Duckworth, "More Than Resisting Temptation: Beneficial Habits Mediate the Relationship between Self-Control and Positive Life Outcomes," *Journal of Personality and Social Psychology* 109, no. 3 (2015): 508–25.

98 **research on the marshmallow test:** Walter Mischel, Yuichi Shoda, and Monica L. Rodriguez, "Delay of Gratification in Children," *Science* 244, no. 4907 (1989): 933–38; Yuichi Shoda, Walter Mischel, and Philip K. Peake, "Predicting Adolescent Cognitive and Self-Regulatory Competencies from Preschool Delay of Gratification: Identifying Diagnostic Conditions," *Developmental Psychology* 26, no. 6 (1990): 978–86.

98 **that's been replicated recently:** Armin Falk, Fabian Kosse, and Pia Pinger, "Re-Revisiting the Marshmallow Test: A Direct Comparison of Studies by Shoda, Mischel, and Peake (1990) and Watts, Duncan, and Quan (2018)," *Psychological Science* 31, no. 1 (2020): 100–104.

98 **a recent replication:** Laura E. Michaelson and Yuko Munakata, "Same Data Set, Different Conclusions: Preschool Delay of Gratification Predicts Later Behavioral Outcomes in a Preregistered Study," *Psychological Science* 31, no. 2 (2020): 193–201.

98 **grow up in a world of scarcity and uncertainty:** Keith Payne and Pascal Sheeran, "Try to Resist Misinterpreting the Marshmallow Test," *Behavioral Scientist*, July 3, 2018.

99 **improve faster when they alternate:** Matthias Brunmair and Tobias Richter, "Similarity Matters: A Meta-Analysis of Interleaved Learning and Its Moderators," *Psychological Bulletin* 145 (2019): 1029–52.

99 **Even small tweaks:** Nicholas F. Wymbs, Amy J. Bastian, and Pablo A. Celnik, "Motor Skills Are Strengthened through Reconsolidation," *Current Biology* 26, no. 3 (2016): 338–43; Johns Hopkins Medicine, "Want to Learn a New Skill? Faster? Change Up Your Practice Sessions," *ScienceDaily*, January 28, 2016.

100 **followed Steph Curry's training regimen:** "I Trained Like Steph Curry for 50 Days to Improve My Shooting," Goal Guys, YouTube, August 18, 2021, youtu.be/2Cf0n7PmMJ0; Philip Ellis, "An Average Guy Trained Like Golden State Warrior Steph Curry for 50 Days to Improve His Shooting," *Men's Health*, August 19, 2021.

102 **micro-breaks of five to ten minutes:** Patricia Albulescu, Irina Macsinga, Andrei Rusu, Coralia Sulea, Alexandra Bodnaru, and Bogdan Tudor Tulbure, "'Give Me a Break!' A Systematic Review and Meta-Analysis on the Efficacy of Micro-Breaks for Increasing Well-Being and Performance," *PLoS ONE* 17, no. 8 (2022): e0272460.

102 **when we work nights and weekends:** Laura M. Giurge and Kaitlin Woolley, "Working during Non-Standard Work Time Undermines Intrinsic Motivation," *Organizational Behavior and Human Decision Processes* 170, no. 1 (2022): 104134.

102 **urged his students not to practice more:** Maddy Shaw Roberts, "How Many Hours a Day Do the World's Greatest Classical Musicians Practice?," Classic FM, June 21, 2021.

102 **breaks unlock fresh ideas:** Ut Na Sio and Thomas C. Ormerod, "Does Incubation Enhance Problem Solving? A Meta-Analytic Review," *Psychological Bulletin* 135 (2009): 94–120.

102 **taking breaks boosts creativity:** Jihae Shin and Adam M. Grant, "When Putting Work Off Pays Off: The Curvilinear Relationship between Procrastination and Creativity," *Academy of Management Journal* 64, no. 3 (2021): 772–98.

103 **dreamed up his blockbuster musical *Hamilton*:** Adam Grant, "Lin-Manuel Miranda Daydreams, and His Dad Gets Things Done," *Re:Thinking*, June 29, 2021.

103 **walks nearly as long as their workdays:** Mason Currey, "Tchaikovsky, Beethoven, Mahler: They All Loved Taking Long Daily Walks," *Slate*, April 25, 2013; Oliver Burkeman, "Rise and Shine: The Daily Routines of History's Most Creative Minds," *The Guardian*, October 5, 2013.

103 **improved recall for students:** Michaela Dewar, Jessica Alber, Christopher Butler, Nelson Cowan, and Sergio Della Sala, "Brief Wakeful Resting Boosts New Memories over the Long Term," *Psychological Science* 23, no. 9 (2012): 955–60; David Robson, "An Effortless Way to Improve Your Memory," BBC, February 12, 2018.

103 **down a forgetting curve:** Jaap M.J. Murre and Joeri Dros, "Replication and Analysis of Ebbinghaus' Forgetting Curve," *PLoS ONE* 10, no. 7 (2015): e0120644.

103 **with spaced repetition:** Nikhil Sonnad, "You Probably Won't Remember This, but the 'Forgetting Curve' Theory Explains Why Learning Is Hard," *Quartz*, February 28, 2018.

CHAPTER 5

105 **"Every limit is a beginning":** George Eliot, *Middlemarch* (London: Pan Macmillan, [1872] 2018).

105 **Baseball was RA's escape:** personal interview, January 2, 2023; R. A. Dickey, *Wherever I Wind Up: My Quest for Truth, Authenticity, and the Perfect Knuckleball* (New York: Plume, 2012) and "Reaching the Summit of Kilimanjaro," *The New York Times*, January 14, 2012; Tim Kurkjian, "The Knuckleball Experiment," ESPN, December 1, 2012; Kevin Bertha, "A Missing Ligament and the Knuckleball: The Story of R. A. Dickey," *Bleacher Report*, April 11, 2010; Alan Schwarz, "New Twist Keeps Dickey's Career Afloat," *The New York Times*, February 27, 2008; Jeremy Stahl, "Master of the Knuckleball," *Slate*, October 29, 2012; Brian Costa, "Knuckleballs of Kilimanjaro: Dickey Plots Ascent," *The Wall Street Journal*, December 27, 2011; Ben Maller, "Mets Pitcher R. A. Dickey Risking $4 Million Salary to Climb Mount Kilimanjaro," ThePostGame, November 2, 2011; Aditi Kinkhabwala, "Rocket Boy vs. the Baffler," *The Wall Street Journal*, July 3, 2010; James Kaminsky, "R. A. Dickey: Did Mt. Kilimanjaro Turn New York Mets Pitcher into an All-Star?," *Bleacher Report*, June 6, 2012; "R. A. Dickey Climbed Mount Kilimanjaro, the Mets' Knuckleballer Again Beats Fear with Staunch Belief," Yahoo! Sports, June 29, 2012.

106 **Pitchers usually peak:** Alex Speier, "What Is a Baseball Player's Prime Age?," *Boston Globe*, January 2, 2015; Rich Hardy, Tiwaloluwa Ajibewa, Ray Bowman, and Jefferson C. Brand,

"Determinants of Major League Baseball Pitchers' Career Length," *Arthroscopy* 33 (2017): 445–49.

108 **before it improves again, it declines:** Wayne D. Gray and John K. Lindstedt, "Plateaus, Dips, and Leaps: Where to Look for Inventions and Discoveries during Skilled Performance," *Cognitive Science* 41, no. 7 (2017): 1838–70.

109 **level off around 30 to 40 words per minute:** Eldad Yechiam, Ido Erev, Vered Yehene, and Daniel Gopher, "Melioration and the Transition from Touch-Typing Training to Everyday Use," *Human Factors* 45, no. 4 (2003): 671–84.

109 **steeper learning curves:** Yoni Donner and Joseph L. Hardy, "Piecewise Power Laws in Individual Learning Curves," *Psychonomic Bulletin & Review* 22, no. 5 (2015): 1308–19.

109 **solving a Rubik's Cube:** Jerry Slocum, David Singmaster, Wei-Hwa Huang, Dieter Gebhardt, and Geert Hellings, *The Cube: The Ultimate Guide to the World's Bestselling Puzzle* (New York: Black Dog & Leventhal, 2009).

109 **after their star players got injured:** John S. Chen and Pranav Garg, "Dancing with the Stars: Benefits of a Star Employee's Temporary Absence for Organizational Performance," *Strategic Management Journal* 39, no. 5 (2018): 1239–67.

110 **The more teams experimented:** H. Colleen Stuart, "Structural Disruption, Relational Experimentation, and Performance in Professional Hockey Teams: A Network Perspective on Member Change," *Organization Science* 28, no. 2 (2017): 283–300.

112 **impossible for humans to drown in quicksand:** Roxanne Khamsi, "Quicksand Can't Suck You Under," *Nature*, September 28, 2005; Asmae Khaldoun, Erika Eiser, Gerard H. Wegdam, and Daniel Bonn, "Liquefaction of Quicksand Under Stress," *Nature* 437, no. 7059 (2005): 635.

113 **That unusual grip takes the rotation off:** Danny Lewis, "Physicists May Have Finally Figured Out Why Knuckleballs Are So Hard to Hit," *Smithsonian*, July 20, 2016.

115 **learned less from introductory classes taught by experts:** David N. Figlio, Morton O. Schapiro, and Kevin B. Soter, "Are Tenure Track Professors Better Teachers?," *The Review of Economics and Statistics* 97, no. 4 (2015): 715–24.

115 **It's called the curse of knowledge:** Colin Camerer, George Loewenstein, and Martin Weber, "The Curse of Knowledge in Economic Settings: An Experimental Analysis," *Journal of Political Economy* 97, no. 5 (1989): 1232–54.

115 **"As you get better and better":** Sian Beilock, "The Best Players Rarely Make the Best Coaches," *Psychology Today*, August 16, 2010.

115 **They're separate skills:** John Hattie and Herbert W. Marsh, "The Relationship between Research and Teaching: A Meta-Analysis," *Review of Educational Research* 66, no. 4 (1996): 507–42.

115 **Einstein's curse in the classroom:** Walter Isaacson, *Einstein: His Life and Universe* (New York: Simon & Schuster, 2007); Dennis Overbye, *Einstein in Love: A Scientific Romance* (New York: Penguin, 2001); Peter Smith, *Einstein* (London: Haus, 2005).

116 **those who can't do, teach:** George Bernard Shaw, *Man and Superman* (New York: Penguin Classics, [1903] 1963).

116 **expert knowledge is tacit:** Asha Thomas and Vikas Gupta, "Tacit Knowledge in Organizations: Bibliometrics and a Framework-Based Systematic Review of Antecedents, Outcomes, Theories, Methods and Future Directions," *Journal of Knowledge Management* 26 (2022): 1014–41.

116 **skilled golfers and wine aficionados:** Kristin E. Flegal and Michael C. Anderson, "Overthinking Skilled Motor Performance: Or Why Those Who Teach Can't Do," *Psychonomic Bulletin & Review* 15 (2008): 927–32; Joseph M. Melcher and Jonathan W. Schooler, "The Misremembrance of Wines Past: Verbal and Perceptual Expertise Differentially Mediate

Verbal Overshadowing of Taste Memory," *Journal of Memory and Language* 35 (1996): 231–45.

116 **struggle to articulate all the steps:** David E. Levari, Daniel T. Gilbert, and Timothy D. Wilson, "Tips from the Top: Do the Best Performers Really Give the Best Advice?," *Psychological Science* 33, no. 5 (2022): 685–98.

117 **single mentor didn't make a difference:** Monica C. Higgins and David A. Thomas, "Constellations and Careers: Toward Understanding the Effects of Multiple Developmental Relationships," *Journal of Organizational Behavior* 22 (2001): 223–47.

117 **greater the range of guides you'll need:** Richard D. Cotton, Yan Shen, and Reut Livne-Tarandach, "On Becoming Extraordinary: The Content and Structure of the Developmental Networks of Major League Baseball Hall of Famers," *Academy of Management Journal* 54, no. 1 (2011): 15–46.

121 **it's called languishing:** Corey L.M. Keyes, "The Mental Health Continuum: From Languishing to Flourishing in Life," *Journal of Health and Social Behavior* 43, no. 2 (2002): 207–22.

122 **neglected middle child of mental health:** Adam Grant, "There's a Name for the Blah You're Feeling: It's Called Languishing," *The New York Times*, April 19, 2021, and "How to Stop Languishing and Start Finding Flow," TED, 2021.

122 *revenge bedtime procrastination:* Vanessa M. Hill, Amanda L. Rebar, Sally A. Ferguson, Alexandra E. Shriane, and Grace E. Vincent, "Go to Bed: A Systematic Review and Meta-Analysis of Bedtime Procrastination Correlates and Sleep Outcomes," *Sleep Medicine Reviews* 66 (2022): 101697; Lui-Hai Liang, "The Psychology behind 'Revenge Bedtime Procrastination,'" BBC, November 25, 2020.

122 **tried calling it a bug:** William K. English, Douglas C. Englebart, and Melvyn L. Berman, "Display-Selection Techniques for Text Manipulation," *IEEE Transactions on Human Factors in Electronics* HFE-8 (1967): 5–15.

123 **engaging evenings on their side hustles:** Hudson Sessions, Jennifer D. Nahrgang, Manuel J. Vaulont, Raseana Williams, and Amy L. Bartels, "Do the Hustle! Empowerment from Side-Hustles and Its Effects on Full-Time Work Performance," *Academy of Management Journal* 64, no. 1 (2021): 235–64.

123 **confidence climbed at work:** Ciara M. Kelly, Karoline Strauss, John Arnold, and Chris Stride, "The Relationship between Leisure Activities and Psychological Resources That Support a Sustainable Career: The Role of Leisure Seriousness and Work-Leisure Similarity," *Journal of Vocational Behavior* 117 (2020): 103340.

123 **strongest known force in daily motivation:** Teresa Amabile and Steven Kramer, *The Progress Principle: Using Small Wins to Ignite Joy, Engagement, and Creativity at Work* (Boston: Harvard Business Review Press, 2011).

124 **Fuel can come from small wins:** Karl E. Weick, "Small Wins: Redefining the Scale of Social Problems," *American Psychologist* 39, no. 1 (1984): 40–49.

126 **Moso bamboo seed:** Zhaohe Yang, Lei Chen, Markus V. Kohnen, Bei Xiong, Xi Zhen, Jiakai Liao, Yoshito Oka, Qiang Zhu, Lianfeng Gu, Chentao Lin, and Bobin Liu, "Identification and Characterization of the PEBP Family Genes in Moso Bamboo (Phyllostachys Heterocycla)," *Scientific Reports* 9, no. 1 (2019): 14998; Abolghaseem Emamverdian, Yulong Ding, Fatemeh Ranaei, and Zishan Ahmad, "Application of Bamboo Plants in Nine Aspects," *Scientific World Journal* (2020): 7284203.

CHAPTER 6

129 **"I believe in pulling yourself up":** Stephen Colbert at the White House Correspondents' Association Dinner, April 29, 2006.

131 **the Golden Thirteen:** Paul Stillwell, *The Golden Thirteen: Recollections of the First Black Naval Officers* (Annapolis: Naval Institute Press, 1993); Dan C. Goldberg, *The Golden 13: How Black Men Won the Right to Wear Navy Gold* (Boston: Beacon, 2020); Ron Grossman, "Breaking a Naval Blockade," *Chicago Tribune*, July 8, 1987; "The Golden Thirteen," Naval History and Heritage Command, November 25, 2020; Kevin Michael Briscoe, "Remembering the Sacrifices of the 'Golden 13,'" *Zenger*, November 26, 2020.

132 **barriers as challenges to conquer:** Nathan P. Podsakoff, Jeffery A. LePine, and Marcie A. LePine, "Differential Challenge Stressor-Hindrance Stressor Relationships with Job Attitudes, Turnover Intentions, Turnover, and Withdrawal Behavior: A Meta-Analysis," *Journal of Applied Psychology* 92, no. 2 (2007): 438–54.

132 **nurturing a growth mindset:** David S. Yeager, Jamie M. Carroll, Jenny Buontempo, Andrei Cimpan, Spencer Woody, Robert Crosnoe, Chandra Muller, Jared Murray, Pratik Mhatre, Nicole Kersting, Christopher Hulleman, Molly Kudym, Mary Murphy, Angela Lee Duckworth, Gregory M. Walton, and Carol S. Dweck, "Teacher Mindsets Help Explain Where a Growth-Mindset Intervention Does and Doesn't Work," *Psychological Science* 33 (2022): 18–32; David S. Yeager, Paul Hanselman, Gregory M. Walton, Jared S. Murray, Robert Crosnoe, Chandra Muller, Elizabeth Tipton, Barbara Schneider, Chris S. Hulleman, Cintia P. Hinojosa, David Paunesku, Carissa Romero, Kate Flint, Alice Roberts, Jill Trott, Ronaldo Iachan, Jenny Buontempo, Sophia Man Yang, Carlos M. Carvalho, P. Richard Hahn, Maithreyi Gopalan, Pratik Mhatre, Ronald Ferguson, Angela L. Duckworth, and Carol S. Dweck, "A National Experiment Reveals Where a Growth Mindset Improves Achievement," *Nature* 573, no. 7774 (2019): 364–69.

134 **how often colleagues teach and coach one another:** J. Richard Hackman and Ruth Wageman, "Asking the Right Questions about Leadership," *American Psychologist* 62 (2007): 43–47; J. Richard Hackman and Michael O'Connor, "What Makes for a Great Analytic Team? Individual vs. Team Approaches to Intelligence Analysis," February 2004.

134 **students learn as much when they're taught by peers:** Eliot L. Rees, Patrick J. Quinn, Benjamin Davies, and Victoria Fotheringham, "How Does Peer Teaching Compare to Faculty Teaching: A Systematic Review and Meta-Analysis," *Medical Teacher* 38, no. 8 (2016): 829–37.

134 **randomly assigned to tutor their peers:** Kim Chau Leung, "An Updated Meta-Analysis on the Effect of Peer Tutoring on Tutors' Achievement," *School Psychology International* 40, no. 2 (2019): 200–14.

134 **"the tutors gained a better understanding":** Peter A. Cohen, James A. Kulik, and Chen-Lin C. Kulik, "Educational Outcomes of Tutoring: A Meta-Analysis of Findings," *American Educational Research Journal* 19 (1982): 237–48.

134 **call this the tutor effect:** Robert B. Zajonc and Frank J. Sulloway, "The Confluence Model: Birth Order as a Within-Family or Between-Family Dynamic?," *Personality and Social Psychology Bulletin* 33, no. 9 (2007): 1187–94.

134 **remember it better after you recall it:** Aloysius Wei Lun Koh, Sze Chi Lee, and Stephen Wee Hun Lim, "The Learning Benefits of Teaching: A Retrieval Practice Hypothesis," *Applied Cognitive Psychology* 32, no. 3 (2018): 401–10.

134 **Even just being told you're going to teach:** John F. Nestojko, Dung C. Bui, Nate Kornell, and Elizabeth Ligon Bjork, "Expecting to Teach Enhances Learning and Organization of Knowledge in Free Recall of Text Passages," *Memory & Cognition* 42, no. 7 (2014): 1038–48.

134 **firstborns have a cognitive edge over laterborns:** Julia M. Rohrer, Boris Egloff, and Stefan C. Schmukle, "Examining the Effects of Birth Order on Personality," *PNAS* 112, no. 46 (2015): 14224–29, and "Probing Birth-Order Effects on Narrow Traits Using Specification-

Curve Analysis," *Psychological Science* 28, no. 12 (2017): 1821–32; Rodica Ioana Damian and Brent W. Roberts, "The Associations of Birth Order with Personality and Intelligence in a Representative Sample of U.S. High School Students," *Journal of Research in Personality* 58 (2015): 96–105; Sandra E. Black, Paul J. Devereux, and Kjell G. Salvanes, "Older and Wiser? Birth Order and IQ of Young Men," *CESifo Economic Studies* 57 (2011): 103–20; Kieron J. Barclay, "A Within-Family Analysis of Birth Order and Intelligence Using Population Conscription Data on Swedish Men," *Intelligence* 49 (2015): 134–143.

134 **We can rule out biological and prenatal causes:** Petter Kristensen and Tor Bjerkedal, "Explaining the Relation between Birth Order and Intelligence," *Science* 316, no. 5832 (2007): 1717.

134 **why only children:** Tor Bjerkedal, Petter Kristensen, Geir A. Skjeret, and John I. Brevik, "Intelligence Test Scores and Birth Order among Young Norwegian Men (Conscripts) Analyzed within and between Families," *Intelligence* 35, no. 5 (2007): 503–14.

134 **benefits of tutoring start to emerge around age 12:** Frank J. Sulloway, "Birth Order and Intelligence," *Science* 316, no. 5832 (2007): 1711–12.

135 **Henry Adams became an expert:** Henry Cabot Lodge, in *Proceedings of the Massachusetts Historical Society* (Cambridge: The University Press, 1918).

135 **The painter Georgia O'Keeffe honed:** Hunter Drohojowska-Philp, *Full Bloom: The Art and Life of Georgia O'Keeffe* (New York: Norton, 2005).

135 **The physicist John Preskill learned quantum computing:** John Preskill, "Celebrating Theoretical Physics at Caltech's Burke Institute," *Quantum Frontiers*, February 24, 2015; "John Preskill on Quantum Computing," *YCombinator*, May 15, 2018.

137 **the coach effect:** Lauren Eskreis-Winkler, Katherine L. Milkman, Dena M. Gromet, and Angela L. Duckworth, "A Large-Scale Field Experiment Shows Giving Advice Improves Academic Outcomes for the Advisor," *PNAS* 116, no. 30 (2019): 14808–810; Lauren Eskreis-Winkler, Ayelet Fishbach, and Angela L. Duckworth, "Dear Abby: Should I Give Advice or Receive It?," *Psychological Science* 29, no. 11 (2018): 1797–1806.

139 **more motivating to be a giver:** Adam Grant, *Give and Take: Why Helping Others Drives Our Success* (New York: Viking, 2013); Adam M. Grant and Jane Dutton, "Beneficiary or Benefactor: Are People More Prosocial When They Reflect on Giving or Receiving?," *Psychological Science* 23, no. 9 (2012): 1033–39; Adam M. Grant, Jane E. Dutton, and Brent D. Rosso, "Giving Commitment: Employee Support Programs and the Prosocial Sensemaking Process," *Academy of Management Journal* 51, no. 5 (2008): 898–918.

140 **Alison Levine wondered:** personal interview, November 28, 2022; Alison Levine, *On the Edge: The Art of High-Impact Leadership* (New York: Grand Central, 2014); Sarah Spain, "Alison Levine Proves She's All Heart," *ESPN*, December 27, 2011; Associated Press, "Climber Conquers Everest and Records Grand Slam," *The New York Times*, August 14, 2010.

142 **leaders hold high expectations:** D. Brian McNatt, "Ancient Pygmalion Joins Contemporary Management: A Meta-Analysis of the Result," *Journal of Applied Psychology* 85, no. 2 (2000): 314–22.

142 **teachers set high expectations:** Robert Rosenthal, "Interpersonal Expectancy Effects: A 30-Year Perspective," *Current Directions in Psychological Science* 3 (1994); 176–79.

142 **when others underestimate us:** Oranit B. Davidson and Dov Eden, "Remedial Self-Fulfilling Prophecy: Two Field Experiments to Prevent Golem Effects among Disadvantaged Women," *Journal of Applied Psychology* 85, no. 3 (2000): 386–98; Dennis Reynolds, "Restraining Golem and Harnessing Pygmalion in the Classroom: A Laboratory Study of Managerial Expectations and Task Design," *Academy of Management Learning & Education* 4 (2007): 475–83.

142 **particularly pronounced among stigmatized groups:** Lee Jussim and Kent D. Harber, "Teacher Expectations and Self-Fulfilling Prophecies: Knowns and Unknowns, Resolved and Unresolved Controversies," *Personality and Social Psychology Review* 9, no. 2 (2005): 131–55

142 **There are times:** Samir Nurmohamed, "The Underdog Effect: When Low Expectations Increase Performance," *Academy of Management Journal* 63, no. 4 (2020): 1106–33.

144 **experiments with job seekers:** Samir Nurmohamed, Timothy G. Kundro, and Christopher G. Myers, "Against the Odds: Developing Underdog versus Favorite Narratives to Offset Prior Experiences of Discrimination," *Organizational Behavior and Human Decision Processes* 167 (2021): 206–21.

144 **"boundaries to bust through":** Michelle Yeoh, "Harvard Law School Class Day," May 24, 2023: youtube.com/watch?v=PZ7YERWPftA.

146 **synchro rather than solo:** Marissa Shandell and Adam M. Grant, "Losing Yourself for the Win: How Interdependence Boosts Performance Under Pressure," working paper, 2023.

146 **deprive another child of an extra cookie:** Rebecca Koomen, Sebastian Grueneisen, and Esther Herrmann, "Children Delay Gratification for Cooperative Ends," *Psychological Science* 31, no. 2 (2020): 139–48.

146 **"counting on you counting on me":** Maya Angelou, *Rainbow in the Cloud: The Wisdom and Spirit of Maya Angelou* (New York: Random House, 2014).

149 **belonging to a group:** Karren Knowlton, "Trailblazing Motivation and Marginalized Group Members: Defying Expectations to Pave the Way for Others" (PhD. diss., University of Pennsylvania, 2021).

PART III

151 **evidence on the impact of opportunity:** Alex Bell, Raj Chetty, Xavier Jaravel, Neviana Petkova, and John Van Reenen, "Who Becomes an Inventor in America? The Importance of Exposure to Innovation," *The Quarterly Journal of Economics* 134, no. 2 (2019): 647–713.

CHAPTER 7

155 **"brilliant child locked inside every student":** Marva Collins and Civia Tamarkin, *Marva Collins' Way* (New York: TarcherPerigee, 1990).

155 **the PISA—a standardized test of their math, reading, and science skills:** OECD, "PISA 2000 Technical Report" (2002), "Learning for Tomorrow's World: First Results from PISA 2003" (2004), and "PISA 2006" (2008), all at pisa.oecd.org.

156 **Finland won the top spot:** Pasi Sahlberg, *Finnish Lessons 3.0: What Can the World Learn from Educational Change in Finland?* (New York: Teachers College Press, 2021) and "The Fourth Way of Finland," *Journal of Educational Change* 12 (2011): 173–85; OECD, "Top-Performer Finland Improves Further in PISA Survey as Gap Between Countries Widens.

156 **OECD gave a different aptitude test:** PIAAC, "International Comparisons of Adult Literacy and Numeracy Skills Over Time," Institute of Education Sciences (NCES 2020-127), nces.ed.gov/surveys/piaac/international_context.asp.

157 **lower child poverty rates and smaller classes:** Dylan Matthews, "Denmark, Finland, and Sweden Are Proof That Poverty in the U.S. Doesn't Have to Be This High," *Vox*, November 11, 2015.

157 **Finland ascended, Norway's test scores plummeted:** Eric A. Hanushek and Ludger Woessmann, *The Knowledge Capital of Nations: Education and the Economics of Growth* (Cambridge, MA: MIT Press, 2015); Amanda Ripley, *The Smartest Kids in the World: And How They Got That Way* (New York: Simon & Schuster, 2013).

158 **"We can't afford to waste a brain"**: Christine Gross-Loh, "Finnish Education Chief: 'We Created School System Based on Equality,'" *The Atlantic*, March 17, 2014.

158 **cultures created in schools and classrooms**: Doris Holzberger, Sarah Reinhold, Oliver Lüdtke, and Tina Seidel, "A Meta-Analysis on the Relationship between School Characteristics and Student Outcomes in Science and Maths: Evidence from Large-Scale Studies," *Studies in Science Education* 56 (2020): 1–34; Faith Bektas, Nazim Çogaltay, Engin Karadag, and Yusuf Ay, "School Culture and Academic Achievement of Students: A Meta-Analysis Study," *The Anthropologist* 21, no. 3 (2015): 482–88; Selen Demirtas-Zorbaz, Cigdem Akin-Arikan, and Ragip Terzi, "Does School Climate That Includes Students' Views Deliver Academic Achievement? A Multilevel Meta-Analysis," *School Effectiveness and School Improvement* 32 (2021): 543–63; Roisin P. Corcoran, Alan C.K. Cheung, Elizabeth Kim, and Chen Xie, "Effective Universal School-Based Social and Emotional Learning Programs for Improving Academic Achievement: A Systematic Review and Meta-Analysis of 50 Years of Research," *Educational Research Review* 25 (2018): 56–72.

158 **culture has three elements**: Edgar H. Schein, "Organizational Culture," *American Psychologist* 45, no. 2 (1990): 109–19; Daniel R. Denison, "What *Is* the Difference between Organizational Culture and Organizational Climate? A Native's Point of View on a Decade of Paradigm Wars," *Academy of Management Review* 21 (1996): 619–54; Charles A. O'Reilly and Jennifer A. Chatman, "Culture as Social Control: Corporations, Cults, and Commitment," *Research in Organizational Behavior* 18 (1996): 157–200.

159 **beliefs about how the world works**: Mark E. Koltko-Rivera, "The Psychology of Worldviews," *Review of General Psychology* 8, no. 1 (2004): 3–58; Jeremy D.W. Clifton, Joshua D. Baker, Crystal L. Park, David B. Yaden, Alicia B.W. Clifton, Paolo Terni, Jessica L. Miller, Guang Zeng, Salvatore Giorgi, H. Andrew Schwartz, and Martin E.P. Seligman, "Primal World Beliefs," 31, no. 1 (2019): 82–99.

159 **culture of winner take all**: Robert Frank and Philip J. Cook, *The Winner-Take-All Society: Why the Few at the Top Get So Much More Than the Rest of Us* (New York: Penguin, 1996); Daniel Markovits, *The Meritocracy Trap: How America's Foundational Myth Feeds Inequality, Dismantles the Middle Class, and Devours the Elite* (New York: Penguin, 2019).

159 **Despite bipartisan support, the plan didn't work**: Lily Eskelsen García and Otha Thornton, "'No Child Left Behind' Has Failed," *The Washington Post*, February 13, 2015; Rajashri Chakrabarti, "Incentives and Responses under *No Child Left Behind*: Credible Threats and the Role of Competition," Federal Reserve Bank of New York Staff Report No. 525, November 2011; Ben Casselman, "No Child Left Behind Worked: At Least in One Important Way," FiveThirtyEight, December 22, 2015; "Achievement Gaps," National Center for Education Statistics, nces.ed.gov/nationsreportcard/studies/gaps/.

159 **central value of educational equity**: Linda Darling-Hammond, *The Flat World and Education: How America's Commitment to Equity Will Determine Our Future* (New York: Teachers College Press, 2015).

160 **what career they respect**: Matthew Smith and Jamie Ballard, "Scientists and Doctors Are the Most Respected Professions Worldwide," YouGovAmerica, February 8, 2021.

160 **most admired profession is often teaching**: Pasi Sahlberg, "The Secret to Finland's Success: Educating Teachers," Stanford Center for Opportunity Policy in Education Research Brief, September 2010.

160 **"education as an instrument for nation building"**: Samuel E. Abrams, *Education and the Commercial Mindset* (Boston: Harvard University Press, 2016).

160 **attracted highly motivated, mission-driven candidates**: Pasi Sahlberg, "Q: What Makes Finnish Teachers So Special? A: It's Not Brains," *The Guardian*, March 31, 2015.

160 **pioneered in other countries**: Valerie Strauss, "Five U.S. Innovations That Helped Finland's

Schools Improve but That American Reformers Now Ignore," *The Washington Post*, July 25, 2014.

160 **"a new culture of education":** Vilho Hirvi, quoted in Sahlberg, 2021.

161 **define their ideal culture:** Pasi Sahlberg and Timothy D. Walker, *In Teachers We Trust: The Finnish Way to World-Class Schools* (New York: W. W. Norton, 2021).

161 **administering standardized tests:** Abrams, 2016.

161 **greater purchasing power:** Abrams, 2016.

162 **same teacher for two years in a row:** Andrew J. Hill and Daniel B. Jones, "A Teacher Who Knows Me: The Academic Benefits of Repeat Student-Teacher Matches," *Economics of Education Review* 64 (2018): 1–12.

162 **replicated the study:** NaYoung Hwang, Brian Kisida, and Cory Koedel, "A Familiar Face: Student-Teacher Rematches and Student Achievement," *Economics of Education Review* 85 (2021): 102194.

162 **same teacher for multiple grades:** Mike Colagrossi, "10 Reasons Why Finland's Education System is the Best in the World," World Economic Forum, September 10, 2018.

164 **school principal, Kari Louhivuori:** personal interview, February 24, 2023; LynNell Hancock, "Why Are Finland's Schools Successful?," *Smithsonian*, September 2011.

164 **"ounce of prevention":** Benjamin Franklin, "On Protections of Towns from Fire," *The Pennsylvania Gazette*, February 4, 1735.

164 **early interventions can help:** Gena Nelson and Kristen L. McMaster, "The Effects of Early Numeracy Interventions for Students in Preschool and Early Elementary: A Meta-Analysis," *Journal of Educational Psychology* 111, no. 6 (2019): 1001–22; Steven M. Ross, Lana J. Smith, Jason Casey, and Robert E. Slavin, "Increasing the Academic Success of Disadvantaged Children: An Examination of Alternative Early Intervention Programs," *American Educational Research Journal* 32, no. 4 (1995): 773–800; Frances A. Campbell and Craig T. Ramey, "Cognitive and School Outcomes for High-Risk African-American Students at Middle Adolescence: Positive Effects of Early Intervention," *American Educational Research Journal* 32, no. 4 (1995): 743–72.

164 **majority of states don't even comply:** John M. McLaughlin, "Most States Fail Education Obligations to Special Needs Students: So, What Else Is New?," *USA Today*, August 10, 2020.

165 **student welfare team:** Timothy D. Walker, *Teach Like Finland: 33 Simple Strategies for Joyful Classrooms* (New York: W. W. Norton, 2017).

165 **leaders who are knowledgeable about the core work:** Amanda H. Goodall, "Physician-Leaders and Hospital Performance: Is There an Association?," *Social Science & Medicine* 73, no. 4 (2011): 535–39, and "Highly Cited Leaders and the Performance of Research Universities," *Research Policy* 38, no. 7 (2009): 1079–92.

165 **leading by doing:** Sigal G. Barsade and Stefan Meisiek, "Leading by Doing," in *Next Generation Business Handbook: New Strategies from Tomorrow's Thought Leaders*, ed. Subir Chowdhury (New York: Wiley, 2004).

166 **alternative to holding students back:** Eva Hjörne and Roger Säljö, "The Pupil Welfare Team as a Discourse Community: Accounting for School Problems," *Linguistics and Education* 15 (2004): 321–38.

166 **30 percent of Finnish students receive extra assistance:** Hancock, 2011.

166 **doesn't do nearly as much early intervention:** Rune Sarromaa Hausstätter and Marjatta Takala, "Can Special Education Make a Difference? Exploring the Differences of Special Educational Systems between Finland and Norway in Relation to the PISA Results," *Scandinavian Journal of Disability Research* 13, no. 4 (2011): 271–81.

166 **intervening early to support freshmen:** Andrew Van Dam, "Why Alabama and West Virginia

Suddenly Have Amazing High-School Graduation Rates," *The Washington Post*, November 18, 2022.

166 **What's distinctive about the Finnish school day:** Sarah D. Sparks, "Do U.S. Teachers Really Teach More Hours?," *EducationWeek*, February 2, 2015; Abrams, 2016.

166 **limiting demands and providing control prevents burnout:** Margot van der Doef and Stan Maes, "The Job-Demand-Control(-Support) Model and Psychological Well-Being: A Review of 20 Years of Empirical Research, *Work & Stress* 13, no. 2 (1999): 87–114; Gene M. Alarcon, "A Meta-Analysis of Burnout with Job Demands, Resources, and Attitudes," *Journal of Vocational Behavior* 79, no. 2 (2011): 549–62; Nina Santavirta, Svetlana Solovieva, and Töres Theorell, "The Association between Job Strain and Emotional Exhaustion in a Cohort of 1,028 Finnish Teachers," *British Journal of Educational Psychology* 77 (2007): 213–28; Adam Grant, "Burnout Is Everyone's Problem," *WorkLife*, March 17, 2020.

167 **clever headline grabbed my attention:** Timothy D. Walker, "The Joyful, Illiterate Kindergartners of Finland," *The Atlantic*, October 1, 2015.

167 **American kindergarten has become more like first grade:** Daphna Bassok, Scott Latham, and Anna Rorem, "Is Kindergarten the New First Grade?," *AERA Open* 1, no. 4 (2016): 1–31.

167 **short activity breaks:** Alvaro Infantes-Paniagua, Ana Filipa Silva, Rodrigo Ramirez-Campillo, Hugo Sarmento, Francisco Tomás González-Fernández, Sixto González-Villora, and Filipe Manuel Clemente, "Active School Breaks and Students' Attention: A Systematic Review with Meta-Analysis," *Brain Sciences* 11, no. 6 (2021): 675; D.L.I.H.K. Peiris, Yanping Duan, Corneel Vandelanotte, Wei Liang, Min Yang, and Julien Steven Baker, "Effects of In-Classroom Physical Activity Breaks on Children's Academic Performance, Cognition, Health Behaviours and Health Outcomes: A Systematic Review and Meta-Analysis of Randomised Controlled Trials," *International Journal of Environmental Research and Public Health* 19, no. 15 (2022): 9479.

167 **clearest talkers and storytellers:** Sebastian Suggate, Elizabeth Schaughency, Helena McAnally, and Elaine Reese, "From Infancy to Adolescence: The Longitudinal Links between Vocabulary, Early Literacy Skills, Oral Narrative, and Reading Comprehension," *Cognitive Development* 47 (2018): 82–95.

167 **taught to read at seven have caught up:** Sebastian P. Suggate, Elizabeth A. Schaughency, and Elaine Reese, "Children Learning to Read Later Catch Up to Children Reading Earlier," *Early Childhood Research Quarterly* 28, no. 1 (2013): 33–48.

167 **haven't yet developed the vocabulary:** Sebastian Paul Suggate, "Does Early Reading Instruction Help Reading in the Long-Term? A Review of Empirical Evidence," *Research on Steiner Education* 4, no. 1 (2019): 123–131.

167 **or the broad knowledge:** Daniel T. Willingham, "How to Get Your Mind to Read," *The New York Times*, November 25, 2017.

167 **might be counterproductive:** Nancy Carlsson-Paige, Geralyn Bywater, and Joan Wolfsheimer Almon, "Reading Instruction in Kindergarten: Little to Gain and Much to Lose," Alliance for Childhood/Defending the Early Years, 2015, available at eric.ed.gov/?id=ED609172.

167 **learn to break down words by sound:** Wolfgang Schneider, Petra Küspert, Ellen Roth, Mechtild Visé, and Harald Marx, "Short- and Long-Term Effects of Training Phonological Awareness in Kindergarten: Evidence from Two German Studies," *Journal of Experimental Child Psychology* 66, no. 3 (1997): 311–40.

168 **students who enjoy school at age six:** Tim T. Morris, Danny Dorling, Neil M. Davies, and George Davey Smith, "Associations between School Enjoyment at Age 6 and Later Educational Achievement: Evidence from a UK Cohort Study," *NPJ Science of Learning* 6 (2021): 18.

168 **"The work of a child is to play":** Pasi Sahlberg and William Doyle, "To Really Learn, Our

Children Need the Power of Play," 2019, pasisahlberg.com/to-really-learn-our-children
-need-the-power-of-play.

168 **deliberate play is more effective than direct instruction:** Kayleigh Skene, Christine M.
O'Farrelly, Elizabeth M. Byrne, Natalie Kirby, Eloise C. Stevens, and Paul G. Ramchandani,
"Can Guidance during Play Enhance Children's Learning and Development in Educational
Contexts? A Systematic Review and Meta-Analysis," *Child Development* 93, no. 4 (2022):
1162–80.

169 **"Don't think you're anything special":** Aksel Sandemose, *A Fugitive Crosses His Tracks*
(New York: Knopf, 1936).

169 **their scores had dipped on all three subjects:** Arto K. Ahonen, "Finland: Success through
Equity—The Trajectories in PISA Performance," in *Improving a Country's Education*, ed.
Nuno Crato (Cham: Springer, 2021).

169 **Estonia had climbed up the charts:** Sarah Butrymowicz, "Is Estonia the New Finland?,"
The Atlantic, June 23, 2016, and "Everyone Aspires to Be Finland, But This Country Beats
Them in Two Out of Three Subjects," *The Hechinger Report*, June 23, 2016; Branwen Jef-
freys, "Pisa Rankings: Why Estonian Pupils Shine in Global Tests," BBC, December 2, 2019;
Rachel Sylvester, "How Estonia Does It: Lessons from Europe's Best School System," *The
Times* (London), January 27, 2022; Thomas Hatch, "10 Surprises in the High-Performing
Estonian Education System," *International Education News*, August 2, 2017; John Roberts,
"Estonia: Pisa's European Success Story," *Tes Magazine*, December 3, 2019; Marri Kangur,
"Estonia's Education Is Accessible to Everyone—Thanks to Social Support and an Adapt-
able System," *Estonian World*, December 27, 2021, and "Kindergarten Teaching in Estonia
Balances between Education Goals and Game-Based Learning," *Estonian World*, October
12, 2021; Alexander Kaffka, "Gunda Tire: 'Estonians Believe in Education, and This Belief
Has Been Essential for Centuries,'" *Caucasian Journal*, April 1, 2021; Adam Grant, "Esto-
nia's Prime Minister Kaja Kallas on Leading with Strength and Sincerity," *Re:Thinking*,
January 31, 2023.

170 **still in the top ten worldwide:** "PISA 2018 Worldwide Ranking," OECD, factsmaps.com
/pisa-2018-worldwide-ranking-average-score-of-mathematics-science-reading.

170 **students had somehow lost a step:** Chester E. Finn Jr. and Brandon L. Wright, "A Different
Kind of Lesson from Finland," *EducationWeek*, November 3, 2015.

170 **many possible reasons for the decline:** Pasi Sahlberg and Andy Hargreaves, "The Leaning
Tower of PISA," *Washington Post*, March 24, 2015; Adam Taylor, "Finland Used to Have
the Best Education System in the World—What Happened?," *Business Insider*, December
3, 2013; Thomas Hatch, "What Can the World Learn from Educational Change in Finland
Now? Pasi Sahlberg on Finnish Lessons 3.0," *International Education News*, February 28,
2021.

170 **challenges with motivation:** Sanna Read, Lauri Hietajärvi, and Katariina Salmela-Aro,
"School Burnout Trends and Sociodemographic Factors in Finland 2006–2019," *Social
Psychiatry and Psychiatric Epidemiology* 57 (2022): 1659–69.

170 **didn't try their best:** Uri Gneezy, John A. List, Jeffrey A. Livingston, Xiangdong Qin, Sally
Sadoff, and Yang Xu, "Measuring Success in Education: The Role of Effort on the Test
Itself," *American Economic Review: Insights* 1, no. 3 (2019): 291–308.

170 **performance is influenced by motivation:** Angela Lee Duckworth, Patrick D. Quinn, Donald
R. Lynam, Rolf Loeber, and Magda Stouthamer-Loeber, "Role of Test Motivation in Intelligence Testing," *PNAS* 108, no. 19 (2011): 7716–20.

171 **lost their love of learning:** Martin Thrupp, Piia Seppänen, Jaakko Kauko, and Sonja
Kosunen, eds., *Finland's Famous Education System: Unvarnished Insights into Finnish
Schooling* (Singapore: Springer, 2023).

171 **wellspring of intrinsic motivation:** Erika A. Patall, Harris Cooper, and Jorgianne Civey Robinson, "The Effects of Choice on Intrinsic Motivation and Related Outcomes: A Meta-Analysis of Research Findings," *Psychological Bulletin* 134, no. 2 (2008): 270–300.

171 **Me & MyCity:** Timothy D. Walker, "Where Sixth-Graders Run Their Own City," *The Atlantic*, September 1, 2016; Eanna Kelly, "How Finland Is Giving 12-Year-Olds the Chance to Be Entrepreneurs," Science|Business, March 22, 2016.

171 **deliberate play for older students:** Olivia Johnston, Helen Wildy, and Jennifer Shand, "Teenagers Learn through Play Too: Communicating High Expectations through a Playful Learning Approach," *The Australian Educational Researcher* (2022).

172 **become more interested in economics:** Panu Kalmi, "The Effects of Me and My City on Primary School Students' Financial Knowledge and Behavior," presented at 4th Cherry Blossom Financial Education Institute, Global Financial Literacy Excellence Center, George Washington University, Washington, DC, April 12–13, 2018.

172 **weren't reading enough to their kids:** "10 Facts about Reading in Finland 2020," Lukukeskus Läscentrum, lukukeskus.fi/en/10-facts-about-reading-in-finland/#fakta-2.

172 **every baby born in Finland:** "Read Aloud-Program and Book Bag to Every Baby Born in Finland," Lue Lapselle, luelapselle.fi/read-aloud/.

172 **make books part of their lives:** Daniel T. Willingham, *Raising Kids Who Read: What Parents and Teachers Can Do* (San Francisco: Jossey-Bass, 2015); Adriana G. Bus, Marinus H. van Ijzendoorn, and Anthony D. Pellegrini, "Joint Book Reading Makes for Success in Learning to Read: A Meta-Analysis on Intergenerational Transmission of Literacy," *Review of Educational Research* 65, no. 1 (1995): 1–21; Joe Pinsker, "Why Some People Become Lifelong Readers," *The Atlantic*, September 19, 2019.

174 **enthusiasm about reading continues to wane:** Daniel Willingham, "Moving Educational Psychology into the Home: The Case of Reading," *Mind Brain and Education* 9, no. 2 (2015): 107–11.

174 **they become more passionate about reading:** Gary P. Moser and Timothy G. Morrison, "Increasing Students' Achievement and Interest in Reading," *Reading Horizons* 38, no. 4 (1998): 233–45.

174 **It's a virtuous cycle:** Jessica R. Toste, Lisa Didion, Peng Peng, Marissa J. Filderman, and Amanda M. McClelland, "A Meta-Analytic Review of the Relations between Motivation and Reading Achievement for K—12 Students," *Review of Educational Research* 90, no. 3 (2020): 420–56; Suzanne E. Mol and Adriana G. Bus, "To Read or Not to Read: A Meta-Analysis of Print Exposure from Infancy to Early Childhood," *Psychological Bulletin* 137, no. 2 (2011): 267–96.

175 **Intrinsic motivation is contagious:** Rémi Radel, Philippe G. Sarrazin, Pascal Legrain, and T. Cameron Wild, "Social Contagion of Motivation between Teacher and Student: Analyzing Underlying Processes," *Journal of Educational Psychology* 102, no. 3 (2010): 577–87.

175 **students sacrifice their mental health for excellence:** Xiaojun Ling, Junjun Chen, Daniel H.K. Chow, Wendan Xu, and Yingxiu Li, "The 'Trade-Off' of Student Well-Being and Academic Achievement: A Perspective of Multidimensional Student Well-Being," *Frontiers in Psychology* 13 (2022): 772653.

175 **students at high-achieving high schools:** Suniya S. Luthar, Nina L. Kumar, and Nicole Zillmer, "High-Achieving Schools Connote Risks for Adolescents: Problems Documented, Processes Implicated, and Directions for Interventions," *American Psychologist* 75 (2020): 983–95.

175 **bottom ten countries on life satisfaction:** Yingyi Ma, "China's Education System Produces Stellar Test Scores. So Why Do 600,000 Students Go Abroad Each Year to Study?," *The Washington Post*, December 17, 2019.

175 **pressure to be perfect:** Andrew S. Quach, Norman B. Epstein, Pamela J. Riley, Mariana K. Falconier, and Xiaoyi Fang, "Effects of Parental Warmth and Academic Pressure on Anxiety and Depression Symptoms in Chinese Adolescents," *Journal of Child and Family Studies* 24 (2015): 106–16.

175 **stress of studying for long hours:** Mark Mohan Kaggwa, Jonathan Kajjimu, Jonathan Sserunkuma, Sarah Maria Najjuka, Letizia Maria Atim, Ronald Olum, Andrew Tagg, and Felix Bongomin, "Prevalence of Burnout among University Students in Low- and Middle-Income Countries: A Systematic Review and Meta-Analysis," *PLoS ONE* 16, no. 8 (2021): e0256402; Xinfeng Tang, Suqin Tang, Zhihong Ren, and Daniel Fu Keung Wong, "Prevalence of Depressive Symptoms among Adolescents in Secondary School in Mainland China: A Systematic Review and Meta-Analysis," *Journal of Affective Disorders* 245 (2019): 498–507; Ziwen Teuber, Fridtjof W. Nussbeck, and Elke Wild, "School Burnout among Chinese High School Students: The Role of Teacher-Student Relationships and Personal Resources," *Educational Psychology* 41, no. 8 (2021): 985–1002; Alan Ye, "Copying the Long Chinese School Day Could Have Unintended Consequences," *The Conversation*, February 24, 2014.

175 **hours of homework per week:** Joyce Chepkemoi, "Countries Who Spend the Most Time Doing Homework," WorldAtlas, July 4, 2017.

175 **ultimate metric for growth:** Jenny Anderson, "Finland Has the Most Efficient Education System in the World," *Quartz*, December 3, 2019.

CHAPTER 8

177 **"Some other eyes will look around":** Malvina Reynolds, "This World" (Schroder Music Company, [1961] 1989).

177 **trapped 2,300 feet underground:** Amy C. Edmondson and Kerry Herman, "The 2010 Chilean Mining Rescue (A) & (B)," Harvard Business School Teaching Plan 613-012, May 2013; Jonathan Franklin, *33 Men: Inside the Miraculous Survival and Dramatic Rescue of the Chilean Miners* (New York: G. P. Putnam's Sons, 2011); Héctor Tobar, *Deep Down Dark: The Untold Stories of 33 Men Buried in a Chilean Mine, and the Miracle That Set Them Free* (New York: Farrar, Straus and Giroux, 2014); Manuel Pino Toro, *Buried Alive: The True Story of the Chilean Mining Disaster and the Extraordinary Rescue at Camp Hope* (New York: St. Martin's Press, 2011); Faazia Rashid, Amy C. Edmondson, and Herman B. Leonard, "Leadership Lessons from the Chilean Mine Rescue," *Harvard Business Review*, July–August 2013,: 113–19; Michael Useem, Rodrigo Jordán, and Matko Koljatic, "How to Lead during Crisis: Lessons from the Rescue of the Chilean Miners," *MIT Sloan Management Review*, August 18, 2011; Korn Ferry, "The Man behind the Miracle": kornferry.com/insights/briefings-magazine/issue-6/34-the-man-behind-the-miracle.

178 **rescue team "drilling blind":** Connie Watson, "The Woman Who Helped Find the Needle in the Haystack," CBC News, October 22, 2010.

180 **studying teams in every field imaginable:** J. Richard Hackman, *Leading Teams: Setting the Stage for Great Performances* (Boston: Harvard Business School Press, 2002) and "Learning More by Crossing Levels: Evidence from Airplanes, Hospitals, and Orchestras," *Journal of Organizational Behavior* 24, no. 8 (2003): 90522.

180 **teamwork failed to make the dream work:** J. Richard Hackman, ed., *Groups That Work (and Those That Don't)* (San Francisco: Jossey-Bass, 1991).

180 **studying how to improve collaboration:** J. Richard Hackman, *Collaborative Intelligence: Using Teams to Solve Hard Problems* (San Francisco: Berrett-Koehler, 2011); Hackman and O'Connor, 2004.

181 **collective intelligence had little to do with individual IQs:** Anita Williams Woolley, Christopher F. Chabris, Alex Pentland, Nada Hashmi, and Thomas W. Malone, "Evidence for a Collective Intelligence Factor in the Performance of Human Groups," *Science* 330, no. 6004 (2010): 686–88.

181 **less on people's cognitive skills than their prosocial skills:** Christoph Riedl, Young Ji Kim, Pranav Gupta, Thomas W. Malone, and Anita Williams Woolley, "Quantifying Collective Intelligence in Human Groups," *PNAS* 118, no. 21 (2021): e2005737118.

181 **bad apple can spoil the barrel:** Patrick D. Dunlop and Kibeom Lee, "Workplace Deviance, Organizational Citizenship Behavior, and Business Unit Performance: The Bad Apples Do Spoil the Whole Barrel," *Journal of Organizational Behavior* 25, no. 1 (2004): 67–80; Will Felps, Terence R. Mitchell, and Eliza Byington, "How, When, and Why Bad Apples Spoil the Barrel: Negative Group Members and Dysfunctional Groups," *Research in Organizational Behavior* 27, no. 3 (2006): 175–22.

181 **one individual fails to act prosocially:** Nicoleta Meslec, Ishani Aggarwal, and Petru L. Curseu, "The Insensitive Ruins It All: Compositional and Compilational Influences of Social Sensitivity on Collective Intelligence in Groups," *Frontiers in Psychology* 7 (2016): 676.

181 **many narcissists or even one extreme narcissist:** Emily Grijalva, Timothy D. Maynes, Katie L. Badura, and Steven W. Whiting, "Examining the 'I' in Team: A Longitudinal Investigation of the Influence of Team Narcissism Composition on Team Outcomes in the NBA," *Academy of Management Journal* 63, no. 1 (2020): 7–33.

182 **undervalued players are the ones who help their teammates:** Peter Arcidiacono, Josh Kinsler, and Joseph Price, "Productivity Spillovers in Team Production: Evidence from Professional Basketball," *Journal of Labor Economics* 35, no. 1 (2017): 191–225.

182 **motivate one another to align their efforts:** Ben Weidmann and David J. Deming, "Team Players: How Social Skills Improve Group Performance," NBER Working Paper 27071, May 2020.

182 **team building and bonding exercises are overrated:** Eduardo Salas, Drew Rozell, Brian Mullen, James E. Driskell, "The Effect of Team Building on Performance: An Integration," *Small Group Research* 30, no. 3 (1999): 309–29; Cameron Klein, Deborah DiazGranados, Eduardo Salas, Huy Le, C. Shawn Burke, Rebecca Lyons, and Gerald F. Goodwin, "Does Team Building Work?," *Small Group Research* 40, no. 2 (2009): 181–222.

183 **groups promote the people who command the most airtime:** Neil G. MacLaren, Francis J. Yammarino, Shelley D. Dionne, Hiroki Sayama, Michael D. Mumford, Shane Connelly, Robert W. Martin, Tyler J. Mulhearn, E. Michelle Todd, Ankita Kulkarni, Yiding Cao, and Gregory A. Ruark, "Testing the Babble Hypothesis: Speaking Time Predicts Leader Emergence in Small Groups," *The Leadership Quarterly* 31 (2020): 101409.

183 **narcissistic people were more likely to rise:** Emily Grijalva, Peter D. Harms, Daniel A. Newman, Blaine H. Gaddis, and R. Chris Fraley, "Narcissism and Leadership: A Meta-Analytic Review of Linear and Nonlinear Relationships," *Personnel Psychology* 68, no. 1 (2015): 1–47.

183 **less effective in those roles:** Eddie Brummelman, Barbara Nevicka, and Joseph M. O'Brien, "Narcissism and Leadership in Children," *Psychological Science* 32, no. 3 (2021): 354–63.

183 **instilled a zero-sum view of success:** Hemant Kakkar and Niro Sivanathan, "The Impact of Leader Dominance on Employees' Zero-Sum Mindset and Helping Behavior," *Journal of Applied Psychology* 107 (2022): 1706–24.

183 **undermining cohesion and collaboration:** Charles A. O'Reilly III, Jennifer A. Chatman, and Bernadette Doerr, "When 'Me' Trumps 'We': Narcissistic Leaders and the Cultures They Create," *Academy of Management Discoveries* 7 (2021): 419–50.

185 **prize results above relationships:** Chad A. Hartnell, Angelo J. Kinicki, Lisa Schurer Lambert,

Mel Fugate, and Patricia Doyle Corner, "Do Similarities or Differences between CEO Leadership and Organizational Culture Have a More Positive Effect on Firm Performance? A Test of Competing Predictions," *Journal of Applied Psychology* 101, no. 6 (2016): 846–61.

186 **the more extraverts you find:** Deniz S. Ones and Stephan Dilchert, "How Special Are Executives? How Special Should Executive Selection Be? Observations and Recommendations," *Industrial and Organizational Psychology* 2 (2009): 163–70.

186 **extraverts are seen as the prototypical leaders:** Sing Lim Leung and Nikos Bozionelos, "Five-Factor Model Traits and the Prototypical Image of the Effective Leader in the Confucian Culture," *Employee Relations* 26 (2004): 62–71.

186 **best leader is not the person who talks the most:** Adam M. Grant, Francesca Gino, and David A. Hofmann, "Reversing the Extraverted Leadership Advantage: The Role of Employee Proactivity," *Academy of Management Journal* 54, no. 3 (2011): 528–50.

187 **In brainstorming meetings, many good ideas are lost:** Brian Mullen, Craig Johnson, and Eduardo Salas, "Productivity Loss in Brainstorming Groups: A Meta-Analytic Integration," *Basic and Applied Social Psychology* 12 (1991): 3–23.

188 **"the human race has not achieved":** Dave Barry, *Dave Barry Turns 50* (New York: Ballantine Books, 1998).

188 **process called brainwriting:** Paul B. Paulus and Huei-Chuan Yang, "Idea Generation in Groups: A Basis for Creativity in Organizations," *Organizational Behavior and Human Decision Processes* 82, no. 1 (2000): 76–87.

189 **another key to collective intelligence is balanced participation:** Anita Williams Woolley, Ishani Aggarwal, and Thomas W. Malone, "Collective Intelligence and Group Performance," *Current Directions in Psychological Science* 24, no. 6 (2015): 420–24.

189 **brainwriting is especially effective in groups that struggle:** Benjamin Ostrowski, Anita Williams Woolley, and Ki-Won Haan, "Translating Member Ability into Group Brainstorming Performance: The Role of Collective Intelligence," *Small Group Research* 53, no. 1 (2022): 3–40.

189 **more brilliant ideas than groups:** Ethan Bernstein, Jesse Shore, and David Lazer, "How Intermittent Breaks in Interaction Improve Collective Intelligence," *PNAS* 115 (2018): 8734–39.

189 **higher proportions of women:** Riedl et al., 2021.

189 **women outperform men:** David Engel, Anita Williams Woolley, Lisa X. Jing, Christopher F. Chabris, and Thomas W. Malone, "Reading the Mind in the Eyes or Reading between the Lines? Theory of Mind Predicts Collective Intelligence Equally Well Online and Face-to-Face," *PLoS ONE* 9 (2014): e115212.

189 **more capable or more motivated:** William Ickes, Paul R. Gesn, and Tiffany Graham, "Gender Differences in Empathic Accuracy: Differential Ability or Differential Motivation?," *Personal Relationships* 7, no. 1 (2000): 95–109.

189 **good team players motivate:** Weidmann and Deming, 2021; J. Mark Weber and J. Keith Murnighan, "Suckers or Saviors? Consistent Contributors in Social Dilemmas," *Journal of Personality and Social Psychology* 95, no. 6 (2008): 1340–53.

189 **as women joined Norwegian boards:** Aaron A. Dhir, *Challenging Boardroom Homogeneity: Corporate Law, Governance, and Diversity* (New York: Cambridge University Press, 2015).

193 **"he would never have spoken up":** Adam Grant, "Is It Safe to Speak Up?," *WorkLife*, July 20, 2021.

193 **climate for voice and psychological safety:** Amy C. Edmondson, *The Fearless Organization: Creating Psychological Safety in the Workplace for Learning, Innovation, and Growth* (New York: Wiley, 2018); Elizabeth W. Morrison, Sara L. Wheeler-Smith, and Dishan Kamdar,

"Speaking Up in Groups: A Cross-Level Study of Group Voice Climate and Voice," *Journal of Applied Psychology* 96, no. 1 (2011): 183–91.

193 **just being looked at by the leader:** So-Hyeon Shim, Robert W. Livingston, Katherine W. Phillips, and Simon S.K. Lam, "The Impact of Leader Eye Gaze on Disparity in Member Influence: Implications for Process and Performance in Diverse Groups," *Academy of Management Journal* 64, no. 6 (2021): 1873–1900.

193 **can't get your boss to hear you out:** James R. Detert, Ethan R. Burris, David A. Harrison, and Sean R. Martin, "Voice Flows to and around Leaders: Understanding When Units Are Helped or Hurt by Employee Voice," *Administrative Science Quarterly* 58, no. 4 (2013): 624–68.

193 **find reasons to say no:** Justin M. Berg, "Balancing on the Creative Highwire: Forecasting the Success of Novel Ideas in Organizations," *Administrative Science Quarterly* 61, no. 3 (2016): 433–68; Jennifer Mueller, Shimul Melwani, Jeffrey Loewenstein, and Jennifer J. Deal, "Reframing the Decision-Makers' Dilemma: Towards a Social Context Model of Creative Idea Recognition," *Academy of Management Journal* 61, no. 1 (2018): 94–110.

193 **Your idea might be a threat:** Nathanael J. Fast, Ethan R. Burris, and Caroline A. Bartel, "Managing to Stay in the Dark: Managerial Self-Efficacy, Ego Defensiveness, and the Aversion to Employee Voice," *Academy of Management Journal* 57, no. 4 (2014): 1013–34; Ethan R. Burris, "The Risks and Rewards of Speaking Up: Managerial Responses to Employee Voice," *Academy of Management Journal* 55, no. 4 (2012): 851–75.

193 **reputation for being prosocial and levelheaded:** Grant, Parker, and Collins, 2009; Adam M. Grant, "Rocking the Boat but Keeping It Steady: The Role of Emotion Regulation in Employee Voice," *Academy of Management Journal* 56, no. 6 (2013): 1703–23.

193 **unproven ideas carry too much risk:** Damon J. Phillips and Ezra W. Zuckerman, "Middle-Status Conformity: Theoretical Restatement and Empirical Demonstration in Two Markets," *American Journal of Sociology* 107, no. 2 (2001): 379–429; Jennifer S. Mueller, Shimul Melwani, and Jack A. Goncalo, "The Bias against Creativity: Why People Desire but Reject Creative Ideas," *Psychological Science* 23, no. 1 (2012): 13–17.

194 **if they perceive leaders above them as opposed:** James R. Detert and Linda K. Treviño, "Speaking Up to Higher-Ups: How Supervisors and Skip-Level Leaders Influence Employee Voice," *Organization Science* 21 (2010): 249–70; Andrea C. Vial, Victoria L. Brescoll, and John F. Dovidio, "Third-Party Prejudice Accommodation Increases Gender Discrimination," *Journal of Personality and Social Psychology* 117, no. 1 (2019): 73–98.

194 **set up to reject ideas with hidden potential:** Charalampos Mainemelis, "Stealing Fire: Creative Deviance in the Evolution of New Ideas," *Academy of Management Review* 35, no. 4 (2010): 558–78.

194 **Xerox programmers pioneered:** Douglas K. Smith and Robert C. Alexander, *Fumbling the Future: How Xerox Invented, Then Ignored, the First Personal Computer* (Lincoln, NE: iUniverse, 1999).

194 **An engineer at Kodak:** Claudia H. Deutsch, "At Kodak, Some Old Things Are New Again," *The New York Times*, May 2, 2008.

195 **best example I've seen of a lattice system:** Adam Grant, "Rethinking Flexibility at Work," *WorkLife*, April 19, 2022.

196 **implicit rules stop many people from speaking up:** James R. Detert and Amy C. Edmondson, "Implicit Voice Theories: Taken-for-Granted Rules of Self-Censorship at Work," *Academy of Management Journal* 54, no. 3 (2011): 461–88.

196 **in innovation tournaments:** "Why Some Innovation Tournaments Succeed and Others Fail," *Knowledge at Wharton*, February 2014.

196 **saved the company:** Christian Terwiesch and Karl T. Ulrich, *Innovation Tournaments: Creating and Selecting Exceptional Opportunities* (Boston: Harvard Business School Press, 2009).

CHAPTER 9

199 **"Success is to be measured":** Booker T. Washington, *Up from Slavery: An Autobiography* (New York: Doubleday, 1907).

199 **José Hernandez kneeled in front:** personal interview, August 31, 2022; José Hernandez, *Reaching for the Stars: The Inspiring Story of a Migrant Farmworker Turned Astronaut* (New York: Center Street, 2012); Jocko Willink, "310: Relish the Struggle and Keep Reaching for the Stars with José Hernandez," *Jocko Podcast*, December 1, 2021; Octavio Blanco, "How This Son of Migrant Farm Workers Became an Astronaut," CNN Business, March 14, 2016; "An Interview with Astronaut José Hernandez," UCSB College of Engineering, YouTube, December 18, 2014, youtu.be/2fLdKrv8zkM; José Hernandez, "Dreaming the Impossible," Talks at Google, YouTube, October 15, 2010, youtu.be/lwVqVu5Tl-k.

203 **rarely make the cut:** Elanor F. Williams and Thomas Gilovich, "The Better-Than-My-Average Effect: The Relative Impact of Peak and Average Performances in Assessments of the Self and Others," *Journal of Experimental Psychology* 48, no. 2 (2012): 556–61.

204 **reduced to thin slices:** Noah Eisenkraft, "Accurate by Way of Aggregation: Should You Trust Your Intuition-Based First Impressions?," *Journal of Experimental Social Psychology* 49, no. 2 (2013): 277–79; Nalini Ambady and Robert Rosenthal, "Thin Slices of Expressive Behavior as Predictors of Interpersonal Consequences: A Meta-Analysis," *Psychological Bulletin* 111, no. 2 (1992): 256–74.

204 **higher-ranking universities performed only slightly better:** Vas Taras, Marjaana Gunkel, Alexander Assouad, Ernesto Tavoletti, Justin Kraemer, Alfredo Jiménez, Anna Svirina, Weng Si Lei, and Grishma Shah, "The Predictive Power of University Pedigree on the Graduate's Performance in Global Virtual Teams," *European Journal of International Management* 16, no. 4 (2021): 555–84.

204 **just 1.9 percent better:** Vasyl Taras, Grishma Shah, Marjaana Gunkel, Ernesto Tavoletti, "Graduates of Elite Universities Get Paid More. Do They Perform Better?," *Harvard Business Review*, September 4, 2020.

204 **skills through alternative routes:** Peter Q. Blair and Shad Ahmed, "The Disparate Racial Impact of Requiring a College Degree," *The Wall Street Journal*, June 28, 2020; Peter Q. Blair, Tomas G. Castagnino, Erica L. Groshen, Papia Debroy, Byron Auguste, Shad Ahmed, Fernando Garcia Diaz, and Cristian Bonavida, "Searching for STARs: Work Experience as a Job Market Signal for Workers without Bachelor's Degrees," NBER Working Paper 26844, March 2020.

204 **work experience had virtually no bearing:** Chad H. Van Iddekinge, John D. Arnold, Rachel E. Frieder, Philip L. Roth, "A Meta-Analysis of the Criterion-Related Validity of Prehire Work Experience," *Personnel Psychology* 72, no. 4 (2019): 571–98.

205 **How well someone has performed in the past:** Leaetta M. Hough, "Development and Evaluation of the 'Accomplishment Record' Method of Selecting and Promoting Professionals," *Journal of Applied Psychology* 69 (1984): 135–46; Charlene Zhang and Nathan R. Kuncel, "Moving beyond the Brag Sheet: A Meta-Analysis of Biodata Measures Predicting Student Outcomes," *Educational Measurement* 39 (2020): 106–21.

205 **were worse at managing people:** Alan Benson, Danielle Li, and Kelly Shue, "Promotions and the Peter Principle," *The Quarterly Journal of Economics* 134, no. 4 (2019): 2085–2134.

205 **phenomenon known as the Peter Principle:** Laurence J. Peter and Raymond Hull, *The Peter Principle: Why Things Always Go Wrong* (New York: Harper Business, [1969] 2014).

206 **scouts didn't account:** Steven Ruiz, "Re-scouting Tom Brady at Michigan: Why NFL Teams Had No Excuse for Passing on Him," *USA Today*, October 20, 2017; ZeeGee Cecilio, "Huge Mistake: Kurt Warner Admits Rams Overlooked Tom Brady in Super Bowl 36," *Blasting News*, December 30, 2019.

206 **dual promotion tracks:** Alan Benson, Danielle Li, and Kelly Shue, "Research: Do People Really Get Promoted to Their Level of Incompetence," *Harvard Business Review*, March 8, 2018.

206 **women are less likely to be promoted:** Alan Benson, Danielle Li, and Kelly Shue, "'Potential' and the Gender Promotion Gap," working paper, June 22, 2022.

207 **candidates with the right stuff:** Duane Ross, personal interviews, August 26, 2022, and April 3, 2023; David J. Shayler and Colin Burgess, *NASA's First Space Shuttle Astronaut Selection* (Switzerland: Springer, 2020); Tom Wolfe, *The Right Stuff* (New York: Farrar, Straus and Giroux, 1979).

209 **different reactions to the same event:** Peggy A. Thoits, "Undesirable Life Events and Psychophysiological Distress: A Problem of Operational Confounding," *American Sociological Review* 46, no. 1 (1981): 97–109.

209 **Liberals and conservatives have heated debates:** Philip E. Tetlock, Ferdinand M. Vieider, Shefali V. Patil, and Adam M. Grant, "Accountability and Ideology: When Left Looks Right and Right Looks Left," *Organizational Behavior and Human Decision Processes* 122 (2013): 22–35.

209 **when their organizations had affirmative action:** Lisa M. Leslie, David M. Mayer, and David A. Kravitz, "The Stigma of Affirmative Action: A Stereotyping-Based Theory and Meta-Analytic Test of the Consequences for Performance," *Academy of Management Journal* 57, no. 4 (2014): 964–89.

210 **improved the odds for women:** Claudia Goldin and Cecilia Rouse, "Orchestrating Impartiality: The Impact of 'Blind' Auditions on Female Musicians," *American Economic Review* 90, no. 4 (2000): 715–41.

210 **advertising their trauma:** Elijah Megginson, "When I Applied to College, I Didn't Want to 'Sell My Pain,'" *The New York Times*, May 9, 2021.

211 **admissions officers pay:** Michael A. Bailey, Jeffrey S. Rosenthal, Albert H. Yoon, "Grades and Incentives: Assessing Competing Grade Point Average Measures and Postgraduate Outcomes," *Studies in Higher Education* 41 (2016): 1548–62; see also Michael N. Bastedo, Joseph E. Howard, and Allyson Flaster, "Holistic Admissions after Affirmative Action: Does "Maximizing" the High School Curriculum Matter?," *Educational Evaluation and Policy Analysis* 38, no. 2 (2016): 389–409.

211 **objectively compare students to their peer group:** Michael N. Bastedo, Nicholas A. Bowman, Kristen M. Glasener, and Jandi L. Kelly, "What Are We Talking about When We Talk about Holistic Review? Selective College Admissions and Its Effects on Low-SES Students," *The Journal of Higher Education* 89, no. 5 (2018): 782–805.

211 **grades relative to their neighborhood:** Michael N. Bastedo, D'Wayne Bell, Jessica S. Howell, Julian Hsu, Michael Hurwitz, Greg Perfetto, and Meredith Welch, "Admitting Students in Context: Field Experiments on Information Dashboards in College Admissions," *The Journal of Higher Education* 93, no. 3 (2022): 327–74; Michael N. Bastedo, Kristen M. Glasener, K.C. Deane, and Nicholas A. Bowman, "Contextualizing the SAT: Experimental Evidence on College Admission Recommendations for Low-SES Applicants," *Educational Policy* 36, no. 2 (2022): 282–311.

212 **signs of economic hardship:** Raphael Mokades, "Only Posh Kids Get City Jobs? This Man Has an Algorithm to Change That," *The Times* (London), April 19, 2022.

213 **neglecting to consider whether they got better or worse:** George Bulman, "Weighting

Recent Performance to Improve College and Labor Market Outcomes," *Journal of Public Economics* 146 (2017): 97–108.

214 **Early failure followed by later success:** Jerker Denrell, Chengwei Liu, David Maslach, "Underdogs and One-Hit Wonders: When Is Overcoming Adversity Impressive?," *Management Science* (2023).

215 **social class achievement gap:** Sarah S. M. Townsend, Nicole M. Stephens, and MaryAm G. Hamedani, "Difference-Education Improves First-Generation Students' Grades throughout College and Increases Comfort with Social Group Difference," *Personality and Social Psychology Bulletin* 47, no. 10 (2021): 1510–19.

215 **discourages them from seeking help:** Nicole M. Stephens, Stephanie A. Fryberg, Hazel Rose Markus, Camille S. Johnson, and Rebecca Covarrubias, "Unseen Disadvantage: How American Universities' Focus on Independence Undermines the Academic Performance of First-Generation College Students," *Journal of Personality and Social Psychology* 102, no. 6 (2012): 1178–97.

215 **absence of belonging:** Mary C. Murphy, Maithreyi Gopalan, Evelyn R. Carter, Katherine T. U. Emerson, Bette L. Bottoms, and Gregory M. Walton, "A Customized Belonging Intervention Improves Retention of Socially Disadvantaged Students at a Broad-Access University," *Science Advances* 6, no. 29 (2020): eaba4677.

217 **Brainteasers don't actually reveal anything:** Adam Pasick, "Google Finally Admits That Its Infamous Brainteasers Were Completely Useless for Hiring," *The Atlantic*, June 20, 2013.

217 **narcissists and sadists:** Scott Highhouse, Christopher D. Nye, and Don C. Zhang, "Dark Motives and Elective Use of Brainteaser Interview Questions," *Applied Psychology: An International Review* 68 (2019): 311–40.

217 **stress created in interviews:** Deborah M. Powell, David J. Stanley, and Kayla N. Brown, "Meta-Analysis of the Relation between Interview Anxiety and Interview Performance," *Canadian Journal of Behavioural Science* 50, no. 4 (2018): 195–207.

217 **fear of confirming negative stereotypes:** Claude M. Steele, "A Threat in the Air: How Stereotypes Shape Intellectual Identity and Performance," *American Psychologist* 52, no. 6 (1997): 613–29; Hannah-Hanh D. Nguyen and Ann Marie Ryan, "Does Stereotype Threat Affect Test Performance of Minorities and Women? A Meta-Analysis of Experimental Evidence," *Journal of Applied Psychology* 93, no. 6 (2008): 1314–34; Markus Appel, Silvana Weber, and Nicole Kronberger, "The Influence of Stereotype Threat on Immigrants: Review and Meta-Analysis," *Frontiers in Psychology* 6 (2015): 900; Claude M. Steele and Joshua Aronson, "Stereotype Threat and the Intellectual Performance of African Americans," *Journal of Personality and Social Psychology* 69 (1995): 797–811; Ruth A. Lamont, Hannah J. Swift, and Dominic Abrams, "A Review and Meta-Analysis of Age-Based Stereotype Threat: Negative Stereotypes, Not Facts, Do the Damage," *Psychology and Aging* 30, no. 1 (2015): 180–93; Stephanie L. Haft, Caroline Greiner de Magalhães, and Fumiko Hoeft, "A Systematic Review of the Consequences of Stigma and Stereotype Threat for Individuals with Specific Learning Disabilities," *Journal of Learning Disabilities* 56, no. 3 (2023): 193–209.

217 **the standard interview process:** Gil Winch, *Winning with Underdogs: How Hiring the Least Likely Candidates Can Spark Creativity, Improve Service, and Boost Profits for Your Business* (New York: McGraw Hill, 2022); Adam Grant, "It's Time to Stop Ignoring Disability," *WorkLife*, June 13, 2022.

218 **work samples can fill gaps in interviews:** Philip L. Roth, Philip Bobko, and Lynn A. McFarland, "A Meta-Analysis of Work Sample Test Validity: Updating and Integrating Some Classic Literature," *Personnel Psychology* 58, no. 4 (2005): 1009–37.

218 **which applicants appreciate:** Neil Anderson, Jesús F. Salgado, and Ute R. Hülsheger, "Applicant Reactions in Selection: Comprehensive Meta-Analysis into Reaction General-

ization versus Situational Specificity," *International Journal of Selection and Assessment* 18, no. 3 (2010): 291–304.

220 **In selection decisions, algorithms generally outperform humans:** Nathan R. Kuncel, David M. Klieger, Brian S. Connelly, and Deniz S. Ones, "Mechanical versus Clinical Data Combination in Selection and Admissions Decisions: A Meta-Analysis," *Journal of Applied Psychology* 98, no. 6 (2013): 1060–72.

220 **than a biased human:** Sendhil Mullainathan, "Biased Algorithms Are Easier to Fix Than Biased People," *The New York Times,* December 6, 2019.

220 **algorithm trained to score character skills and values:** Benjamin Lira, Margo Gardner, Abigail Quirk, Cathlyn Stone, Arjun Rao, Lyle Ungar, Stephen Hutt, Sidney K. D'Mello, and Angela L. Duckworth, "Using Human-Centered Artificial Intelligence to Assess Personal Qualities in College Admissions," working paper (2023).

220 **An algorithm is an input:** Adam Grant, "Reinventing the Job Interview," *WorkLife,* April 21, 2020.

EPILOGUE

225 **"Hold fast to dreams":** Langston Hughes, *The Collected Poems of Langston Hughes* (New York: Knopf, 1994).

225 *King's advisors feared*: Jim Polk and Alicia Stewart, "9 Things about MLK's Speech and the March on Washington," CNN, January 21, 2019.

225 **Young people with grander dreams:** Warn N. Lekfuangfu and Reto Odermatt, "All I Have to Do Is Dream? The Role of Aspirations in Intergenerational Mobility and Well-Being," *European Economic Review* 148 (2022): 104193.

IMAGE CREDITS

Graph Source Credits

Page 8: Raj Chetty, John N. Friedman, and Jonah E. Rockoff, "Measuring the Impacts of Teachers II: Teacher Value Added and Student Outcomes in Adulthood," *American Economic Review* 104, no. 9 (2014): 2633–79.

10: Raj Chetty et al., "How Does Your Kindergarten Classroom Affect Your Earnings? Evidence from Project Star," *The Quarterly Journal of Economics* 126, no. 4 (2011): 1593–1660; "$320,000 Kindergarten Teachers," *Kappan*, November 2010.

46 and 47: Sascha O. Becker and Ludger Woessmann, "Was Weber Wrong? A Human Capital Theory of Protestant Economic History," *The Quarterly Journal of Economics* 124, no. 2 (2009): 531–96.

110: John S. Chen and Pranav Garg, "Dancing with the Stars: Benefits of a Star Employee's Temporary Absence for Organizational Performance," *Strategic Management Journal* 39, no. 5 (2018): 1239–67.

169: Arto K. Ahonen, "Finland: Success through Equity—The Trajectories in PISA Performance," in *Improving a Country's Education*, ed. Nuno Crato (Cham, Switzerland: Springer, 2021).

215: George Bulman, "Weighting Recent Performance to Improve College and Labor Market Outcomes," *Journal of Public Economics* 146 (2017): 97–108.

INDEX

Italic page numbers indicate charts and illustrations